Brazil's International Ethanol Strategy

Brazil's International Ethanol Strategy

Lula's Quest for a Global Biofuels Market

Thomas Fröhlich

ANTHEM PRESS

Anthem Press
An imprint of Wimbledon Publishing Company
www.anthempress.com

This edition first published in UK and USA 2022
by ANTHEM PRESS
75–76 Blackfriars Road, London SE1 8HA, UK
or PO Box 9779, London SW19 7ZG, UK
and
244 Madison Ave #116, New York, NY 10016, USA

British Library Cataloguing-in-Publication Data
A catalogue record for this book is available from the British Library.

Library of Congress Control Number: 2021948444

ISBN-13: 978-1-83998-024-4 (Hbk)
ISBN-10: 1-83998-024-9 (Hbk)

Cover credit: sugar cane industry. By mailsonpignata/Shutterstock.com

This title is also available as an e-book.

CONTENTS

ILLUSTRATIONS

Figures

Tables

PREFACE

Brazil, the world's largest sugar producer, fulfils 16 per cent of its energy consumption and approximately three quarters of its transport fuels with sugarcane-based ethanol. During Brazil's internationalisation under President Lula da Silva, and to a lesser extent in President Rousseff's first term, the country aimed at creating a global market for ethanol. The time seemed right to steer foreign policy towards this goal due to a benevolent structural environment with global discussions about energy security, climate change and South–South cooperation.

Within a Neoclassical Realist framework, I show how Brazil failed to bring its ethanol diplomacy to success and to create a global market for ethanol. Neoclassical Realism sheds light on the area of energy security. This is an approach that so far has mainly been applied to hard security questions.

The analysis covers three analytical levels: the bilateral with Brazil in power deficit, the bilateral with Brazil in power surplus and the multilateral, represented in three empirical chapters: Brazil–US, Brazil–Mozambique and Brazil's multilateral ethanol diplomacy.

Process tracing based on primary-source research and expert interviews leads to the conclusion that the Brazilian foreign policy complex (FPC) failed to formulate and implement a coherent ethanol strategy. Ethanol diplomacy was never a top priority for Brazil's Ministry of Foreign Affairs, representing a lack of cohesion in the FPC. In international negotiations, Brazil has deficits in predicting its negotiating partners' preferences and therefore lacks the ability to form long-term alliances with converging interests, rather than merely convening disruptive ad hoc coalitions.

This study shows that Neoclassical Realism can combine foreign policy output with international politics outcome research and is useful to analyse policy outside the hard security realm. It offers a basis for further research towards an understanding of Brazil's overall foreign policy and the foreign policies of other emerging powers.

ACKNOWLEDGEMENTS

This book is based on my doctoral research that I concluded by submitting a version of this manuscript in August 2017. With the support of the team at Anthem and the insights of my anonymous reviewers, we managed to successfully conclude this fascinating project.

I would like to express my special appreciation and thanks to my PhD supervisors, Anthony Pereira, Jeff Garmany and Álvaro Comim, for their guidance, support and patience.

I gratefully acknowledge the support of a King's College Global Research Grant, a King's College London Small Research Bursary Award, a King's College London Study Abroad Student Award, a KCL PI Incentivisation Grant, an ESRC-funded postdoctoral fellowship (grant ref ES/T00892X/1), a visiting fellowship at the Fundação Getúlio Vargas in São Paulo and several King's Interdisciplinary Social Sciences Doctoral Training Centre travel and conference awards.

I highly appreciate the time and commitment of all my interviewees, in particular former foreign minister Celso Amorim; the former heads of renewable energy at Itamaraty, Claudia Santos and Emerson Kloss; Counsellor Joaquim Pedro Penna at the Brazilian Permanent Representation to the International Organisations in London; the Africa and Asia manager at Agência Brasileira de Cooperação, Paulo Roberto Barbosa Lima; the general coordinator for ethanol at the Brazilian Ministry for Mines and Energy Marlon, Arraes Jardim; the ethanol coordinator at the Brazilian Ministry of Agriculture, Cid Caldas; the former ethanol coordinator at the Brazilian Ministry of Agriculture, Alexandre Strapasson; the adviser at the Brazilian Ministry of Agriculture, Luis Job; the president of the International Sugar Organisation, José Orive; the former president of the International Sugar Organisation, Peter Baron; the chief economist of the International Sugar Organisation, Leonardo Rocha; the ethanol expert at the Inter-American Development Bank in Washington, DC, Arnaldo Vieira; experts from the US Department of Commerce, Maria Cameron, Braeden Young and Cora Dickinson; the executive director of the Brazil Industries Coalition in Washington, DC, Antonio Josino Meirelles; Laís

Thomaz and Dawn Alexandra Brown, who helped facilitate many interviews in Washington, DC; the president and CEO of UNICA (*União da Indústria de Cana-de-Açúcar* (Brazilian Sugarcane Industry Association)) in São Paulo, Elisabeth Farina; the head of international affairs and senior international adviser to the president of UNICA, Geraldine Kutas; the president of ED&F Man Brasil, S. A. Carlos Guimarães; the head of ethanol at ED&F Man Brasil, S. A. Eduardo Puertas; the president of bioagencia, Tarcilo Rodrigues; the sugar expert at bioagencia, Paulo Trucco; and all the other interviewees who donated their time and knowledge but asked to remain anonymous.

I would furthermore thank my friends in the Brazilian diplomatic service, Bruno Quadros e Quadros, Leonardo Azevedo and Rafael Prince; my friends at the Friedrich-Ebert-Foundation's offices in Latin America and Mozambique, Claudia Detsch, Thomas Manz and Tina Henneken; my friends and colleagues at *Fundação Getúlio Vargas* (Getulio Vargas Foundation), Oliver Stuenkel, Matias Spektor, Guilherme Casarões and Vinícius Rodrigues Vieira, who provided valuable insights for my understanding of Brazilian politics and foreign policy; and my friends and colleagues at UN Development Program International Policy Center for Inclusive Growth in Brasília who are too many to name.

I am grateful for the support of my friends and colleagues at King's Brazil Institute, Michael St Aldwyn and Vinicius Mariano de Carvalho, who facilitated a number of interviews.

A special thanks to my fellow PhD students at King's College London, who are a constant source of funspiration.

Finally, I would like to thank my family, Anja, Barbara, Werner, and Edith and John, without whose support in every life situation, I would not have been able to go through with this project.

Words cannot express how grateful I am to my partner, Nikki Shure, who encouraged me to take a risk and start this project and supported me with her sweat and tears. I owe this to you!

ABBREVIATIONS

ABBC	Advanced Biofuels Business Council (formerly Advanced Ethanol Council)
ABC	*Agência Brasileira de Cooperação* (Brazilian Cooperation Agency)
ABFA	Advanced Biofuels Association
ACORE	American Coalition on Renewable Fuels
ACP	African, Caribbean and Pacific Group of States
AmCham	American Chamber of Commerce
AMS	Aggregate Measure of Support (in the WTO system)
ANFAVEA	*Associação Nacional dos Fabricantes de Veículos Automotores* (Brazilian Automotive Association)
ANP	*Agência Nacional do Petróleo, Gás Natural e Biocombustíveis* (Brazilian National Agency of Petroleum, Natural Gas and Biofuels)
APEX-Brasil	*Agência Brasileira de Promoção de Exportações e Investimentos* (Brazilian Trade and Investment Promotion Agency)
ATACs	Agricultural Technical Advisory Committees
ATO	US Agricultural Trade Office
BIC	Brazil Industries Coalition
BNDES	*Banco Nacional de Desenvolvimento Econômico e Social* (Brazilian National Bank for Economic and Social Development)
BRDI	Biomass Research and Development Initiative
BRICS	group of countries including Brazil, Russia, India, China and, since 2010, South Africa
CAFTA	Central American Free Trade Agreement
CBI	Caribbean Basin Initiative
CCA	Consultative Committee on Agriculture between USDA and MAPA
CDM	Clean Development Mechanism
CEBEU	*Conselho Empresarial Brasil-Estados Unidos* (Brazil–US Business Council)
CEPAL	*La Comisión Económica para América Latina y el Caribe* (UN Economic Commission for Latin America and the Caribbean)

CFR	Council on Foreign Relations
Commerce	US Department of Commerce
CTESS	Committee on Trade and Environment in Special Session
DAC	Organisation for Economic Co-operation and Development's Development Assistance Committee
DoE	US Department of Energy
ECPA	Energy and Climate Partnership of the Americas
EERE	US Office of Energy Efficiency and Renewable Energy
EGA	Environmental Goods Agreement
EGS	Environmental Goods and Services
EIA	US Energy Information Agency
Embrapa	*Empresa Brasileira de Pesquisa Agropecuária* (Brazilian Agricultural Research Corporation)
EPA	US Environmental Protection Agency
EPP	environmentally preferable product
EWG	Environmental Working Group
FAO	Food and Agriculture Organization
FASE	*Federação de Órgãos para Assistência Social e Educacional* (Brazilian Federation of Organs for Social and Educational Assistance)
FFV	flex-fuel vehicles
FGV	*Fundação Getúlio Vargas* (Getulio Vargas Foundation)
FPA	foreign policy analysis
FPC	foreign policy complex
FPE	foreign policy executive
FTAA	Free Trade Agreement of the Americas
FUNAG	*Fundação Alexandre de Gusmão* (Foundation Alexandre de Gusmão, MRE's in-house think tank)
GBEP	Global Bioenergy Partnership
GHG	greenhouse gas
GMOs	genetically modified organisms
GPD	Global Partnership Dialogue
IBF	International Biofuels Forum
IBSA	India, Brazil, South Africa
IPE	international political economy
IR	international relations
ISO	International Sugar Organisation
ITA	US International Trade Administration
JICA	Japan International Cooperation Agency
LDC	Least Developed Countries Group
MAPA	*Ministério da Agricultura, Pecuária e Abastecimento* (Brazilian Ministry of Agriculture, Livestock and Supply)

MinAg	Mozambican Ministry of Agriculture
MinFaz	*Ministério da Fazenda* (Brazilian Ministry of Finance)
MMA	*Ministério do Meio Ambiente* (Brazilian Ministry for the Environment)
MME	*Ministerio de Minas e Energia* (Brazilian Ministry of Mines and Energy)
MoU	memorandum of understanding
MRE	*Ministério das Relações Exteriores Itamaraty* (Brazilian Ministry of Foreign Affairs)
MTBE	methyl tert-butyl ether
NAMA	non-agricultural market access negotiations at the World Trade Organization
NAMA-11	a group of 11 developing countries participating in non-agricultural market access negotiations at the World Trade Organization: Argentina, Venezuela, Brazil, Egypt, India, Indonesia, Namibia, Philippines, South Africa, Pakistan and Tunisia
NCR	Neoclassical Realism
NGO	non-governmental organisation
NPA	necessary points of analysis
NSA	US National Security Agency
ODI	Overseas Development Institute
OECD	Organisation for Economic Co-operation and Development
OEPNU	US Office of Energy Policy and New Uses
PDP	*Política de Desenvolvimento Produtivo* (Productive Development Policy)
Petrobras	*Petróleo Brasileiro S.A.* (Brazil's National Oil Company)
Proálcool	*Programa Nacional do Álcool* (National Program for Alcohol)
PRODECER	*Programa de Cooperação Nipo-Brasileira para o Desenvolvimento dos Cerrados* (Japanese development project in Brazil)
ProSavana	triangular co-operation programme for agricultural development of the tropical savannah in Mozambique
PT	*Partido dos Trabalhadores* (Workers' Party)
RFA	Renewable Fuels Association
RFS	Renewable Fuel Standard
SADC	Southern African Development Community
SDGs	sustainable development goals
SRB	Sociedade Rural Brasileira
TRIPS	Agreement on Trade-Related Aspects of Intellectual Property Rights
TRQ	tariff rate quota

UN	United Nations
UNASUR	Union of South American Nations
UNCED	UN Conference on Environment and Development
UNCSD	UN Conference on Sustainable Development
UNCTAD	UN Conference on Trade and Development
UNFCCC	UN Framework Convention on Climate Change
UNGA	UN General Assembly
UNICA	*União da Indústria de Cana-de-Açúcar* (Brazilian Sugarcane Industry Association)
UNSC	UN Security Council
UNSG	UN Secretary-General
USDA	US Department of Agriculture
WTO	World Trade Organization
WTO AoA	World Trade Organization's Agreement on Agriculture

INTRODUCTION

Brazilian ethanol has been a strategic energy commodity in the South American country since the 1970s. The efficiency of sugarcane-based ethanol and the abundance of its primary resource convinced the military leadership of the 1970s to use this commodity to supplement the national gasoline market and thereby decrease the dependency on international oil markets.

After the 2003 introduction of the flex fuel engine, a car engine that can run on any mixture of ethanol and gasoline, ethanol expanded its market reach and thereby increased its strategic value for Brazil's energy mix. The Brazilian government that came into power in 2003 under the presidency of Lula da Silva understood the implications of this rise in internal ethanol consumption and saw the international potential that sugarcane-based ethanol offered for Brazil.

For one thing, with a consumption rate that equalled that of gasoline in 2010 (about two billion litres), ethanol provided a suitable substitute for fossil fuels and decreased dependence on international oil markets; however, at the same time, it created a new dependence on domestic production capacities. As the world's largest producer of sugarcane-based ethanol, Brazil cannot count on an international market to supplement the consumption of domestic production in the case of low production caused by droughts, flooding or other unforeseeable events.

Hence, Brazil has been working towards creating an international market for ethanol that would both reduce Brazil's dependency on the internal market and leave the country in a position as the technological leader in an increasingly important economic sector. To achieve this, it is important to broaden the consumer base of ethanol as a fuel as well as to increase the number of producers internationally. Furthermore, ethanol lacks international standardisation, which is one of the main reasons why the World Trade Organization (WTO) has not yet specifically addressed the product.

Additionally, promoting ethanol internationally gave Brazil the opportunity to position itself at the pinnacle of the climate change discourse of the 2000s and develop strong ties, mainly with other developing nations, through new 'South–South cooperation' that has gained importance since the rise of the emerging markets and their turn to the 'Global South' in the early 2000s. The rise of South–South cooperation has laid the foundation for Brazil to convince other states from the Global South of the merits of sugar-based ethanol and broaden ethanol's consumer base.

Brazil has pursued the issue on several levels: the bilateral level (and trilateral level in development cooperation), en bloc – or regional level – within MercoSul, and the multilateral level within the WTO and other fora. All these state-sanctioned actions, whether carried out by the Brazilian diplomatic service, the presidency or other government agencies as well as the actions carried out internationally by the respective industrial corporations or their associations will be summarised under the term 'ethanol diplomacy'. Understanding the strategy and methods applied by the Brazilian government to this issue also helps to paint a broader picture of the Brazilian approach to foreign policy and to conceptualise it within the framework of international relations theory.

Despite the efforts undergone within the framework of ethanol diplomacy, Brazil has not achieved its explicit goal to create a global ethanol market in the two terms of the Lula government and the first term of the Dilma government. The research question therefore is: Why has Brazil failed to create a global ethanol market despite the beneficial international context?

To answer this question, I will bring together Brazil's multilevelled international ethanol strategy in one coherent analysis and apply the approach of Neoclassical Realism (NCR) to understand the way foreign policy decisions have come to play. This will be guided by the following sub-questions:

- What is Brazil's international ethanol strategy?
- How was Brazil's international ethanol strategy elaborated and by whom?
- Who are the central stakeholders within Brazil and abroad that are involved in the process of implementing Brazil's international ethanol strategy?
- What power relationships are at play within Brazil and towards its partners that influence the implementation of Brazil's international ethanol strategy?
- What are the turning points in Brazil's ethanol diplomacy and how did these happen?
- How can the processes and outcomes be explained within the realm of international relations theory?

Hypotheses

This study will apply a Neoclassical Realist approach of foreign policy analysis (FPA) to answer these research questions. The analysis will be guided by the following hypotheses, which may be deducted from the main strands of international relations theory (Table 1).

How these hypotheses were derived and why the Neoclassical Realist approach to FPA seems most appropriate for the case at hand will be discussed later in the section on the theoretical framework.

NCR enhances the structural (neo-)Realist argument that international constraints shape foreign policy with the understanding that sub-state actors influence the way the international context is understood and to how it is reacted (modelled as an intervening variable). The study will follow a case study design with three empirical chapters (Brazil–United States, Brazil–Mozambique and Brazil's multilateral ethanol diplomacy) that analyse the critical junctures of each of the examples at hand according to George and Bennett's (2005) approach to theory-guided process tracing.

Background: A Brief History of Ethanol in Brazil

With its vast arable land and its history of sugarcane cultivation, Brazil entered the production of ethanol as a fuel before World War II. It was not, however, until the oil crisis of 1973 that Brazil started to fully take advantage of this resource.

In 1975, the military government introduced the National Program for Alcohol (Programa Nacional do Álcool – 'Proálcool') which had four explicit goals: first, to even out the trade balance by reducing the demand for fossil fuel imports; secondly, to create agricultural income in underdeveloped areas of the country; thirdly, to create growth by increasing the use of agricultural land and labour; and finally, to increase the demand for technological products in the sector (Hira and de Oliveira 2009: 2452).

The four main political tools of Proálcool, which enabled Brazil to pursue these goals, were: the guaranteed purchase of ethanol by Brazil's national oil company Petrobras, low-interest loans for ethanol producers, a price control for the consumer market and a production quota as well as export controls for sugar (Hira and de Oliveira 2009: 2452).

Puppim de Oliveira analyses the formation of these policies with the concepts of 'interests, values and knowledge'. Surprisingly, he portrays this policy as a 'result of interest groups in an appropriate occasion' – an implicit description of a bottom-up policy-making process (2002: 137). However, it becomes clear in the study that the reference point for all decisions was indeed

Table 1 Hypotheses

	Classical Realism	**Liberalism**	**Constructivism**	**Neoclassical Realism**
General Hypothesis	Structural environment causes political outcomes	Actors' preferences and the decision-making process cause political outcomes	Actors' attitudes and values create a cooperative environment for political outcomes	Structural pressures are the main driver for political outcomes and the interpretation of those by the foreign policy complex (FPC) defines political output
Case Study 1: Brazil–United States	In a structurally subordinated position, Brazil is not able to reach its goals in the negotiations	The preferences of Brazilian and US political actors do not align, and the negotiation process gives them too much veto power	The epistemic communities in both countries cannot overcome the differences in values, especially in terms of the corn- vs. sugar-based ethanol question, and cannot reach agreement in terms of renewable energy preferences	The Brazilian FPC underestimates the power gap between the two countries and therefore cannot prepare an adequate negotiation strategy to achieve their goals
Case Study 2: Brazil–Mozambique	Brazil is structurally in a better position than Mozambique and can achieve most of its demands	The preferences of political actors from Brazil and Mozambique do not align, and the negotiation process gives them too much veto power	Brazil's epistemic community is not able to understand the values and ideas of their counterpart from Mozambique, which results in suboptimal negotiation results	The Brazilian FPC is able to reach an agreement with their Mozambican counterpart but does not take into account the domestic pressures that will result from the elite decision in Mozambique
Case Study 3: Brazil's multilateral ethanol diplomacy	Brazil achieves an alliance to counter the traditional hegemon but struggles to advance an agenda that goes beyond balancing	The interests of the participants in the negotiations do not align, especially in terms of preference order between market protection and opening of the economies, and due to the high number of veto points, no agreement can be reached	Brazil's epistemic community is partially able to convince enough states to stop the traditional ideological course of the WTO, but cannot succeed in creating new values for the further trajectory of the organisation	Multilateral negotiations with their complex power architecture are structurally prone to failure. The Brazilian FPC manages to successfully adjust the agenda and block an agreement that would have been unfavourable to the country, yet they fail to create a constructive alliance within the WTO and other fora

the military government and its genuine interests, values and knowledge, which unintentionally makes the case for a top-down policy-making process – a fact that is important to keep in mind when putting ethanol diplomacy in an international relations context. To anticipate the theoretical understanding of the matter at hand, NCR seems to fit both the assumption that the international context defines political options to a great extent and the understanding that national stakeholders can influence decision making to a certain degree (modelled as an intervening variable).

Hira and de Olivera (2009: 2453) call the years between 1979 and 1985 the 'honeymoon phase' of Proálcool. After the second oil crisis in 1979, the decision of the military government to focus on fossil fuel substitution proved right. The automotive industry started manufacturing alcohol-fuelled cars, which in December 1980 accounted for over 70 per cent of new cars sold (Hira and de Oliveira 2009: 2453). The mandatory blend remained above 20 per cent (Goldemberg 2013: 17), so by the mid-1980s ethanol accounted for about 50 per cent of Brazil's liquid fuel supply (Sandalow 2006: 2).

After the drop in oil prices and the increase in sugar prices in the late 1980s, however, the situation changed; the government phased out subsidies and gradually opened up the sugar market (Hira and de Oliveira 2009: 2454; Goldemberg 2013: 18). In 1990, the sale of alcohol-fuelled cars dropped by almost 80 per cent (Hira and de Oliveira 2009: 2455) due to the shortage of 'appropriate' fuel (Goldemberg 2013: 18).

The 1990s were characterised by low oil prices and market deregulation. By 1999, the Brazilian government had deregulated sugarcane, ethanol – including the expensive guaranteed purchase by Petrobras, and gasoline prices (Hira and de Oliveira 2009: 2454), which resulted in a comparative disadvantage for ethanol.

This brief history of ethanol in Brazil demonstrates how the international context, and in particular the exogenous shock of the oil crisis, prompted the military government to adjust its domestic policy and install a regime to support the domestic ethanol industry. The decision to diversify the energy mix towards ethanol was based on the existing knowledge and interests of national stakeholders, which helped to shape the direction of the reorientation of the official policy.

Background: The Comeback of Ethanol in Brazil

In 2003, driven by tax incentives of the Brazilian government (Hira and de Oliveira 2009: 2454), the automotive industry presented the first cars that could run on any blend of gasoline and ethanol, so-called flex-fuel vehicles (FFV). The high oil prices of the time facilitated the acceptance

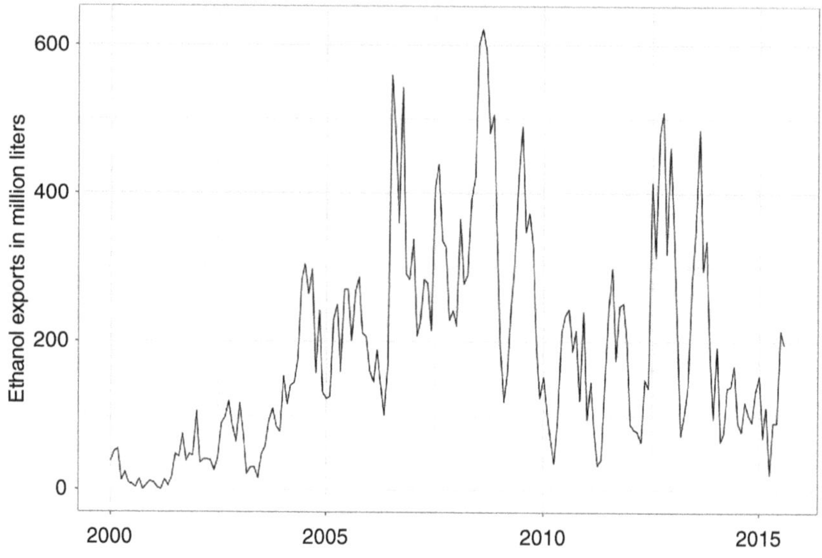

Figure 1 Brazilian ethanol exports, 2000–15 (*Source*: UNICA (2015)).

of FFV by consumers, and by 2005, the numbers of FFV sold surpassed the combined numbers of gasoline- and alcohol-fuelled cars (Hira and de Oliveira 2009: 2455). According to the Brazilian Automotive Association – ANFAVEA – , FFV accounted for 87 per cent of new cars sold as of January 2013, a number which had been fairly constant since the beginning of 2006 (see Joseph 2013: 13). This trend will increase the share of FFV in the Brazilian automobile fleet, which was at about 60 per cent in 2011 (2013: 5), and reflects the consumer side of the internal ethanol market. It is noteworthy that the increase in FFV accounts for the growth of the ethanol industry, while the ethanol/gasoline blend of over 20 per cent guarantees a constant minimum demand for the industry. In the 2012–13 farming season, Brazil produced 23.2 billion litres of ethanol, of which 19.7 billion litres were dedicated to domestic consumption and 3.5 billion litres to export (UNICA 2013: 17). FFV have clearly played a major role in the comeback of ethanol as a crucial commodity in the Brazilian energy mix (Figure 1).

Background: The International Environment

In many ways, the international environment has been highly favourable for the development of an international biofuels market. This is due to the combination of the market's nascent state coupled with increasing demand for biofuels, which creates large growth potential and high returns for the countries that invest early.

Internationally, the market for ethanol is underdeveloped. According to the Renewable Fuels Association, in 2013, the three biggest producers of fuel ethanol were the United States (59 billion litres), Brazil (28.5 billion litres) and the European Union (6.2 billion litres), followed by China (3.2 billion litres), India (2.5 billion litres) and Canada (2.4 billion litres), each of them producing only slightly less than the rest of the world combined (3.3 billion litres). There is room for growth, and as the second largest producer, Brazil, could capitalise quite a lot on this, hence the Brazilian government's focus on ethanol diplomacy.

The market also shows promise due to the growing importance of three major global themes: climate change, energy security in an era of rising oil prices and the emancipation of the Global South, including the new era of South–South cooperation. In the following paragraphs, I will discuss each of these trends in detail and show how they have helped to foster a positive environment for the development of an international biofuels market (Figure 2).

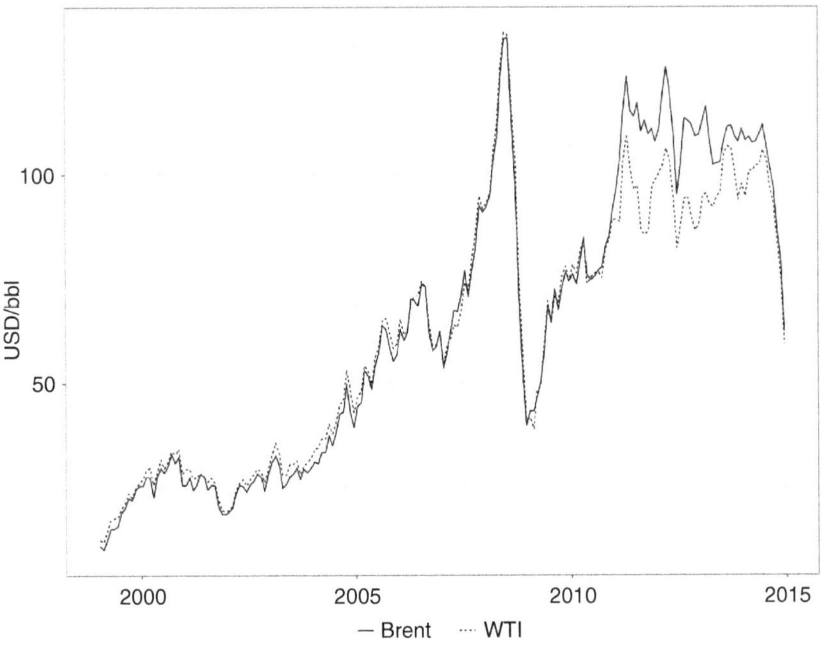

Figure 2 Spot oil prices, 2000–15 (*Source*: US Energy Information Agency (2016)).

Climate Change

Since the 1992 United Nations 'Conference on Environment and Development' (UNCED) – also known as the Rio Earth Summit – the question of global warming and climate change caused by humans has been on the international agenda. UNCED produced two documents that influence the framework in which Brazil's ethanol diplomacy is embedded: Agenda 21, a non-binding document outlining a plan for sustainable development, and more importantly, the Rio Declaration on Environment and Development, which describes the principles of sustainable development. Particularly relevant for Brazilian foreign policy are Principles 2–5 (state sovereignty, the right to development, environmental protection as an integral part of the development process and the eradication of poverty as a requirement for sustainable development). President Lula continuously referred to those principles on his missions abroad, for example, at his first speech before the UN General Assembly 2003, when he demanded

> leadership [...] in guiding the political process towards the restoration of Iraqi sovereignty, as soon as possible [because] peace, security, development and social justice are indivisible. (Lula UN General Assembly Speech, 23 September 2003)

and further that

> [trade] liberalisation should not require countries to abandon the prerogative of formulating industrial, technological, social and environmental policy. [...] From this standpoint, trade negotiations are not an end in themselves, but rather a means to foster development and overcome poverty [when] hunger is an emergency and should be dealt with as such. (Lula UN General Assembly Speech, 23 September 2003)

This is coherent with one of the continuities in Brazilian foreign policy, the strife for autonomy. Silva (2013: 23; following Vigevani e Cepaluni (2007)) outlines the idea that Brazil has been seeking autonomy in its foreign policy since the times of the military government, be it through distance from the United States (*autonomia pela distância*) in the beginning, later under President Cardoso through integration into the world economy (*autonomia pela integração*) and then under Lula through diversification of its foreign relations (*autonomia pela diversificação*).

The third outcome of UNCED that is relevant to this topic was the opening of discussions on the UN Framework Convention on Climate Change, which resulted in the so-called Kyoto Protocol to reduce greenhouse gas (GHG) emissions. One major innovation that the Kyoto Protocol introduced is Article 12, the 'Clean Development Mechanism' (CDM), a flexibility mechanism which allows developed countries to offset their GHG quota with investments in sustainable development projects for GHG reduction in developing countries (Wittger 2010: 8). Brazil, in this context, is not part of Annex 1, the list of signatory states that are defined as developed, and it does not come as a surprise that the first registered CDM project was based in Brazil (2010: 34) and that Brazil continues to take advantage of this framework. In 2010, Brazil was the country with the third largest number of CDM projects after China and India (2010: 35), and this experience helps Brazil promote ethanol-related projects in developing countries within the CDM. It is important to point out, though, that not many ethanol-related CDM projects – such as the Africa Ethanol Stove Program – have been realised due to the complexity of the certification process (Atkinson 2004: 3); therefore, CDM is primarily used as a narrative to open doors for Brazil to other developing markets, but not actually implemented.

The discussion on climate change reached a peak between 2007 and 2009, when the UN Security Council (UNSC) initially discussed the nexus between climate change and security in 2007, and in 2009, when the UN General Assembly (UNGA) demanded a concise report of climate change and security from the UN Secretary-General (UNSG), which was then presented in September 2009 as Document A/64/350 (Adriázola et al. 2013: 16). With this, the connection between climate change and international security was established and Brazil was able to add its idea of a renewable energy policy to the discussion leading up to the 2012 United Nations Conference on Sustainable Development in Rio de Janeiro (also known as 'Rio +20'). The main outcome of Rio +20 was the working document 'The Future We Want', which established the global community's commitment to develop sustainable means of energy generation and transport, including the phase-out of fossil fuel subsidies (UN 2012: 29). The document also reaffirmed the need to combat climate change and put this in the context of global food security – a criticism that has been raised towards the Brazilian ethanol program and biofuels in general through the 'food vs. fuel' debate; however, Brazil continuously rejects this criticism with respect to its own experience (Salifu and Masters 2011: 6) where plantations for biofuels do not directly compete with plantations for food. This issue needs to be taken more seriously, however, in the African context.

Another criticism that Brazil has had to face is deforestation in the Amazon, which according to some authors is indirectly caused by the expansion of sugarcane plantations (Vieira 2012: 28). While representatives of the sugarcane industry (UNICA 2013: 8) argue that sugarcane occupies only 1 per cent of Brazil's land, other authors argue that while sugarcane does not directly contribute to deforestation, it might cause livestock to move further towards the Amazon and thereby expand the agricultural frontier (Rodrigues de Castro et al. 2012). Even though the case is not clear-cut and experts do not share a common point of view on the issue, the Brazilian government needs to address these questions in a global context, especially when promoting sugar-based ethanol abroad and in countries where food security is of high concern. The same accounts for the question of food security as raised by authors like Procópio (2007). While this does not constitute a pressing problem in Brazil, especially African countries might be more vary about the distribution of agricultural production between food and fuel. The outcome of these discussions on a global scale reflects Brazil's soft power as well as its ability to shape international discourses. Medeiros (2010: 145) suggests that the main task of Itamaraty in this issue is to 'desmistificar as informações em relação ao etanol'.[1]

With these questions in mind, Brazil continues to advocate for biofuels and sees its achievements in the global climate change debate as a diplomatic victory (Mello and Toni 2013: 16) that combined a traditional emphasis on sovereignty and a more Liberal position that favoured collective solutions to sustainability (Vieira 2012: 30). Brazil is continuously trying to capitalise on this leadership position.

Climate Change and Energy Security

Brazil successfully managed to embed the question of climate change and sustainability into the discourse about energy security, partially due to strong national stakeholders, in order to increase the country's leverage in international politics (Vieira and Dalgaard 2013: 612). During the period of rising oil prices coinciding with the first Lula government in 2003 and structural insecurities in oil-producing countries, it was opportune for Brazil to connect ethanol with a more secure diversification of energy resources to comply with the two main factors of energy security, availability and reliability (Vieira and Dalgaard 2013: 612), not only domestically but also on the international level.

The connection between security and climate change becomes clear when analysing the elite discourses in major economies, even though many countries still view these issues as quite separate (Toke and Vezirgiannidou 2013: 547). Brazil has supported the creation of the Energy and Climate Partnership of the Americas (ECPA) at the 2012 Summit of the Americas in Cartagena and promoted this institutional linkage between the two issues on a regional level within and through the Union of South American Nations (UNASUR) (O'Keefe and Negroponte 2012: 45). The fact that energy security

1. "demystify the information regarding ethanol" (author's own translation).

is of strategic concern for the definition of most countries' foreign policies underlines the importance of climate change for national strategies on top of the immediate concern of damages caused by adverse weather or social costs caused by climate migration. It proves the point that divestment from climate change causing technologies and carbon fuels is more than an ecologic concern but lies at the centre of national strategic planning.

Brazil has successfully raised awareness about these issues in international fora. However, the output of concrete policy measures by such fora is low, and while climate change is being addressed multilaterally, energy security seems to remain the remit of the national governments (O'Keefe and Negroponte 2012: 54). If energy security is defined three-dimensionally, as suggested by Vieira and Dalgaard (2013: 612) through the factors of availability, reliability and sustainability, even Brazil focuses less on sustainability when the exploration of pre-salt oil fields receives more investment than the other two pillars of its national energy strategy: hydro- and bioenergy (Vieira and Dalgaard 2013: 615). Hence, Brazil faces a dilemma and to a certain extent a crisis of credibility when its investments are mainly geared towards fossil fuels even if it maintains a high degree of renewables in its energy mix. On the one hand, Brazil managed to connect climate change and energy security within the narratives of international fora; on the other hand, it cannot adhere to this high and hard-to-achieve standard. Brazil focuses on narratives of solidarity when dealing with countries from the Global South, but it is unclear where this new South–South cooperation will lead (Figure 3).

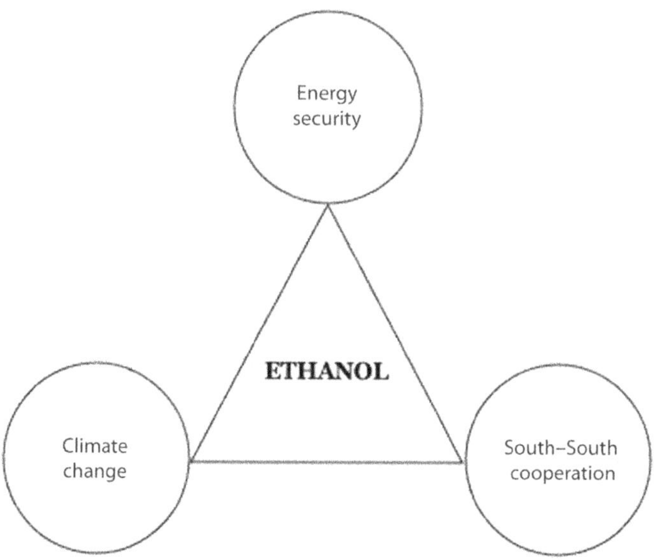

Figure 3 Ethanol at the centre of international discourses (*Source*: Author's own).

South–South Cooperation

South–South cooperation between countries in the Global South, or developing countries, dates back to at least 1978, when the UN Office for South–South Cooperation was founded. However, the term gained relevance at the beginning of the 21st century with the establishment of the term 'BRICS group' (Brazil, Russia, India, China, and since 2010 South Africa), first as a description of strong economies from the Global South, then after the institutionalisation of the group in 2008 and recently with the creation of the BRICS development bank. The creation of the bank has manifested the existence of a new structure of donors in international cooperation and development.

In addition to the budget provided for investment by the BRICS bank, direct investment and cooperation between these emerging markets and developing countries are on the rise (Burges 2012: 229), as is trade between these countries. Since 2008–9, the South has been exporting more to the South than to the North (UNCTAD 2013), mainly due to the extraordinary growth of China. Both China and India now comprise large internal markets for production and consumption of goods. This increased trade volume shows that the new form of South–South cooperation puts a central focus on trade as opposed to the more traditional forms of development aid.

Thanks to the increased importance of trade and the resulting economic growth, the BRICS countries are now mostly classified as 'upper middle-income countries' or 'high income country' in the case of Russia, with the exception of India, which still counts as a 'low middle-income country', according to the World Bank's Development Indicators (2015). This has enabled them to open the channels of development aid to other countries as part of South–South cooperation. The question that has been raised by many researchers is whether these new donors act differently from the traditional donors (Lechini 2012; Alden and Vieira 2005; Tiburcia and Lira 2010; Romano-Schutte 2012; Sotero 2009; Rodriguez 2014; Stolte and de la Fontaine 2012). While interests might be the same as of traditional donors, Burges (2012: 228) outlines two differences that characterise South–South cooperation. First, since it is mainly carried out directly by the respective governments, the cost is lower than in traditional cooperation work. Secondly, the discourse of solidarity with an 'idea of collective advancement' serves domestic political interests and facilitates access to developing markets.

After a relatively isolationist period in the 1980s that was followed by a period of orientation towards the North in the 1990s, President Lula changed direction and oriented the country towards increased South–South cooperation. While this process had started under Lula's predecessor, Fernando Henrique Cardoso, due to systemic changes, as Rodrigues Vieira (2014) argues, the Lula government understood South–South cooperation as a political strategy. This was due to the political program of his Workers' Party, but also due to the lack of opportunities to further elaborate ties with the North, especially within the framework of trade (Ondetti and Rhodes 2010: 7).

Within the South–South framework, Brazil supports other developing countries through its own development agency (Agência Brasileira de Cooperação – ABC) and through credit lines by the national development bank BNDES. The fact that ABC forms part of the Ministry of Foreign Affairs (MRE) underlines the strategic use of development cooperation by the Brazilian government. Even though ABC has risen from the third-tier administrative unit subordinated to the Fundação Alexandre de Gusmão (FUNAG) – MRE's in-house think tank – at the time of its founding, to departmental status within the MRE, ABC cannot claim independence or pursue projects outside of MRE's strategic interests. In this respect, Brazil models its policies after the United States, Canada and Russia, contrasting the European trend to give more autonomy to national development agencies (e.g. France, Germany, Sweden).

Both, the budget of ABC and the activity in foreign investment by BNDES have constantly been increasing throughout the two Lula presidencies until the first half of the Dilma presidency with a greater focus on South–South cooperation. However, ABC pursues an additional method of implementing technical cooperation, through so-called trilateral cooperation. This mode of cooperation combines North–South and South–South cooperation. It includes one of the traditional donors from the Organisation for Economic Cooperation and Development's (OECD) Development Assistance Committee (DAC) or another international organisation, a technical partner from the emerging donor countries in the South and a less-developed beneficiary country from the South (Ashoff 2010: 23).

The main argument in favour of trilateral cooperation is that the assistance from a traditional donor can leverage the effects of South–South cooperation. However, there are risks involved, such as the decrease of procedural standards, an increase in transaction costs and the possibility of neglecting the needs of the beneficiary due to the interests of the other two, stronger partners (Ashoff 2010: 24). According to the ABC website, at its peak in November 2014, Brazil was engaged in 23 trilateral projects with international organisations as partners and in 21 trilateral projects with donor countries from the North as partners, among them projects with Mozambique, including the ProSavana program (with Japan), which will be subject to a deeper investigation later in this study.

It becomes clear that Brazil's international ethanol strategy cannot be understood without the national experience of the successful substitution away from gasoline as an energy source or without the international context that raised awareness for alternatives to fossil fuels due to the climate change debate, the strategic considerations of future energy security in times of high oil prices and the new instruments of South–South and trilateral cooperation.

To understand how and why Brazil failed at creating an international market for ethanol despite the beneficial structural conditions – the questions of energy security, climate change, new South–South cooperation – requires the assessment of how actors such as the president, Itamaraty and the Brazilian Sugarcane Industry Association (União da Indústria de Cana-de-Açúcar – UNICA) developed their preferences and intermediate goals with regard to the international ethanol market and how those were transformed into policy.

The following chapter will elaborate a theoretical framework for understanding the actions of states in International Relations.

Chapter 1

THEORETICAL FRAMEWORK

Introduction: How to Explain State Behaviour in International Relations?

How can we understand and conceptualise processes, actions, outputs and outcomes within international relations (IR)? Two paradigms have dominated how scholars have approached this question in the past: political Realism and the idea of Liberalism (with the constructivist idea gaining momentum since the 1990s). There is still debate about the number of ideas in IR theory, for example, Legro and Moravcsik count 'at least three paradigmatic alternatives' to Realism (1999: 10). One approach to understand the differences and the different usages of the theoretical approaches is to look at the variables under consideration in each strain of thought.

Rose (1998: 146) argues that the main difference in explaining state behaviour lies in the dichotomy between Realist approaches that see international pressures and structures as the driving force in international politics, whereas 'Innenpolitik' approaches like Liberalism and Constructivism focus on domestic pressures. Sterling-Folker (1997) identifies the difference between environment-based Realist approaches and process-based Liberal approaches. While the assessment of the Realist approach coincides with Rose's, her focus on process is not necessarily confined to domestic politics, but can rather be applied to international organisations and institutions as well. Legro and Moravcsik, on the other hand, equally claim that the central variable defines the respective paradigm in IR theory. 'Power, preferences, beliefs, and information [...] correspond to the four major categories of modern rationalist International Relations theory, namely realist, liberal, epistemic, and institutionalist theories' (1999: 46–47).

Taking a step back from this theoretical discussion, what are the problems we are trying to analyse using these approaches? The main questions raised by the two dominant schools of thought are how states act in the international arena and what their motives are. Or to simply put it in Moravcsik's (1992) words, 'to explain what states do.' Deducted from these general considerations, the question of war, peace and security is dominant in the literature – indeed it has been a driving force of the normative ideas behind Liberalism – and has been extended by the question of how cooperation in IR works and what role do norms and institutions play.

New forms of coordination between states, international organisations and non-state actors have increasingly become subjects of research within the concept of governance (e.g. Rosenau/Czempiel 1992), but the results in huge parts can be subsumed within the classical paradigms or their adaptations. The increasing complexity of the world requires different, less-purist and more-inclusive theoretical approaches than ever before. Slaughter (1995: 731) warns of 'artificial' analyses when pressing real-world events into mono-theoretic corsets, because 'the actual international system naturally contains Realist, Institutionalist, and Liberal elements [and] state behaviour is the product of a complex web of factors'.

The most suitable approach to answering these questions is the recently developed framework of NCR. This particular school of thought within Realism considers the main aspects of the aforementioned theoretical approaches and therefore seems most appropriate to explain why Brazil has so far failed to implement an international ethanol market.

Neoclassical Realism

This particular strain of Realism evolved after the end of the Cold War, when more detailed insight into the unit level seemed appropriate to initially explain only specific foreign policies but was later developed into a theory of international politics. The term 'Neoclassical Realism' was coined by Rose (1998) in a review essay in which he identified a shift away from the purely structural perspective of the Neorealism of the 1970s/80s to an increasing interest in domestic factors to explain 'the behaviour of individual states' (1998: 145). This branch of Realism explicitly includes internal and external factors to properly explain the foreign policy outputs of states (1998: 146). While structural Realists focus merely on states seeking security, Neoclassical Realists assume that states strive to expand their ability to influence their environment irrespective of their concrete interests and how these came about (1998: 152). These structural aspects form the first pillar (the independent variable) of NCR, and the way decision-makers interpret external pressures forms the second pillar (unit-level intervening variable), so that in the 'Neoclassical Realist world leaders can be constrained by both international and domestic politics' (1998: 152). The following paragraphs outline the development of NCR from a second-image theory of foreign policy to a fully-fledged theory of international politics by presenting the main steps and thinkers for the development of this theoretical approach. This section will be concluded by the role of the intervening variable in NCR and the usefulness of the approach to explain Brazil's international ethanol strategy.

A Neoclassical Realist Theory of Foreign Policy

In 1998, Rose coined the term 'Neoclassical Realism', but it took until 2009, when Norrin Ripsman, Jeffrey Taliaferro and Steven Lobell published a first collection of NCR research into foreign policy, that an attempt was made to coherently organise this stream of research and to map its unique contributions to previous Realist works as well as to differentiate it from Liberal and Constructivist approaches. At that point, Ripsman et al. (2009: 3–4, 10) are still humble about the reach of NCR and only propose it as a collection of theories to explain foreign policy changes and decisions. In their view, NCR 'seeks to explain variation in the foreign policies of the same state over time or across different states facing similar external constraints [...] [and] makes no pretense about explaining broad patterns of systemic or recurring outcomes' (2009: 21). The goal is to offer solutions to the shortcomings of exclusively structural approaches while maintaining the criticism of solely actor-focused approaches that deny an autonomous role of the state (2009: 298). In their volume, the authors collected a number of articles that cover threat assessment, strategic adjustment and questions regarding resource extraction, domestic mobilisation and policy implementation (2009: 31). In the volume, the authors put particular emphasis on the question of clarity in the international context and what that means for the impact of the domestic-level intervening variable. When there is a clear threat, there is less domestic inference, the same as when there is a broader perception of instability, while 'in contrast, when the security environment is more stable, domestic interests have greater latitude to shape the content of foreign policy' (2009: 286). The contributions of Lobell (2009), Brawley (2009b) and Sterling-Folker (2009) focus on threat assessment and how the perception of the international system by the foreign policy executive (FPE) can shape policy decisions depending on who is involved in decision-making (Lobell 2009: 73), what domestic situation the decision-makers face (Brawley 2009b: 97–98) and how identity can shape strategic decisions (Sterling-Folker 2009: 114–115). These three authors focus on what can be understood as a constructivist element of the intervening variable: ideas and perceptions. The contributions of Dueck (2009) and Ripsman (2009), on the other hand, put an institutionalist element into the analysis by examining how domestic set-ups and interest groups shape strategic decision making. While Dueck refines the understanding of the tension between the FPE's strategic view of the national interest and the personal interests of influential domestic stakeholders (2009: 145), Ripsman (2009: 177, 185) claims that democratically organised states impede the FPE's autonomy as opposed to autocratic states since democratic leaders depend on the vote-mobilising ability of collective societal actors. The contributions of Taliaferro (2009) and Schweller (2009) focus on the question of domestic resource mobilisation, which essentially is a qualification of the concept of power. Taliaferro (2009: 213) develops a resource-extraction model, where the 'level of external threat or vulnerability is the independent variable [...], the intervening variable is state power [and] the dependent variable is the variation in the types and intensity of the adaptive strategies the state will pursue'. This enables the researcher to account for strategic decisions unforeseen by purely structural approaches. Schweller (2009: 227, 249) presents a provocative position where he attributes ideal resource mobilisation capacity to monarchies from the 16th century until the Napoleonic era and fascist regimes in the early 20th century. While his argument might be seen critically, Schweller makes the valid point that political life has changed with mass politics and media. Leaders can no longer afford to float above the people and make elite decisions, a crucial insight and justification for the deployment of domestic variables in Realist analyses.

With their volume, Ripsman et al. (2009) inspired a wave of IR studies that followed the principles of NCR. The following sections will present the main thinkers behind these studies.

A Wave of NCR Research

The main works dealing with NCR in one way or another can be classified into three categories: (1) works that locate NCR within the spectrum of IR theories, (2) works that introduce new or refine existing intervening variables and (3) works that develop new strategies or international patterns based on NCR analysis.

In the first category, we find Adam Quinn and Tudor Onea. Quinn approaches the debate whether NCR deserves to be classified as a research paradigm per se from a theoretical perspective. He comes to the conclusion that 'neoclassical realists could argue that these divergences between systemic imperatives and state behaviour are not merely anomalous occurrences, but rather are regular, consistent and lasting patterns of state behaviour' (Quinn 2013: 160), which justifies NCR's positioning as a separate rather than a complementing theory to Neorealism. Berenskoetter and Quinn (2012: 216) therefore argue that soft power 'phenomena' should be incorporated into a Neoclassical Realist theory of international politics. With this claim, Quinn (2014: 253) argues to overcome the 'failures of insight' of Neorealism by reintroducing classical Realist categories of inquiry into a more positivist research agenda. In a very useful essay, Onea classifies Neoclassical Realist research streams in 'orthodox', 'semi-orthodox' and 'revivalism,' where the first merely aims to 'refine, not refute Waltz' (2012: 143), the second understands NCR as a theory to explain anomalies in structural Realist theories (2012: 144) and the third 'emphasizes the role of international interactions in shaping foreign policy' (2012: 155). Onea (2014) furthermore introduces the category of international status and a new understanding of prestige into NCR research through the examples of the *American Empire* (2009) and the *US Foreign Policy after the Cold War* (2013). His work can therefore be seen as covering categories 1 and 2. In addition to Onea, the second category encompasses the works of Dueck and Brawley. Besides his contribution to the Ripsman et al. (2009) volume, Colin Dueck (2004, 2005) explained US strategic decisions with ideas and strategic culture. Brawley (2009a: 3) developed an NCR model based on principles of political economy that combines the distribution of power in the system, the time horizon for responding to a threat and the rate at which domestic economic resources can be converted into military power. The main representative of the third category is Victor Cha (1997, 2000, 2009) who examines US alliance building in Asia and develops a 'quasi-alliance model' (2000) and the concept of 'powerplay' (2009). Cha (1997: 620) first pointed out coordination issues in the Asian security arrangement after World War II, which ultimately lead him to introduce the concept of a quasi-alliance 'as the relationship between two states that are un-allied but share a third great power patron as a common ally' (2000: 262). From the perspective of that patron, Cha (2009: 158) describes that strategy as powerplay, 'the construction of an asymmetric alliance designed to exert maximum control over the smaller ally's actions'. Shiping Tang's contribution is threefold and therefore represented in all three categories. He takes stock of current developments in NCR theory development (Tang 2009a) and also further adjusts Realist concepts within an NCR framework, like the security dilemma (2009b), defensive Realism (2010), offence–defence theory (2008b) as well as fear (2008a) and reputation (2006) as intervening variables in the analysis of international politics. Tang convincingly refuted the established notions of reputation, fear and the offence–defence balance while making the case that the world fundamentally changed in the second half of the 20th century, which makes offensive Realism obsolete, and the new security dilemma, including nuclear threats and international institutions, can only be accounted for by means of defensive Realist approaches. As Tang (2008a: 468) puts it, 'Offensive realism's stand was the right stand for a bygone era of offensive realism world, whereas non-offensive realism stand is the right stand for the present defensive realism world, although a more-or-less rule-based future may already be in the making'.

A Neoclassical Realist Theory of International Politics

After roughly two decades when NCR was seen as a useful approach towards explaining foreign policy either as a refinement of Waltz' structural Realism or as an appropriate way of explaining outlier cases, and even as its own approach, Norrin Ripsman, Jeffrey Taliaferro and Steven Lobell elevated NCR from a second-image theory to the level of third-image theory with the publication of their book *Neoclassical Realist Theory of International Politics* in 2016. Based on previous empirical work, the authors mainly engage in a theoretical discourse about the need for a more granular yet sufficiently parsimonious theory of international politics than structural Realism offered. They elaborate a coherent framework covering the delimitation from other Realist (structural) and Liberal and Constructivist (*Innenpolitik*) approaches; the definition of independent, intervening and dependent variables; as well as questions of NCR methodology, its contribution to IR research so far and the set-up of a future NCR research agenda.

Motivated by the lack of explanatory power in IR of purely structural and purely domestic approaches, the authors (Ripsman et al. 2016: 5) locate the vast majority of research cases in IR at a level where causes are 'primarily systemic but moderated by domestic-level intervening variables'. The concrete limitations of structural Realism that can be overcome by NCR are problems of perception by leaders, the lack of clarity of the international system, the problem of leaders' rationality as well as resource extraction and mobilisation (2016: 20).

In a typically Realist manner, the authors identify the system structure (anarchy, power relations) and system modifiers (e.g. geography, hierarchy, clarity) as independent variables that set the parameters for states' actions (Ripsman et al. 2016: 56–57). The influence of these systemic stimuli is subsequently determined by domestic-level intervening variables. Due to the prominent position of the intervening variable in NCR, a separate paragraph will address its meaning in the theoretical approach as well as in the concrete empirical case of Brazil's international ethanol strategy. The dependent variable, finally, is essentially defined by the researcher. The dependent variable can reach from foreign policy choices to international outcomes (2016: 80). As foreign policy choices have important and decisive effects on the international outcomes and structure, Ripsman et al. (2016: 81) reject Waltz's strict separation between the two levels. The appropriateness of the dependent variable depends to a large extent on the number of cases and the timeframe under examination. The authors are clear that NCR is a useful and appropriate approach to explain particular outputs and outcomes but rather 'an inefficient explanation of recurring patterns, such as why wars occur in general'

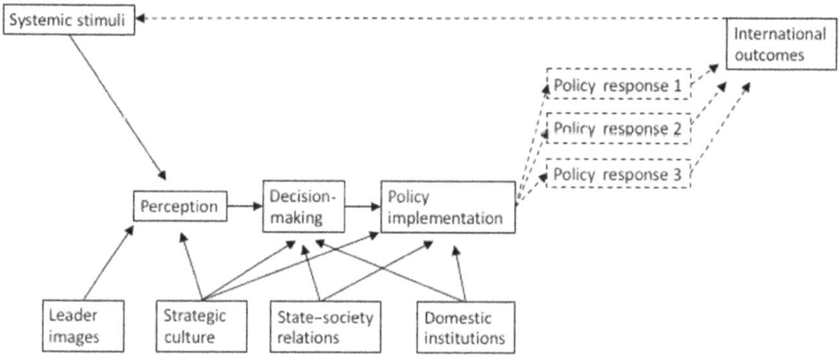

Figure 4 Neoclassical Realist model of international politics (*Source*: Ripsman et al. (2016: 34)).

(2016: 96). The authors subsequently give examples of theoretical debates where NCR could offer new insights. These include a more sophisticated understanding of the balancing versus bandwagoning debate (2016: 142–46) where states actually decide based on anticipated shifts in the international power distribution and follow their ability to mobilise domestically. NCR can also add to the question of hegemony: whether it is more stable than other set-ups in the international system or whether it leads to balancing. The insight that NCR can offer is that not every hegemon is perceived the same and that the domestic set-up of the hegemon influences their expansionary aspirations and hence the stability of a unipolar system (2016: 150–52). With particular relevance for this study, the authors (2016: 153–56) also included an assessment of international trade as one significant contribution of NCR to the understanding of international politics. While the primary factor is the system's level of security at that particular time, domestic factors can lead to preference setting in favour or against international trade. In a scarce-security set-up, the primacy of the FPE is clearer than in a set-up with abundant security. Decisions in both situations, however, can be directed by domestic ideas, a clear contrast to structural arguments that would suggest an omnipresent primacy of security over trade, whereas Liberal approaches would discount the importance of the international security structure in any way (Figure 4).

The Intervening Variable

Introducing domestic factors as an intervening variable in the analysis of both foreign policy decisions and international outcomes is the core contribution of NCR. Ripsman et al. (2016) dedicate an entire chapter to define the intervening variable and structure it in a form that makes it convenient to replicate. The development of policy responses to systemic stimuli follows through three stages of processes and mechanisms within the domestic sphere, the perception of the external stimulus, the decision-making about it and the policy implementation. These processes are influenced by intervening variables that Ripsman et al. (2016: 59–60) cluster in four categories: leader images, strategic culture, state–society relations and domestic institutions. The level of inference by each of these categories depends on the stage in the decision-making process as well as the timeframe and the level of clarity of the international environment.

Leaders' images are defined by the 'beliefs or images of individual decision-makers who sit at the helm of the state' (Ripsman et al. 2016: 61) and mainly influence the perception of the systemic stimulus. In the case at hand, the leaders' image can be neglected as one central argument is that the international system was permissive to the creation of a global market for ethanol. There is no indication that the Brazilian foreign policy complex misinterpreted this situation; the perception of the situation is therefore not the subject of this inquiry. The key insights therefore should be located in the decision-making process and/or the policy implementation. The strategic culture of Brazil does include its tendency towards autonomy and a desire and claim to be recognised as a world power. This certainly had an influence on decision-making and policy implementation. Particularly, policy implementation in the Mozambique case was heavily influenced by this Brazilian peculiarity, as will be shown. The state–society relations within Brazil will be under scrutiny as well. Ripsman et al. (2016: 71) describe this cluster of intervening variables as 'the degree of harmony between state and society, [...] distributional competition among societal coalitions, [...] the level of political and social cohesion, [as well as] public support for general foreign policy'. In the Brazilian context, most of these factors inhibit both coherent decision-making and efficient policy implementation. Particularly, the contrast between the Workers Party government and the rather conservative agricultural elites influenced coherence and efficiency in adjusting Brazil's foreign policy responses. The institutional set-up with a splintered Congress and a high number of ministries and agencies involved had a similar effect. While there is no explicit infighting between government agencies, coherence and efficiency suffer from an institutional set-up with many stakeholders. With Brazil's strategic culture in mind, this study will therefore put a strong focus on how state–society relations and the institutional set-up influenced the development and implementation of Brazil's international ethanol strategy.

NCR's Explanatory Value for Brazil's International Ethanol Strategy

Sterling-Folker elaborates how, despite the common narrative, Realist systemic-level analysis is more suitable to domestic-level variables than Liberal theory and how domestic and systemic variables can best be combined to achieve the highest level of explanation. While Liberalism can be seen as a process-based theory where domestic processes are independent variables, Realism can be understood as an environment-based theory where both environment and processes act as independent variables (Sterling-Folker 1997: 4). Sterling-Folker's central argument is that the Liberal focus on process is the primary determinant (independent variable) for actors' interests, behaviour and outcomes (1997: 4–5).

The difficulty arises when weighing domestic versus systemic processes. Sterling-Folker elaborates how systemic processes are implicitly weighed heavier than their domestic counterparts (1997: 11), which results in a 'causal flexibility' (1997: 12) that might interpret domestic processes as independent or dependent variable without methodological rigor. Realism, on the other hand, understands 'process as a means to an end' (1997: 18) and can therefore integrate systemic environment and domestic process as simultaneous independent variables in the Realist argument (1997: 22).

Randall Schweller, according to Caverley (2013: 158), was 'one of the first to embrace the neoclassical label'. In a widely cited 2003 essay, Schweller examines the progressiveness, that is, the potential for advancement of IR research, of Neoclassical Realism. According to Schweller (2003: 317), Neoclassical Realism proves useful to expand on classical and Neorealist ideas and to apply to case studies to test and generate hypotheses and explanations, while incorporating first-, second- and third-image variables, that is, the individual, state and international system levels (following the concept of Waltz 1959). Schweller (2003: 336) makes the point that the inclusion of state-level variables does not contradict the structural Realist proposition, as shown by Sterling-Folker, but rather brings out the non-structural arguments, including the role of ideas (Caverley 2013: 158), causal processes and linkages at the domestic and international levels; these are already implied in the more traditional approaches. Additionally, by making sense of a state's decision-making process, Neoclassical Realism offers a framework to counter the typical errors of evaluation as described by Morgenthau (Schweller 2003: 339). Recently, Neoclassical Realism has been applied to some useful examples. Kitchen (2010) uses NCR to explain grand strategy formation, while Dyson (2010) and Purdon (2014) give accounts of how to apply Neoclassical Realist theory within the policy areas of defence and climate change, respectively. This is the realm within which this study is located.

In the particular case of Brazil, I will develop a Neoclassical Realist explanation for why the Brazilian state has failed thus far to implement a global market for ethanol despite the favourable structural environment. This includes understanding the way in which the foreign policy complex in Brazil has perceived the structural situation and how decisions and assessments have been realised. Neoclassical Realism as an approach to explain Brazil's foreign policy and its results in the global context seems most appropriate due to its focus on both international and domestic variables with an emphasis on structural constraints.

As explained in the introduction section, the international environment was welcoming towards the increased use of biofuels, especially due to the rise in the importance of climate change, energy security and South–South cooperation. This limits structural explanations as to why the global market was not created. Since government negotiations are not participatory processes and we can assume that governments only negotiate with the goal of concrete outcomes, Liberal approaches towards the research question fail to offer a suitable explanation for why the global biofuels market was not created. Therefore, I focus on the way Brazilian foreign policy is implemented and how the actors involved filter outside information, as suggested by the Neoclassical Realist approach.

Concepts in Realist IR

After this introduction to NCR, it is prudent to clarify the central concepts that will be dealt with in this study. While several have been mentioned in the paragraphs above, it is worthwhile to clarify discussions surrounding these concepts and define them where needed.

Soft Power

The concept of soft power – which has frequently been attributed to Brazil (e.g. Visentini 2010; Flemes 2007) – was developed by Nye (1990) and has since then found its way, often unreflected, into popular discourse. While some might claim that soft power is inconsistent with the Realist approach, I argue that it is a modern form of politics of prestige (discussed later), which has been described by Morgenthau. While in ancient times, leaders would send each other messages through envoys, in today's interconnected world, with the increasing accountability of leaders, sending messages through their respective constituencies is a new way – but not inconsistent with Realism – of executing power politics.

According to Nye (1990: 155), power needs to be assessed not by measuring the resources of a country, but rather by its 'ability to change the behaviour of states'. This does not contradict Morgenthau's idea of power, but rather adapts it to the reality of the late 20th and early 21st centuries.

Although Nye emphasises shaping the preferences of countries, his concept of soft power is not necessarily applicable only within a Liberal framework. It may be argued that aiming at the hearts and minds of people in order to influence their leaders would coincide with a Liberal concept of foreign policy deliberation; however, soft power can also be understood within a Realist framework. If the process of shaping preferences of other countries is understood as part of successful diplomacy, Morgenthau would agree that this concept of soft power complements rather than contradicts his ideas of foreign policy. On top of that, soft power is compatible with the concept of Neoclassical Realism, the main theoretical approach of this research project.

Political Strategies Based on Realism

Morgenthau (1978: 50) describes three ideal strategies that states can follow when they understand international politics in Realist terms: (1) politics to keep power or politics of status quo, (2) politics to increase power or imperialism and (3) politics to demonstrate power or politics of prestige. Deduced from these strategies, there can be two dominant actions to stabilise the political situation: balancing of power by expanding domestic capabilities and 'bandwagoning,' the tendency of smaller powers not to go into an alliance with the dominant but instead with a secondary power (Marx 2010: 48).

Status Quo

Morgenthau identifies two 'ideologies' that can be understood as symptoms of a status quo policy: peace and international law. While pacifism and the rejection of war as a political means is a rather common claim in IR in the late 20th and early 21st centuries, it is worth understanding international law as a status quo force. According to Morgenthau (1978: 103), it 'defines a certain distribution of power and offers standards and processes to ascertain and maintain it in concrete situations'. Given the expansion of international law in the second half of the 20th century, and Brazil's role in international negotiations on multilateral institutions and trade codification, one question to be asked is whether Brazil can be conceptualised as a status quo power. This is something that will be addressed through the case studies explored in this work.

Imperialism

The second grand strategy Morgenthau describes is imperialism. It is defined as 'a policy that aims at the overthrow of the status quo, at a reversal of the power relations between two or more nations' (Morgenthau 1978: 57) and it is important to point out the meaning of this. It does not mean that every policy that aims at expanding power is imperialism, but rather imperialism is defined by seeking a significant change in relative power. Relative power is a crucial concept in this context.

There are three types of imperialism: military, economic and cultural (Morgenthau 1978: 69). Here, military imperialism (i.e. military conquest) is 'the most obvious, the most ancient, and also the crudest' (1978: 70). Hence, it is easy to identify, while economic imperialism is an 'unobtrusive, indirect, but fairly effective method of gaining and maintaining domination' (1978: 71), with President Taft's 'dollar diplomacy' as an example. Within the context of Brazil's international ethanol strategy, economic imperialism is one strategy that must be considered as being applied by the Brazilian government.

The form of imperialism most difficult to identify is cultural imperialism. This is because it is the subtlest, but potentially most successful, aiming 'at the conquest and control of the minds of men as an instrument for changing the power relations' (Morgenthau 1978: 72). This is an accurate description of Nye's definition of soft power. While Morgenthau probably considered mainly the minds of decision-makers, Nye takes a more inclusive approach; however, in modern democratic societies with higher levels of political accountability and media scrutiny, where ordinary citizens can rise to powerful positions, this is not necessarily a contradiction.

Politics of Prestige

The 'third of the basic manifestations of the struggle for power on the international scene' (Morgenthau 1978: 84) consists of 'demonstrating the power a nation has' (1978: 89). This can be an objective in itself but more often supports policies of imperialism or status quo (1978: 91).

Just as in domestic politics, prestige serves as an indicator of dominance and therefore provides its holder with a certain form of legitimisation. In international politics, this means that a nation has a 'reputation for unchallengeable power and [a] reputation for self-restraint in using it' (Morgenthau 1978: 93). This, again, can be conceptualised within a soft power framework – especially the second part concerning the reputation of self-restraint – and also coincides with both possible paradigms: Liberalism and Realism. This work will investigate whether Brazil is applying policies of prestige to convince other nations to join its efforts in creating an international ethanol market and whether such policies prove successful. Again, it is noteworthy that these concepts cannot be sharply distinguished, often overlap and require a fair amount of interpretation. It is noteworthy that the term *prestige* has altered its meaning since Morgenthau first developed the concept. Nowadays, it is commonly used not only in the meaning of displayed power but also in terms of moral legitimacy (as seen in Silva 2013: 26; following Ricupero 2010).

With regard to politics of prestige – but also regarding the other strategies mentioned earlier – the first step in the analysis will be to understand the actions and outcomes of Brazilian policies towards other countries. The second step will be to understand the position of the decision-makers, their scope of action and finally their declared intentions. The third step will be to understand the action and response of the actors in the receiving country. The synthesis of these steps will allow judgement as to whether or not the respective policy falls into one of the categories mentioned earlier and reflects more of a Realist or Liberal approach to foreign policy.

Balance of Power/Stability

A result of these different forms of power strategies is a 'configuration that is called the balance of power and [...] policies that aim at preserving it' (Morgenthau 1978: 183). A balance of power is the only way of guaranteeing stability within this system of autonomous states (1978: 184). When power aspirations collide, there are two ways to resolve this conflict: direct opposition and competition (1978: 188). Direct opposition is 'the desire of either nation to see its policies prevail over the policies of the other' (1978: 189) and competition aims at including third parties, which can lead to the formation of alliances.

Alliances

When two nations compete with each other, they have three options to increase their relative power: they can increase their own power, which would lead to an arms race; form an alliance to add other nations' power resources to their own; or form an alliance to withhold these resources from the competitor (Morgenthau 1978: 197). Depending on the level of coherence of interests between the parties in an alliance, Morgenthau (1978: 199) elaborates five criteria to classify alliances:

1. the intrinsic nature and relationship of the partners (whether the alliance is serving identical, complementary or ideological interests and policies),

2. the distribution of benefits and power (whether the alliance is mutual or one-sided),
3. the coverage of interests of members (whether the alliance is general or limited),
4. the coverage with relation to time (whether the alliance is temporal or permanent), and
5. the effectiveness of policies and actions carried out by the alliance (whether the alliance is operative or inoperative).

Points 1, 2 and 5 seem particularly relevant for the analysis of Brazil's foreign policy. While Morgenthau (1978: 201) states that typically alliances transform a 'small fraction of total interests into common policies', this seems to be an important point of analysis to determine whether an alliance is operative or not, which might be the case for some of Brazil's endeavours. Also important to note is that complementary alliances tend towards a disproportion of benefits (1978: 200). Because of the different value that each party attributes to the received benefits, they are by definition not directly comparable; this will lead to a benefit surplus of the more powerful ally. It therefore seems appropriate to identify 'complementary' elements in Brazil's foreign policy initiatives and to critically assess those. Official statements can serve as resources for this identification strategy.

With regard to Brazil's approaches in the so-called triangular cooperation, the role of a third party within Morgenthau's idea of balance of power is noteworthy. The so-called balancer (1978: 209), 'holder of the balance' or 'arbiter' (1978: 210) has a powerful position in this system. Its options are to join an alliance, to make support conditional or to simply follow its own interests. Granted, the arbiter needs to dispose of a certain basic amount of power to ensure its own integrity, but, for example, African countries could fulfil such a role and enhance their negotiating position towards traditional donors like the World Bank. And finally, as Morgenthau (1978: 213) notes, alliances are usually complex systems with a plethora of subsystems. Brazil's position within this conundrum is one parameter to determine the political framework in which it can pursue actions.

Diplomacy

Apart from the structural balance of power method to stabilise the international environment, Morgenthau emphasises the power of diplomacy as a stabilising tool in interstate relations. It is noteworthy that many critiques of classical Realism emphasise the capabilities and structural constraints, while

Morgenthau himself dedicates a considerable amount of his thought to the definition and explanation of successful diplomacy.

Diplomacy is a tool of international politics that defines the national interest in order to make compromises on non-vital issues and interact emphatically with other nations (Kaufman 2006: 27). Morgenthau (1978: 361) defines diplomacy as a fourfold process of the formation and execution of foreign policy, in which its objectives depending on available and potential power are determined, the objectives of other nations under the same aspects are assessed, the correlation or divergence between the two of them is determined and finally the strategies to pursue the state's objectives are developed.

Morgenthau (1978: 363) further outlines three tools of diplomacy: persuasion, compromise and threat of force. The statesman – or diplomat – has to be able to understand the thinking of the other power as well as overcome popular 'simple moralistic and legalistic terms' of thinking in order to achieve the national interest (1978: 161). Since the pursuit of military power might lead to arms races that in the end could jeopardise a nation's survival, its prime interest, diplomacy is a central tool in the Realist understanding of IR (Keaney 2006: 44). This is why the focus on Brazilian ethanol diplomacy is so fundamental to this work.

Theoretical Framework – Conclusion

This section presented the core points of NCR, its development over time and the core concepts that will be applied in this study. It seems suitable to focus on a Neoclassical Realist approach in the analysis of the case at hand, since this approach offers the analytical combination of structural restrictions and an insight into the policy-making process. Finally, it seems appropriate to use the Realist paradigm because of the focus on the power of the Brazilian foreign policy complex, the shape of foreign policy actors in Brazil, the willingness for institutional cooperation and the strategic relevance of ethanol diplomacy during the Lula administration. As Legro and Moravcsik (1999: 52) point out, 'Liberalism explains preferences, [constructivist] theories explain beliefs, whereas Realism [helps] explain strategic interaction based on resources and information.' This makes the Neoclassical Realist approach most suitable for the purpose of explaining Brazil's international ethanol strategy, as we will focus on strategic interactions on different levels that have to do with both resources and information.

At the same time, we will follow Nye's (1990: 170) advice to take political ideas – like sustainability – that serve as sources of power into account but understand them in a structural way in order to adequately deal with the

Table 2 Overview of Classical Realism, Liberalism, and Neoclassical Realism (adapted from Rose (1998: 154))

	Classical Realism	**Liberalism**	**Neoclassical Realism**
Theoretical reach	Systemic (macro-level)	Unit (micro-level)	Connecting unit-level analysis with systemic reach (meso-level)
International environment	Anarchy	Anarchy	Anarchy
Agency	States/governments	Governments and societal interest groups	Governments and societal interest groups (foreign policy complex)
Goal of action	Power	Realisation of particular interests; exchange/trade	Primarily power but depending on the filter by the foreign policy complex
Means	Expansion of power	Negotiations	Choice of means is dependent on the foreign policy complex
Structural pressures	Power politics	Societal interests and pressure groups	Subject to filter by the foreign policy complex
Security	Balance of power	Interdependence	Choice of means is dependent on the foreign policy complex
Cooperation	Limited cooperation and tendency towards bilateral agreements	Possibility of enduring cooperation through multilateral institutions	Cooperation possible
Level of Analysis	System	Process	Primary system, secondary process, tertiary policies
Gains	Relative (bigger piece)	Absolute (bigger cake)	Depending on the elites
Hypothesis (why did Brazil's ethanol diplomacy fail?)	Systemic causes prevented Brazil from initiating cooperation between potential partner nations. The lack of cooperation could have been predicted based on the lack of relative gains that other countries saw in Brazil's initiative despite the welcoming conditions within the discourses of energy security, climate change and South–South cooperation.	The process of creating an international biofuels market offered too much influence to actors whose preferences were opposed to this political goal.	While the systemic circumstances were as beneficial as possible and there was a general consensus in favour of this market, the Brazilian foreign policy complex misjudged the degree of support from foreign actors and systemic factors.

blurred line between Realism and Liberalism (Moravcsik 1992: 4). The inter-paradigm debate between Realism and Liberalism has dominated 'since the infancy of the organised study of international affairs' (Mononen 2008: 1, following Carr 2001), which means it is important to understand the main differences between the two ideas. This is why we summarise the previous discussion on these theories in Table 2.

Chapter 2

METHODOLOGY

Methodology is about defining the research process in order to come to meaningful results. In the present case, it will be used to explain Brazil's foreign policy actions by understanding its ethanol diplomacy during the two terms of the Lula government and Dilma's first term as president. This chapter will cover the variety of methods used to explain and analyse Brazil's international ethanol strategy.

The discussion of the methods in use serves to enable other academics to reproduce and therefore validate the results of research, which therefore need to follow rules that are 'intersubjectively communicable' (Gläser and Laudel 2009: 31). How the researcher obtained her results needs to be clear to academic peers. The minimum amount of reproducibility that should be sought consists of a description of the steps to be taken and the rules to be followed to achieve the results (2009: 32). This chapter will lay out the methods I use to explore Brazil's international ethanol strategy in a coherent manner that will allow for transparency and possible reproduction by other researchers.

Transparency of research is even more important when applying and combining a multitude of methods. The use of different methods and theories within one study is called 'triangulation' (Gläser and Laudel 2009: 105). Given the complex nature of social processes and the limitations of methodological purism, Flick argues, 'it is becoming more fruitful to combine different theoretical approaches or to take these into account in combining methods' (2002: 16). This study will follow this recommendation.

Flick further advocates for a 'pragmatic use of methods', while keeping in mind the dilemma between 'pragmatic but nevertheless methodologically acceptable short-cut strategies for collecting, transcribing, and analysing qualitative data' (2002: 19). This general stream of thought is supported by Gerring's view, that a 'good enough' research design that has been developed 'after a theory and hypothesis has been formulated' can be judged by six general criteria: 'theoretical fit, cumulation, the treatment, the outcome, the sample, and practical constraints' (2011: 627).

The following paragraphs will therefore describe the pragmatic combination of case study research and process tracing, while keeping in mind the goal of reproducibility. After the discussion of methods, the means of data collection, construction of variables and research design of the study will be presented. First, we will examine why 'Brazil's international ethanol strategy' is a suitable case study for understanding Brazil's foreign policy and why qualitative methods are appropriate in this context.

Quantitative versus Qualitative Social Science Research

Whether to apply quantitative or qualitative methods in social science research depends on the subject in question. What is the aim of the research and what questions does the researcher want to answer? Does the researcher dispose of a large-n data set, or does the data consist of only a few or even just one case?

The argument in question is that correlation needs to be proven before causation can be established (Hall 2006: 26), which gives a small-n research design a disadvantage over a large-n design. Furthermore, critiques of qualitative, small-n research claim that both data collection and data analysis are not reproducible and therefore not reliable (Gläser and Laudel 2009: 25).

The main misunderstanding, however, is based on the fact that proponents of 'quantitative, nomothetic-deductive, or theory-testing' researchers are looking for causal inference (Gläser and Laudel 2009: 26). While some people might claim 'that "small-n" research designs can be valuable for causal inference' (Hall 2006: 24), because they 'allow scholars to assess more complex causal processes in a much richer set of observations' (Falleti 2006: 4), the difference lies in the research strategy. Researchers who follow a 'qualitative, inductive, or theory generating' strategy are looking for causal mechanisms rather than causal inference (Gläser and Laudel 2009: 26). To follow this standard, however, seems equally useful for qualitative research that aims at theory amendment. Theory testing in a unique case of foreign policy by analysing causal mechanisms makes an appropriate approach to embedding theory into political contexts.

Hall (2006: 27) proposes that when applying the method of process tracing (to be discussed later) on a small set of cases, observations can be drawn that are 'especially well-suited to assessing the complex causal theories' that explain social interaction with causal mechanisms rather than describe with causal inference. Caporaso makes a strong point that a single case can be sufficient to explain causality in that respective case by stating:

> The historian is not philosophically embarrassed when she says that 'the assassination of the Austrian Archduke Franz Ferdinand by the Serbian

> nationalist Gavrilo Princip was a cause (precipitant, catalyst) of World War I'. There is no distribution here. Causal status is attributed to an event, not to a covariance structure. (2007: 7)

Following Gläser and Laudel (2009: 27), it is important to understand that within qualitative research, the information about the event under investigation is not standardised at the beginning. Its complexity will be reduced only during the analysis of the case. The benefit of a case study is to gain a deeper understanding of not only why things happen but also how they happen, the causal mechanisms.

Case Study Research

Current social science discourse has no general definition or understanding of what a case study is or what the general criteria for its application should be; however, this does not spoil a lively debate among scholars of social science methodology.

Gerring asks the question 'what is a case study and what is it good for?' and comes to the conclusion that a case study is 'an intensive study of a single unit with an aim to generalise across a larger set of units' while being 'a particular way of defining cases, not a way of analysing cases or a way of modelling causal relations' (2004: 341). While this emphasises the narrative and descriptive elements of case studies, Gerring stresses that 'the primary virtues of the case study method are the depth of analysis that it offers' as well as the 'detail, richness, completeness, wholeness, or degree of variance that is accounted for by an explanation' (2004: 348). He concludes that

> case studies are generally more useful [...] when inferences are descriptive rather than causal, [...] when insight into causal mechanisms is more important than insight into causal effects, [and] when the strategy of research is exploratory, rather than confirmatory. (2004: 352)

This is the case for the Neoclassical Realist approach towards Brazil's international ethanol strategy in this study. The question why Brazil has failed thus far to implement an international market for biofuels and ethanol in particular represents a puzzle that can be solved with a Neoclassical Realist approach using dense description (following Geertz 2008) of the processes and investigating the causal mechanisms that guide Brazilian foreign policy.

Levy goes further and offers a categorisation of types of case studies with different aims and uses. While it is important to note that 'these are ideal types, and in practice case studies often combine several of these aims, often (and preferably) in sequence as a part of a multi-stage research program, one that may involve other methods' (2008: 3), it seems appropriate to classify this work within Levy's categories.

The case of 'Brazil's international ethanol strategy' certainly needs to be described and interpreted well within the outlined theoretical framework of Neoclassical Realism, as it exhibits certain aspects of a theory-guided historiographical case study.

Case Selection

Since the goal of this case study is to describe Brazil's international ethanol strategy, and examine why it has failed to implement a global market for biofuels, some thought needs to be put into how to select the case and the crucial sequences for identifying the underlying causal mechanisms. Following Levy (2008: 7), 'considerations of "intrinsic interest" or "historical importance" are no longer regarded acceptable criteria for case selection, unless the aim is [...] purely idiographic', and therefore, a strong argument needs to be made for selecting one particular case. This might be difficult when one accepts that 'in most circumstances, there is no justification for a stand-alone case study' (Gerring 2007: 249).

Generally speaking, as Gläser and Laudel (2009: 98–99) point out, the researcher should aim to select either a typical case that represents the characteristics of the subject of research well or an extreme case, in the sense that it contains either indicators that are distinctive or a blocked intervening variable. Levy (2008: 7, citing Popper 1965) identifies the possible value of such a selection strategy of 'extreme values' for hypothesis generation rather than testing, which corresponds 'to the notion that there is a logic of scientific confirmation but not of scientific discovery'.

One advantage of the case at hand is that it is the first example of Brazil trying to promote ethanol as a commodity abroad. This is therefore likely to show the working mechanisms within the Brazilian administration and the 'ethanol complex' with a lessened risk of distorted results due to path dependency, which might be the case in other policy areas with an extensive institutional memory. Path dependency itself is not an analytical impediment per se; however, the case of Brazil's international ethanol strategy offers the advantage that within the administration the internal distribution of competences and vested interests can be observed in a relatively short period of time and its outcome reflects the positioning of the respective actors within the Brazilian foreign policy complex.

While there might be another case of a unique foreign policy in the Brazilian context, for example, the UN military mission to Haiti, the case of ethanol diplomacy carries a number of analytical advantages. This includes that Brazil is less constrained by international rules in this particular case (i.e. acting in an anarchic scenario), that ethanol diplomacy can be understood as an example of Brazilian soft power in action, that military foreign policy follows a clearer path of internal responsibility and, finally, that non-traditional foreign policy actors play a more important role in ethanol diplomacy.

Gerring develops criteria to identify a 'pathway case' with 'the purpose of an intensive analysis of an individual case to elucidate causal mechanisms (i.e., to clarify a theory) rather than to confirm or disconfirm a general theory' (2007: 233). He develops this concept on the basis of the 'crucial case concept' by political scientist Harry Eckstein, which has been seen as 'the most methodologically defensible approach to single-case analysis' (2007: 232). This means that a 'case is crucial if the facts of that case are central to the confirmation or disconfirmation of a theory' (2007: 231) and 'crucial in the strongest sense when it can be explained precisely by a theory; no other theory can explain the facts of that case, and the theory is invariant' (2007: 232). Gerring therefore calls the crucial case research design a 'highly deductive enterprise' with a high dependency 'on the quality of the theory under investigation' since the aim is to confirm or disconfirm the hypotheses (2007: 235).

The pathway case, on the other hand, aims to detect the causal mechanisms that underlie the well-established hypotheses (Gerring 2007: 238). In this methodology, a cross-case examination establishes the general causal relationships prior to the case investigation, whereas 'in the crucial case method, by contrast, these expectations are deductive rather than empirical' (2007: 241). This makes the pathway case more suitable to detect causal mechanisms, but as Gerring (2007: 245) warns, this 'is no guarantee that the researcher will gain insight into general causal mechanisms' and still 'requires considerable interpretation on the part of the researcher' to detect those causal mechanisms. We can understand Brazil's international ethanol strategy as a pathway case to test and expand the Neoclassical Realist framework.

Another issue that should be addressed is 'selection bias', namely the problem of selecting based on the dependent variable, which can be highly problematic for hypothesis testing (Levy 2008: 8). In the case of Brazil's international ethanol strategy, a partial selection based on the dependent variable, that is, the different efforts Brazil's ethanol complex is undertaking to achieve the international biofuels market, is given, but according to George and Bennett (2005: 22–23) does not pose a problem to an inductive or theory-expanding case study. Brazil's international ethanol strategy serves as a case to test and expand the Neoclassical Realist framework. Case studies with carefully applied process tracing avoid the issues with selection based on the dependent variable since this kind of case study 'does not involve comparisons and [and follow a] different inferential logic' (Levy 2008: 8, following George and Bennett 2005: 22–25; Collier, Mahoney and Seawright 2004: 96; Bennett and Elman 2006: 460–63). The case at hand will be hypothesis testing within the Neoclassical Realist framework.

Definition of Variables

Since the concepts of dependent and independent variables have been mentioned in the preceding paragraph, it is worth defining variables in order to clarify some of those concepts. Gläser and Laudel (2009: 79) define variables generally as 'constructs that describe changeable aspects of social reality'. Caporaso argues that variables are the main ingredient for theoretical work 'in mainstream social science' while the cases 'are either unproblematic givens or deep reservoirs from which one can draw variables' (2007: 6).

The main distinction lies between dependent variables and independent variables. Gläser and Laudel (2009: 81) rely on a strict definition of their variables when they say that for independent variables, only their effect matters, rather than their causes, and the opposite holds for dependent variables. While this is certainly true in a strict sense, different analytical frameworks require some flexibility in that respect since, for example, a structural condition might influence an actor in one sequence, while this actor has a causal effect on another matter in the next sequence. The problem of reverse causality or endogeneity needs to be taken seriously. The answer to my research question, however, can be found by identifying the intervening variables that define the causal mechanism that causes the change in the dependent variable.

Hall (2006: 27) puts special emphasis on the role of intervening variables in theory formation, where these intervening variables can be included into a set of theories to explain 'how those and other variables interact in the causal chain that leads to the outcome' and his method of choice in theory (hypothesis) generating research design is process tracing.

Qualitative research in general and case studies in particular face a common problem, the degrees-of-freedom problem. It arises 'when a researcher has many independent variables but only one or a few observations on the dependent variable, the research design is indeterminate, and there is a very limited basis for causal inferences apart from simple tests of necessity or sufficiency' (Bennett and George 1997: 10). In order to minimise this problem, the main theoretical approaches in IR (Realism and Liberalism) will be taken into consideration as well as a wide range of analytical frameworks, which will be discussed later. In this, I follow Bennett and George's recommendation: 'In contrast to research using statistical methods, case study research should in general err on the side of including too many theories and variables rather than too few' (1997: 16).

In the context of this study and the theoretical framework that has been discussed earlier, the primary independent variables consist of the structural conditions that both the international environment and the domestic polity offer. The dependent variables are the respective policies and interactions that the actors of the foreign policy and ethanol complex implement towards their respective partners. According to the Neoclassical Realist framework, a substantial part of this research will be dedicated to deciphering the intervening variables, that is, the way the foreign policy and ethanol complex filters and processes information and comes to decisions.

Process Tracing

Process tracing has become one of the mainstream methods in qualitative social science and case study research. There seems to be a consensus that process tracing is a 'fundamental tool of qualitative analysis' (Collier 2011: 823) and 'an invaluable method that should be included in every researcher's repertoire' (Bennett and George 1997: 21). It is 'particularly well-suited to the task of uncovering intervening causal mechanisms and exploring reciprocal causation and endogeneity effects' (Levy 2008: 6).

Process tracing is 'the appropriate method to be used to generate data on causal mechanisms, events, actions and other kinds of intervening variables or context conditions that link arguing to observed effects' (Ulbert et al. 2004: 20) because of its focus on identifying the intervening variables 'that link putative causes to observed effects' (Bennett and George 1997: 5).

Collier defines process tracing as 'the systematic examination of diagnostic evidence selected and analysed in light of research questions and hypotheses posed by the investigator' (2011: 823) and as 'an analytic tool for drawing descriptive and causal inferences from diagnostic pieces of evidence – often understood as part of a temporal sequence of events or phenomena' (2011: 824). Levy (2008: 11) sees a comparative advantage when using process tracing 'in the empirical analysis of decision making at the individual, small group, and organisational levels, including the analysis of leaders' perceptions, judgments, preferences, internal decision-making environment, and choices'. This is mainly due to the understanding of detail that is involved in process tracing, but also the focus on the critical junctures that define processes.

Process tracing is a crucial method to assess causal mechanisms – while covariance (i.e. quantitative) tests address causal effects – and 'can identify different causal paths to an outcome, point out variables that otherwise might be left out, check for spuriousness, and allow causal inferences' (Bennett and George 1997: 5, 14) and therefore is well suited to single-case studies (1997: 21).

According to George and Bennett (1997: 5), there are two main approaches to applying process tracing that also follow the classification of case studies we saw earlier: 'process verification' (hypothesis testing) and 'process induction' (hypothesis generating). While they insist on a clear distinction between the two approaches, it might be useful in the case of Brazil's international ethanol strategy to principally apply hypothesis testing but also be open to process induction when necessary. This means that while I am looking to understand and conceptualise the way decisions are formed and policies are implemented, I am also looking for indicators that confirm or invalidate the notion that foreign policy is driven by structural pressures rather than the bottom-up process.

After dividing the case into subsets, 'an intensive analysis of the development of a sequence of events over time' (Levy 2008: 6) will be conducted. As Collier (2011: 828–29) points out:

> It can therefore be productive to start with a good narrative or with a timeline that lists the sequence of events. One can then explore the causal ideas embedded in the narratives, consider the kinds of evidence that may confirm or disconfirm these ideas, and identify the tests appropriate for evaluating this evidence.

The 'fine-grained specification of this process will not only increase the number of observations but also enrich our theory by helping us to discover causal mechanisms' (Caporaso 2007: 7), which means that despite the focus on critical junctures, a detailed rich narrative of the processes will contribute to the understanding of the causal mechanisms.

Bennett and George (1997: 15–16) discuss in depth the questions of where and how to draw theories. They suggest three possible sources – existing theories, expert opinions and explanations of participants – and advise to apply more rather than less of these possible sources to both test and induct theory into the analysed cases. They additionally say it is desirable to transform potential causal paths without pre-existing theory into specified and operationalised assumptions that can undergo a plausibility probe in order to contribute to a new theory (1997: 18).

In practical terms, this means that after the case at hand, Brazil's international ethanol strategy, has been divided into subsets (multilateral, bilateral – the United States, bilateral – Mozambique), the respective processes will be described and subdivided into sequences that lie between critical junctures in the process. According to George and Bennett (1997), the critical juncture is usually the point in a process where a decision is made, a point where hypotheses can be generated and adapted according to the mechanism in place. It is crucial to specify 'theoretically well-defined alternative causal paths in advance' – one could say counterfactuals – to 'guard against the common cognitive bias to see patterns where none exist' (1997: 17).

Definition of the Critical Junctures – Necessary Points of Analysis

Collier and Collier most notably applied the concept of 'critical junctures' to describe the points of institutional change in Latin American history. They relate this back to Max Weber, who described 'sharp disjunctures [...] that reshape established social relations' (1991: 28) when describing critical junctures as points of academic enquiry. They provide us with four descriptions of critical junctures: 'crucial choices and their legacies', 'major watersheds in political life', 'transitions that establish certain directions' and 'period[s] of significant change' (1991: 27–29), which leave quite a broad understanding of the concept. Analytically, Collier and Collier (1991: 30) focus on three central elements that they see in critical junctures in their comparative study: significant change must have happened, different cases must result in distinct ways for comparison and the critical juncture must offer an explanatory hypothesis about the consequences. Furthermore, Collier and Collier (1991: 28–29) find critical junctures most meaningful when considered in the context of societal cleavages, the big divisive issues of a society. This point is valid in a sense that structural changes will be more significant if a great conflict such as one between labour and capital is involved; however, this yields a high threshold for the application of the concept of critical junctures.

Rodrigues Vieira operationalised the concept by differentiating between two levels: the institutional and the organisational. He then analyses the transition on each level in three realms: the political, the economic and the social. This way, Rodrigues Vieira offers a stringent measure for critical junctures, which he visualises in diagrams (e.g. Rodrigues Vieira 2013: 170). This makes the process of analysis transparent and comprehensible. This approach – much like Collier and Collier's – seems appropriate for comparative analysis in a most-similar research design that spans long periods of time. It seems useful, however, to transfer the concept of critical junctures to a case study design, with several cases, each with shorter time frames. The advantage is to define criteria a priori to identify the relevant points of interest in a process to limit the dense description to the necessary minimum.

This study, therefore, applies a wider understanding of the concept, which will be called 'necessary points of analysis' (NPA). An NPA occurs when the course of direction has been significantly changed in the process (e.g. the suspension of talks between Brazil and the United States in face of the US National Security Agency scandal), when a sub-process has been concluded (the 2007 memorandum of understanding on biofuels) or when the basis for the subject matter, the rules of the game, have changed significantly (the initiation of the Strategic Energy Dialogue). These NPAs will then be analysed in terms of the factors leading up to them, the structural and procedural changes they initiated and how they were implemented in the follow-up.

Information Gathering

In order to define the relevant structures, institutions and actors, a three-step information-gathering process was applied. After a systematic literature review that focused on ethanol diplomacy in the context of general Brazilian foreign policy, as well as South–South cooperation and climate change policy, the main documents relevant for the process were reviewed. These documents are crucial to reconstruct the implementation process (Roos 2012: 11) of Brazil's ethanol strategy and focus on the 'three great regulatory systems [regional, bilateral, non-reciprocal]' that affect the trade governance of ethanol (Thorstensen 2012: 85).

The third step of the information-gathering process was conducting expert interviews to close gaps in the knowledge and understanding of the subject.

Document Research

A large quantity of documents are available on the topic of international ethanol negotiations. Many international organisations and fora (World Trade Organization, European Union, MercoSul, Global Bioenergy Partnership, International Sugar Organisation, etc.) offer access to their publications and, more importantly, working documents and minutes of their meetings. Here, access to information does not pose a significant challenge to the research.

It is more difficult to gain access to information of the national administrations. In Brazil, the publicly available documents, such as laws, parliamentary discussion minutes and press statements cover the relevant events for this research. With regard to the United States, the documentation of the State Department is ample, as is the documentation of Congress. With regard to Mozambique, the access to official documents is more restricted. While their congress passed a freedom of information bill in November 2014, and the president signed it in January 2015, the practical application of the law is still unclear. I had to rely on publicly available (leaked) information and documents passed on by interview partners.

In addition to officially released documents, I also took into account recent publications by WikiLeaks and similar organisations. In any case, the limitations of access to public documentation did not pose a threat to the findings of this study. Moreover, one cannot expect official documents to retrace processes; they rather represent results. This means their use is limited and needs to be enhanced and triangulated with other sources of information anyways.

Expert Interviews

The way expert interviews are understood and applied in this research is mainly based on the concept elaborated by Gläser and Laudel (2009). The central idea is to access the knowledge of experts on a defined topic (2009: 12). There are different types of interviews according to their degree of standardisation. While highly standardised interviews are mainly applied in conjunction with quantitative methods, semi-standardised or non-standardised interviews are more useful within the context of qualitative research (2009: 41). Non-standardised interviews can again be categorised as semi-structured (*Leitfaden-*) interviews, open interviews and narrative interviews (2009: 42). Following the argument of Gläser and Laudel (2009: 43), semi-structured interviews are the best option for this work because of their ability to cover a range of loosely connected topics within an interview setting with time constraints. Apart from this, an advantage of semi-structured interviews lies in the ability to cover a broad spectrum of topics and accommodate the need of the researcher to gather very specific information (2009: 111).

Gläser and Laudel (2009: 199–212) further suggest their own method to analyse and interpret the gathered information: the qualitative content analysis (*qualitative Inhaltsanalyse*). With this method, the text is not coded, but rather the authors suggest a process of 'information extraction', which aims at gathering the information from the text rather than analysing meta-information through an index (2009: 199). This extracted information is then stored with the appropriate citation (2009: 201) and entered into a structured information base (2009: 202). Gläser and Laudel (2009: 204) furthermore recommend the use of electronic tools, with the analytical program MIA in particular.

While this process seems suitable for large research projects with several researchers and a magnitude of interviews, the number of interviews and the information gathered from them will be manageable without electronic tools for the purpose of this work. One central aim of the interviews was to gather concrete information that was not available through literature or document research. Therefore, the method of information extraction is used in selected critical cases but will mainly remain in the background for understanding the process of interpreting the information. This follows the notion of theoretical sampling, which was developed by Glaser and Strauss (2017), to allow the researcher to form categories during the process of interpretation rather than pre-define those and hence hedge possible findings (Roos 2012: 17).

The total number of interviews in this work was just under 80, for methodological and practical considerations. With this number, I covered several representatives from all major institutions involved (discussed later); allowing for several interview partners from the different institutional actors means I cross-checked critical information. Theoretical saturation, the point when additional data collection and analysis no longer contribute any new information and all aspects of the theory have been addressed, is difficult to achieve (Guest et al. 2006: 76), but this number should guarantee a good standard for the generalisation of findings because it includes all relevant institutions and stakeholders and offers the possibility to cross-check claims made by interviewees on several levels.

The Selection of Interviewees

People are considered 'experts' when they have gathered inside knowledge through participation in the process to be reconstructed (Gläser and Laudel 2009: 13) or using the broader definition of Belting (2008): 'a person who has a high degree of skill and knowledge in a certain domain, field or industry due to long-time experience' (Belting 2008: 2). For this study, a broad definition of 'expert' is applied in order to gain insight from academics working on the topic, political decision makers, industry representatives and activists from non-governmental organisations.

The recruitment of interviewees in the initial phase was done through an analysis of the institutions involved in the respective processes. Within the Brazilian administration, most government departments and ministries have one assigned focal point for ethanol. These were the initial points of contact, from where I enlarged my target group through the recommendations of previous interview partners (similar to a snowball system). I also attended industry events and talked to representatives of the British Foreign Office and the German Foreign Service as well as representatives of the European Commission.

Research Design

This methodology section described my approach to answering the question why Brazil has thus far failed to establish a global ethanol market. The theoretical approaches of IR suggest that the reason for this can be found in the

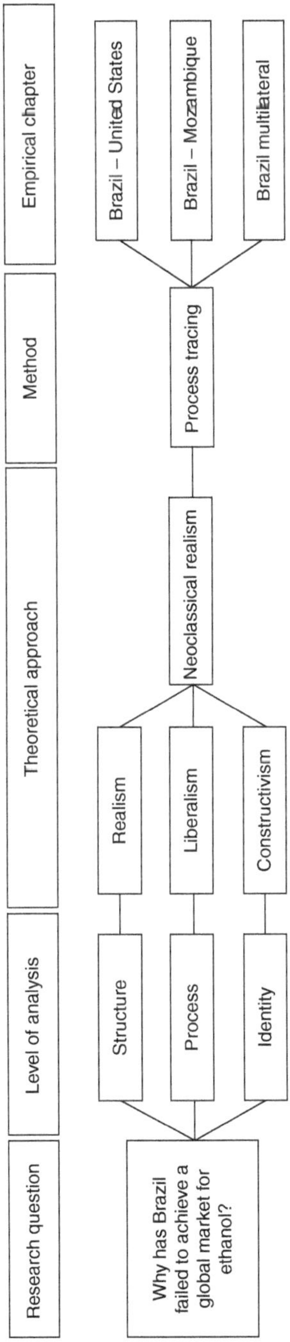

Figure 5 Research design (*Source*: Author's own).

structural environment and actions of administrations (Neoclassical Realist explanation) or in the processes and preferences that lead up to the respective foreign policies (Liberal explanation). The Neoclassical Realist approach can shed light on both spheres of arguments by first examining the structural conditions and then the internal processes. This is taking into account the beneficial structural conditions and then analysing how the Brazilian foreign policy complex interpreted these and adjusted their policy decisions accordingly. At this point, we know that the Brazilian foreign policy complex did not manage to transform the structural environment into successful political outcomes, and we can assume that they either misjudged the structural environment and/or the preferences of their partners but also that the internal cooperation between the Brazilian actors was hindering a coherent policy output.

To reach a conclusion on this question, I reconstructed the case of Brazil's international ethanol strategy and tested these hypotheses within the theoretical background of Neoclassical Realist IR theory. The hypotheses will be mapped onto actions taken by the actors at the NPA or, using Risse and Müller's (2001: 8) dramatic words, at the 'moments of crises, of surprising and counterintuitive developments' during the analysed processes.

By the method of process tracing, I identified the actions that defined the outcomes of the respective processes in each of the three case studies with the goal in mind, 'to see if the multiple actions and statements of the actors at each stage of the causal process are consistent with the image of the world implied by the theory' (Hall 2006: 28).

Given this information, Figure 5 presents a structure of the research design applied in this study.

Following Gerring's insight, this chapter outlined 'the process by which data [is] generated' (2011: 625) that complies with the 'multiple and diverse' criteria applicable to social science research designs and follows a 'realistic standard' (2011: 632) from which to draw conclusions. The following chapters will apply the aforementioned methodologies in order to understand why Brazil has not been able to establish a global market for ethanol, explore the Brazilian foreign policy complex and explain Brazil's international ethanol strategy.

Chapter 3

LITERATURE REVIEW

This is the first comprehensive work on Brazil's international ethanol strategy or ethanol diplomacy that has focused on the question of whether or not this particular policy achieved success at creating an international ethanol market. Fagundes (2013) offers an output-oriented overview of the major initiatives and suggests an unusual perspective on interdependence in the global biofuels sector. On the other hand, useful research has been undertaken on parts of the issue and several sub-topics. As a result, this literature review is divided into three major sections: research on global biofuel markets, research that has been done on Brazil's ethanol diplomacy in general and research that refers to specific geographical or organisational levels.

The research on global biofuel markets reflects the optimistic notion of the mid-2000s, outlining several of the structural assumptions that have been made before in this study. The research on Brazil's ethanol diplomacy in general will be further divided into three blocks: studies that focus on the actors involved in the process (the 'ethanol complex'), studies that deliver a strategic assessment of ethanol diplomacy and studies that put ethanol diplomacy in the context of South–South cooperation.

The section on specific geographical or organisational levels will focus on literature that looks at the cases that are investigated in this study: the relationship between the United States and Brazil with respect to ethanol, between Brazil and Mozambique, and at the multilateral level with a primary focus on the WTO.

Literature on Global Biofuel Markets

During the second half of the first decade of the 2000s, the question of prospective biofuel markets was raised in a number of research centres. Most prominently, the UN Economic Commission for Latin America and the Caribbean (CEPAL) and the 'Task 40' group of the International Energy Agency researched these issues. While these studies are fairly optimistic about future biofuels markets and lay out quantitative projections and regulatory as well as material requirements for the creation of such markets, they do not explain why this endeavour has failed thus far. They do, however, outline areas of contention that we need to refer to when looking for possible mistakes in the Brazilian strategy.

CEPAL's André Furtado sees the main obstacle in the current WTO classification of ethanol as an agricultural product. This means it does not fall under the General Agreement, but rather under the Agreement on Agriculture (AoA), which allows for a higher level of tariffs. Furtado (2009: 31) points out Brazil's initiative to reclassify ethanol as an 'environmental good' in 2005 as an intelligent step towards abandoning trade barriers despite its apparent lack of success. One question that will be addressed in the section about Brazil and the WTO will be whether Brazil should have aimed for a reclassification of ethanol as an 'industrial product', which has initial import tariffs, but this could have been a more successful reclassification strategy.

Anil Hira delves deeper into the problem and asks what the issues are that prevent a global agreement. He identifies five central obstacles to the creation of the market: lack of standards, lack of commodities exchange, lack of infrastructure, lack of flex fuel vehicles and the question of sustainability (Hira 2011). While Matzenberger et al. (2015: 936) see 'sustainability considerations, especially carbon balance of biomass, trade limitations as well as time and scope of policy implementation' as the central issues to tackle. This view is supported by Junginger's excellent study that found that technical barriers are not a major problem for ethanol trade (2011: 2032) and can easily be overcome just like logistical and infrastructure challenges with other sources of energy (2011: 2036). Furthermore, Junginger affirms that tariff barriers and concerns of sustainability and certification are seen as the central blockages for a maturation of the ethanol market (2011: 2031, 2033).

Lamers et al. give an interesting account of how market forces circumvent existing trade barriers, for example, the import to the United States through the countries of the Caribbean Basin Initiative (CBI) and the Central American Free Trade Agreement (CAFTA) and through the 'Swedish loophole' to the European Union (2011: 2665–68). The former two enabled Brazil to export anhydrous ethanol to Central American and Caribbean countries, where it was processed into hydrous ethanol, which in turn could be exported to the United States without tariffs. The latter applied a similar logic to exports to the European Union. It is noteworthy that the Swedish loophole was closed in 2006, while the trade through Central America and the Caribbean is being tolerated.

These examples show that the market is mainly hindered through tariff barriers and that an economically sustainable trade would flourish if these barriers were abolished. This being said, we need to evaluate the Brazilian strategy under the premise of whether it actually focused on the appropriate arena for negotiation. While multilateral approaches towards standardisation and the focus on the WTO get an 'A for effort', the smarter approach might have been to solely focus on bilateral agreements with the United States and exert more pressure on the partners in MercoSul to reach an agreement with the European Union. These questions will be raised in the respective sections of this study.

Rosillo-Calle and Walter find that one central political force that has been blocking the creation of an international ethanol market is the preference to first satisfy the domestic demand before creating export facilities. They further suggest switching the negotiating arena towards the international institutions for climate change mitigation, which so far has not been reflected in official arrangements. For example, the Brazilian Ministry for the Environment (MMA) is not part of the informal 'Council of Four' that decides on Brazil's international ethanol policies (more on this in the section on stakeholders) (2006: 27).

While the literature on biofuel markets does not give an explicit explanation for the ongoing infancy of this sector, it raises important questions that should be asked when assessing Brazil's international ethanol strategy: Did Brazil focus on the pressing problems, tariff barriers and sustainability concerns, to advance its plans; did Brazil choose the appropriate arenas to address these; and finally, did Brazil act appropriately towards the concerns and preferences of its negotiating partners?

To get closer to answering these questions, we must look at the official strategy.

Outlining the Official Strategy

There are two publications that outline the official Brazilian ethanol strategy, both written by Brazilian diplomats. Ambassador Antônio José Ferreira Simões (2007) explains the background and the strategic importance of the country's initiative to realise the global market for ethanol. Ambassador Simões has been sub-secretary general for South and Central America and the Caribbean at Itamaraty since 2010 and served as Brazilian ambassador to Venezuela from 2008 to 2010. Before that, he was director of the energy department at Itamaraty from 2006 to 2008 and secretary for planning from 2005 to 2006. In these functions, he has been crucial in developing Brazil's international ethanol strategy.

The second official account is given by Emerson Coraiola Kloss, who headed the division for new and renewable energy resources at Itamaraty (2011–15) and was stationed at the Brazilian Embassy in Washington, DC, during the negotiations that lead to the Brazil–US biofuels MoU in 2007. He gives an account of what has been done to establish an international market for ethanol and focuses on the actions Brazil should take to transform ethanol into a global commodity. It is interesting to observe that Kloss (2012: 185–86) sees little room for influencing the bigger partners, the United States and the European Union, directly, but instead recommends the multilateral way in arenas outside the Doha Round, like the International Sugar Organisation (ISO) or the Global Bioenergy Partnership (GBEP).

Ferreira Simões (2007) represents the opinion that energy security is a strategic issue and has been militarised since before World War I. Countries that have diversified their energy matrices when structural change happened are, as a result, in an advantageous position; however, in order to reap the full benefits of biofuels, an international market needs to be created. Ferreira Simões (2007) points out that Brazil has a three-level (global, regional and bilateral) strategy to achieve this. Globally, the producer base needs to be extended and international standards introduced, and for this reason, Brazil also supports research in technology and studies on the sustainability of biofuels. On the regional level, Brazil is working towards energy integration and to use comparative advantages in production to provide better energy, including through the MercoSul MoU on energy integration. Bilaterally, Brazil is using technical cooperation to advance biofuels. Ferreira Simões's (2007) analysis inspired the structure of this study.

The question remains as to whether or not these two high-level diplomats actually have the power to implement the strategies they created or are there other actors involved who can alter Brazil's international ethanol strategy? The following section will take a look at the stakeholders involved in Brazil's international ethanol strategy.

The Ethanol Complex

In this section, I summarise the actors and institutions involved in the development and implementation of Brazil's international ethanol strategy.[1] This reflects the wide network of actors and the entangled nature of their respective responsibilities and competencies, which have led to a lack of systematic, comprehensive overviews of this policy area. Many authors instead focus on a subset of actors and/or institutions according to their (research) agenda.

Schlesinger (2012) delivers an initial mapping of the actors in the Brazilian ethanol complex. He focuses on the Brazilian government and sees the leading role being played by the Ministry of Foreign Affairs (MRE, or Itamaraty), with

1. For a more convenient overview, please see a list of the actors and institutions involved in the subject of study in the appendix.

its development agency Brazilian Cooperation Agency (ABC) as the facilitator for international ethanol projects in the field of development. Furthermore, the state agency for agricultural research, Embrapa, delivers technological know-how in agricultural science, while Petrobras, the national oil company, supports the installation of ethanol infrastructure. The credit lines provided by the national development bank (BNDES) support private sector investments that otherwise would not be feasible. Organisations like the think tank and research institution Getulio Vargas Foundation (FGV) are mentioned as domestic beneficiaries, due to feasibility studies that they conduct. One interview partner from ABC made critical remarks about FGV's role in rebranding the ProSavana project in Mozambique, a problematic relationship that will be subject to deeper enquiry in the chapter on Brazil–Mozambique relations.

The Brazilian export agency, APEX-Brasil, supports Brazilian companies in entering foreign markets by connecting the private sector of Brazil with the private sector in the receiving country and the necessary political decision-makers. Several Brazilian ethanol producers are invested in Africa and cooperate with other Brazilian companies whenever suitable, such as the construction giant Odebrecht. Schlesinger (2012: 33) states,

> Brazilian cooperation is reproducing the North–South cooperation mistakes and tends to operate South–South cooperation as a subsidiary line and a support to the expansion of corporate interests of big national corporations.

Schlesinger's criticism reflects the notion that Brazil's ethanol diplomacy has been primarily defined by particular interest groups from the beginning and sheds light on the influence these actors have in policy making. While this suggests a rather cynical version of Liberalism, one should not forget that trade diplomacy and ethanol diplomacy in particular were central projects of the first left-wing government under president Lula and the Workers' Party (PT) that were embedded in their political strategy (Ondetti and Rhodes 2010: 6). While some authors (e.g. Rodrigues Vieira 2014) and interview partners (Trindade) claim that ethanol diplomacy already had been developed and applied under President Cardoso, the results in terms of international agreements signed in that area suggest that President Lula made it a government priority (see the list of agreements in the appendix).

Ferreira Capellaro et al. put ethanol diplomacy into context with Brazil's domestic 'Productive Development Policy' (PDP) and provide a good overview of the tasks and actors involved. PDP is a governmental growth program that applies to 25 strategic sectors in Brazil, including biofuels. The program covers four areas of instruments: financial incentives; government purchasing power; economic, technical and competition regulation; and technical support regarding trade issues (2012: 10678). The authors identify BNDES, MRE, Petrobras, APEX-BRASIL and the National Agency of Petroleum, Natural Gas and Biofuels (ANP) as actors who can apply instruments for international trade promotion (2012: 10679).

While these are the primary actors in the international side of PDP, the authors also recognise that other entities, such as the Brazilian Sugarcane Industry Association (União da Indústria de Cana-de-Açúcar – UNICA), the state government of São Paulo, the biggest sugar and ethanol exporter COPERSUCAR, Petrobras and the commodities and futures exchange are involved in the promotion of ethanol from a non-regulatory side (Ferreira Capellaro et al. 2012: 10680). Only close interaction between these agents would ensure the successful implementation of international ethanol projects, but it becomes clear that the role of state actors outweighs the role of non-regulatory actors.

While the aforementioned authors list a number of actors that are commonly referred to in the literature, I want to add to the list the Casa Civil (the president's office) and the informal 'council of four', with which I became acquainted during my research interviews. The former was central in initiating Brazil's ethanol strategy, and the latter is the informal decision-making body coordinated by the Casa Civil, which brings together the Ministry of Agriculture (Ministério da Agricultura, Pecuária e Abastecimento – MAPA), the Finance Ministry (Ministério da Fazenda – MinFaz), the Ministry of Mining and Energy (Ministério de Minas e Energia – MME) as well as the Foreign Ministry (Ministério das Relações Exteriores – MRE, or Itamaraty). Since many authors suggest switching arenas from trade to climate-related issues – a strategy that is even adopted by UNICA, as confirmed by its president during one of my interviews – one wonders whether this will actually be successful since MMA is not represented in this central body. I will refer to this question and the role of the environmental argument throughout the different chapters.

This leads directly to the central issue at hand: why has Brazil's international ethanol strategy not been successful, specifically why has there not been a significant increase in the production, consumption and trade in ethanol, and why is there still a lack of international regulation in this field?

Strategic Assessment of Ethanol Diplomacy

Several authors attempt to assess Brazil's international ethanol strategy on a strategic level. This proves useful for this study because these authors give blueprints for such a strategic assessment but have also already shed light on the issue from different angles. Their results, however, vary in quality and depth.

Dalgaard, for example, provides an initial description of the main actors, which includes a summary of the creation of the energy department in the MRE in 2006, with interesting information about the internal relations within the early Lula government. He also attributes strong influence to private actors and external actors within trilateral cooperation projects and makes the government seem like a coordinating force that was riding a wave in a benevolent international context (2012: 206). He comes to the conclusion that ethanol diplomacy needs to be seen within the context of a broader soft power strategy that did not yield short-term success, but might have positive effects on Brazil internationally in the long term. We will refer to this question when analysing in later chapters the failure of several initiatives: was ethanol diplomacy just a stone in a broader plan of soft power or was soft power the means to achieve the goals of the ethanol strategy?

Stephanie Hanson (2007) from the Council on Foreign Relations, provides a much more positive perspective on this. She calls ethanol diplomacy 'Lula's most important foreign policy initiative', because of its prominence in presidential diplomacy and due to the achievements in terms of signed agreements (see the list of agreements in the appendix). She agrees that the creation of an international ethanol market is crucial for Brazil not only to achieve its goals of internationalizing its ethanol industry but also to gain political weight and support internationally to improve Brazil's position globally with the long-term goal of becoming a more powerful player in a future UN governance framework. A high-level official in the MRE confirmed this second priority in one of the interviews conducted for this research.

While it is clear that the seat in the UNSC is a higher ranking goal of Brazilian diplomacy than a global ethanol market, Ubiraci-Sennes and Narciso (2008) find yet another surprising explanation for ethanol diplomacy. They analyse Brazil's energy mix of the mid-2000s and deduce a strong dependency on fossil fuels. The authors are unsure whether state or private sector dominates biofuels but choose to focus on the hybrid role of Petrobras in the ethanol sector. This hybrid function of Petrobras as an actor between government and markets that mainly focuses on fossil fuels production and distribution, but also on the organisation of the ethanol market, makes it an interesting case for further analysis. The authors deliver a comprehensive description of the organisational role of Petrobras but fall short in analysing its qualities as both an actor and an institution.

While I intended to close this gap in the literature, it was very difficult to gain insight into or comments on Petrobras, which can be partially explained by the current corruption scandal. It seems unreasonable to take the state oil company completely out of the equation for the purpose of analysis, so I included Petrobras in my analysis as relevant to my cases but did not rely on primary data collection due to the lack of insights gained from interview partners. At the same time, any official information on Petrobras needs to be seen critically due to the ongoing corruption scandal.

At this point, two aspects should be mentioned: the official strategy of Petrobras (and other Brazilian multinationals) to expand their markets globally and the potential role in the corruption scandal. The former indicates again that ethanol diplomacy might have been a vehicle rather than a goal, while the latter is difficult to take into account at this point while investigations are still going on. One might consider the possibility, however, that questionable business practices have been exported from Brazil through the Petrobras network, which might explain reluctance by some African partners to fully engage with Brazilian ideas. At the same time, the obvious mismanagement of Petrobras also compromises the company as a source for data, especially when it comes to financial assets and investment, which has to be taken into account when assessing Brazil's engagement in Africa.

But not only the role of the national oil company needs to be critically assessed within the broader question of how decisions are being made. In their detailed historic overview, Medeiros and Froio (2012) elaborate a strong argument for the importance of the biofuels sector in the Brazilian political system by tracing campaign donations of sugar refinery owners (*usineiros*) to political parties. These strong actors can not only create political pressure domestically but might also play a role as political proxies internationally, who, for example, support the Brazilian state informally to reach decisions in African countries.

These sources are connected by three common threads: that ethanol diplomacy was an appropriate measure in the international context, that it was not successful in the short or medium term and that in some instances the creation of a global market for ethanol was a tool to achieve higher ranking goals rather than a primary goal on its own. Interview partners at MAPA and MRE carefully confirmed this last point. We will now turn to the literature on the appropriateness of Brazil's ethanol diplomacy in international contexts.

The South–South Context

The Brazilian discourse on South–South cooperation has been marked by strong notions of solidarity and a claim of mutual benefit. A closer examination of South–South cooperation, however, shows that the net interests of Brazilian foreign policy depend on it.

Visentini sees Brazil's agenda in Africa as entailing more than the 'obvious material interests' (2010: 71), such as resources and influence, but rather the goal of being a leader and a respectable mid-size power. Visentini comes to the conclusion that Brazil is engaging in a political discourse, which aims at raising its reputation among developing countries and calls this 'prestige diplomacy', while the country at the same time pursues a 'soft imperialism' in economic terms (2010: 80). This means that, on the one hand, Brazil creates a narrative to align the preferences of African countries with those of Brazil and, on the other hand, incentivises desired action by creating economic and financial (inter-)dependence.

According to White (2013), Brazil's strategy in Africa is based on three pillars: political diplomacy, strategic commercial interests and development cooperation. The country got a head-start over other emerging economies because of Lula's presidential diplomacy – a sign that prestige diplomacy is working – and while some criticise the 'non-political' involvement of Brazil in Africa, White (2013) sees it simply as a new reality where cooperation cannot be conditioned (on, e.g. certain internal governance standards) due to the competition between the new donors.

Stolte (2013) claims that Brazil's engagement in Africa is relatively invisible in the media because it is status-seeking as opposed to resource-seeking. Brazil still has a negative trade balance with Africa due to oil imports, yet the difference between Brazil and other BRICS is that Brazil does not depend on the African resources and it does not directly tie its development aid to extraction rights. Brazil actually views Africa as a potential consumer market for ethanol, as evidenced by the free sharing of technologies to open these markets, and the regional presence of Embrapa.

Stolte and de la Fontaine (2012) see the new actors in Africa as mainly having gained influence through their own growth and, therefore, their size in terms of trade and investment. The 'Beijing Consensus' as a development model is oriented towards trade and pursues an idea of non-interference. Stolte and de la Fontaine (2012) classify Brazil's cooperation accordingly, but unlike China and India, Brazil aims to internationalise its big corporations rather than only seeking access to resources. Additionally, the regular summits with African leaders are used to gain international influence and secure support in questions of global governance (i.e. UNSC reform).

Burges (2012) views South–South cooperation as an explicit tool of Lula's foreign policy strategy. This type of cooperation is not new; it was introduced in the late 1970s by countries that were not members of the traditional donors' clubs, such as the OECD's DAC, the OECD's Export Credits Group or the Paris Club of creditor countries. These countries do not give infrastructure development as foreign aid, but instead organise such projects as commercial investments, supported by export-financing loans from state-owned development banks (like BNDES). In the Brazilian case, ABC is the facilitator that engages with the local and domestic stakeholders. Thematic priorities for

Brazilian development projects are biofuels, agriculture, health and professional education.

Burges (2012: 243–45) concludes that countries that are not members of the traditional clubs can successfully implement development cooperation projects and have been doing so for quite some time. A convergence between development and national interest is useful and the result can be seen in Lula's strong rhetoric of solidarity.

Within the South–South context, the literature is clear that the primary goal is status seeking and prestige diplomacy. Ethanol diplomacy within Brazil's South–South efforts serves not only as a vehicle to garner support for Brazil's main global diplomacy goals but also the purpose of boosting the domestic economy through new markets for Brazilian multinationals. In the respective chapter, I will investigate whether this preferential treatment of private interests has hurt Brazil's success in the region, as Visentini (2010) suggests.

The structural environment for a successful implementation of Brazil's ethanol diplomacy in the South–South context seems permissive. Brazil can dispose of more power resources than its partners in the Global South and should ultimately be able to prevail with its vision in terms of direction of development and alliance formation for higher levels of global governance.

United States–Brazil

Literature on the US–Brazil Relationship

The relationship between the United States and Brazil has been studied extensively. Both countries have had a special relationship right from the start when the United States was the first state to recognise Brazil's independence. Burns describes the admiration that Brazil's doyen of foreign policy, Baron Rio Branco, had for the United States and his desire for a close, yet levelled relationship. He organises the 'reasons for Brazil's approximation with the United States [at that time in] three categories: historical, commercial, and political' (1966: 178). Despite the obvious similarities and some overlapping interests between the two countries, the relationship was characterised by ups and downs. Guided by the 'four cardinal points of a new foreign policy', Brazil was aiming for 'Pan-Americanism, close relations with the United States, Latin American leadership, and international prestige' (Burns 1993: 284) once Rio Branco became foreign minister in 1902. One can see the seed for Brazil's later international engagement under the guidance of President Lula and Foreign Minister Amorim. Another recurring theme of US–Brazilian relations was identified by Burns (1966: 122) regarding the 1907 Hague Conference, when

Brazil 'failed to find out the intentions of the United States beforehand and [was] caught unprepared [...], at odds with his ally and for the time being in a humiliating position.' Monica Hirst describes this relationship as a 'long road of unmet expectations' and as an ebb and flow between good and cool but never hostile' (2005: xvii). She gives a historic overview of the phases that the relation has undergone from alliance in the early years of Brazil's republic (1889–1930), to alignment (1943–74), through autonomy (1974–85) until adjustment (since 1990). Her in-depth account starts with this period of adjustment. In particular with regard to trade, Brazil was able to emancipate from the United States and diversify its exports through the membership in and active support for multilateral trade regimes, particularly the WTO, while maintaining a critical position towards the creation of the Free Trade Agreement of the Americas (FTAA) (2005: 29–30, 33). In the political realm, Brazil chose not to bandwagon with the United States in major international situations like the Gulf War(s) and the Kosovo intervention, and presented differing opinions regarding UN peace-keeping missions, while criticising the US influence in the Southern Hemisphere (2005: 41, 44, 48). The assessment is similar in lower ranked issues such as human rights, environmental policies and mutual perceptions. In this sense, the Brazil–US ethanol diplomacy could be either a case of unmet expectations or the lighthouse project that brings together the agendas of the two countries. Joseph Smith approached the relationship between the two *Unequal Giants* (1991) from a historical-structural perspective. He understands the relationship between the United States and Brazil at the beginning of the 20th century as mainly commercial (1991: 43) with only 'minimal diplomatic consultation' around and during World War I (1991: 106). The 'high point of diplomatic collaboration between Brazil and the United States was the period of "approximation" associated with' Rio Branco and Joaquin Nabucco (Smith 2010: 2). After this Pan-American period, Brazil supported the United States in both world wars mainly due to an alignment of economic interests. Brazil's participation in the Versailles Conference is a story 'of increasing irritation and bruised feelings' (Smith 1991: 127) while the 'relationship was not merely sentimental, but reflected mutual interests' (1991: 204). During the interwar period, trade between the two countries grew, but Brazil's Great Power aspirations, particularly in the League of Nations, were not supported by the United States (Smith 2010: 88). On top of that, the United States had doubts about Brazil's political instability and subsequent inward turn as well as Vargas's 'Estado Novo' political program. Vargas understood to respond 'favourably' (2010: 5) to FDR's Good Neighbour Policy. With the rise of the United States as the world's superpower, 'the relationship was more unequal than ever' (Smith 1991: 205). Brazil's entry into World War II according to Smith (2010: 123) ultimately resulted from the United States' reaction to the coup in Bolivia to send military aid to Brazil. At this point officially aligned with the United States but not yet involved in the war, Brazil re-assessed its interests and now saw enormous benefit in closer military cooperation with the United States , including the sending of an expeditionary force to Europe. After World War II, Brazil embarked into a new Pan-American project that was rejected by the United States at the time (2010: 5). The North American scepticism increased due to Brazil's independent foreign policy stand and ultimately led the United States to support political opposition and the subsequent coup in 1964 on the basis of counter-communism (2010: 5), which led to 'close and friendly relations [...] in diplomatic affairs' (2010: 170). With the military government following a more nationalist approach and Brazil's economy diversifying away from the United States in the 1970s, the two countries began to estrange again (2010: 174). Questions regarding human rights and nuclear non-proliferation in the late 1970s opened Brazil up to extensive criticism from the Carter White House onwards (2010: 178–79). Democratic opening in Brazil, the end of the Cold War and the arrival of the Washington Consensus led to a phase of renewed interest between the two countries in the 1990s (2010: 188–96). Britta Crandall identifies a 'misunderstood history' between the two *Hemispheric Giants* (2011) instead of misunderstandings between them. She indeed states that since the early days of the Brazilian dictatorship in the 1970s, the United States has not prioritised Brazil but also never neglected the southern giant (Crandall 2011: 2–3). Cooperation between the two countries varies and is issue driven, while

> the degree to which common issues exist is driven by both 'structural' and 'agency' factors. The structural factors affecting the existence of common concerns are (1) the degree of relative power disparity between the two countries, and (2) their foreign policy traditions. The agency factor comprises the presence of policy makers interested in and capable of effecting closer engagement between the two countries. (Crandall 2011: 5)

Unsurprisingly, this leads to the conclusion that in the early 2000s, 'engagement between Washington and Brasilia on the two issues of the G-20 and ethanol occurred because both countries deemed them important' (2011: 243); however, the two countries' priorities barely ever overlap, so there is limited space for high-level interaction (2011: 192). This pragmatic approach is not shared by Moniz-Bandeira (2006), who sees Brazil rise *from dependency to equality*. Brazil's foremost public intellectual understands the rise of Brazil in the 1990s and early 2000s as a liberation from US dependency and sees the country on its way to become an equal partner to the United States with the backing of Mercosul and the international community as well as at that point its apparently consolidated democracy and growing economy. Brazil's former ambassador to the United States, Rubens Barbosa (2011, 2015) adds to the understanding of the US–Brazil relationship with his unique experience but sees the relationship in a less-positive light. Barbosa identifies three challenges to the bilateral relationship: 'connecting Brazil-U.S. interests; altering U.S. perceptions of Brazil; and imposing greater clarity on the question of what Brazil expects from its relationship with the United States'. In his 2015 review of his time as Brazilian ambassador to the United States, he can only find a *Washington Dissensus*. Due to the overwhelming number of opposing interests, Barbosa (2015: 16–17) calls his time in Washington undiplomatically 'a difficult period'. From global security to international trade and the political engagement of the United States in Latin America, the two countries did not share common ground on central political issues. Barbosa (2015: 236–37) closes his account with a call to leave this period of 'a certain disharmony' behind and to 'take measures to protect against future disagreements'. Finally, Sean Burges takes measure of *Brazil in the World*. His account touches upon all aspects of Brazil's foreign relations by aiming for a comprehensive theory of Brazil's foreign policy since the 1990s. A recurring theme in the book is Brazil's well-known quest for autonomy and its disdain for 'contests of relational power' (2017: 25). The relation between the United States and Brazil since the 1990s and in particular during the PT administrations is characterised by a contrast between ideology and pragmatism and ultimately leaves Brazil in the position as 'junior partner' (2017: 243, 254).

Literature on the US–Brazil Biofuels Partnership

Particular focus has been placed on the realm of ethanol diplomacy, where researchers have explored the lead-up to the 2007 MoU on biofuels between the two countries and the results of this cooperation in the following years. Paiva Benevides (2011) offers a very detailed work on the process of negotiating the 2007 biofuels MoU, starting with the consultation mechanism that was agreed upon in 2003. This research goes through the different stages of negotiations, citing documents, diplomatic cables and actors who were involved.

Nolte and Stolte (2007) analyse the biofuels MoU between the United States and Brazil and come to the conclusion that it aims at counterbalancing the growing influence of Venezuela, helps Brazil to find international markets for its ethanol and might support the US strategy to diversify its energy imports. It is more pragmatic than idealistic. Sotero (2007), on the other hand, calls the MoU 'symbolic' despite his optimism about the future of biofuels. He agrees with the assessment that the strategic value of potentially containing Venezuela is higher than the actual gains through the half-hearted biofuels cooperation.

Logan (2007) calls ethanol diplomacy a 'hoax' because the interests of the United States and Brazil diverge too much – Brazil wants international markets, while the United States wants to protect its own agricultural market. Although he does not focus on the question of Venezuela, it becomes clear that the MoU in itself does not contain very concrete steps for enhancing trade between the two countries – or even third parties.

Wright (2008) assesses the MoU one year after its signing in a conference proceeding. While the MoU is a success with regard to building trust between the United States and Brazil, it lacks technical success in terms of research output and trade promotion. Wright mentions the small role of the International Biofuels Forum (IBF), a discussion platform consisting of Brazil, China, the European Commission, India, South Africa and the United States with the aim of developing standards for biofuels, and underlines the need for standardisation. The IBF will be considered in the chapter on Brazil's multilateral ethanol diplomacy.

W. Almeida (2009) points out that international investment in Brazilian biofuels increased after the signing of the MoU. In his view, the Central American countries especially profited by receiving a higher rate of investment in research and technological capabilities with regard to ethanol. Hollander (2010) presents an interesting view by highlighting the connection between the negotiations on the FTAA and the 2007 biofuels MoU, and how influential lobbying groups – including the Inter-American Commission on Ethanol (IACE) – worked towards the agreement. He outlines the interests and connections between agro-business in Florida and Brazil and unveils the role of Jeb Bush leading up to the MoU.

Romano Schutte (2012) provides the most recent analysis of Brazil–US relations in the ethanol sector, by looking at the period right before the ongoing crisis hit the industry. He comes to the conclusion that external factors play a minor role in the success of ethanol diplomacy. He attributes a possible success to the performance of the domestic ethanol market and asks whether the industry can meet increased demand in the long run.

From this overview, we can deduce several conclusions. On the one hand, it is clear that the 2007 MoU between Brazil and the United States is the central event that will be scrutinised in the further analysis. Even if this did not yield the expected (or hoped for) profits, the benefit of increased trust between the two partners (until the US National Security Agency (NSA) spy scandal) was of value. For the United States, just as for Brazil, ethanol diplomacy seems to play a minor role and mainly serves higher-ranking goals, such as balancing Venezuela. In the chapter on Brazil's relationship with the United States, I clarify to what extent Brazil was pursuing an opening of the US market for Brazilian ethanol as a primary goal and what other higher-ranking goals might have been involved. I also explore how Brazil performed in assessing its partners' positions in the negotiations and how Brazil's behaviour in international politics varies depending on the relative power of its partner.

The Neoclassical Realist approach would suggest that we consider the structural setting first. In this circumstance, Brazil and the United States can be seen as competing actors who would reach an agreement only if the relative balance of power would not be disturbed. However, the problems of climate change and energy security pressure the two countries to enter into negotiations, and the question at this point is whether each of the countries – with Brazil having less leverage – assesses its counterpart's preferences and capabilities appropriately to reach a viable agreement. With the 2007 MoU, such an agreement has been reached; the implementation, however, has been very poor, something that the Neoclassical approach would predict if the partners were not very successful at interpreting their respective counterparts. Additionally, the power balance between Brazil and the United States adds to the difficulty of finding a working agreement since the two countries are regional leaders and yet face a strong asymmetry of power. The case of Brazil and Mozambique will further assess how such power asymmetries affected the outcome of Brazil's ethanol diplomacy.

Brazil–Mozambique

The relationship between Brazil and Mozambique is special because it is one of the closest that Brazil has with any African country. Mozambique is one of the biggest beneficiaries of Brazilian foreign aid and state investment. The cooperation includes the trilateral project ProSavana (with Japan) to develop agricultural capabilities in the tropical savannah in Mozambique. Parts of the newly developed capabilities will be used for sugarcane production to develop a national ethanol industry. Bambo (2014: 52) understands the cooperation between Brazil and Mozambique as a flagship project with high hopes of spill-over effects to neighbouring countries.

Atanassov assesses the state of biofuels projects in Mozambique for the Overseas Development Institute (ODI) and shows that only three of six authorised projects have been implemented, with the current ethanol output at less than 1 per cent (3,500 tonnes in 2012–13) (2013: 3) of the projected output in those years. This project has had a rocky start not only in terms of project implementation but also in social terms. Gunter (2010) raises concerns about negative social, environmental and energy security consequences of 'agrofuels' in Mozambique. She points out that the ethanol from ProSavana would be for export and therefore would not lower Mozambique's dependence on oil imports. As a result, the consumer base for ethanol would not be expanded, which is one of Brazil's goals. Whether this focus on economic diversification rather than on strategic energy security explains the lack of success of the program is explored in this section, as are Brazil's potential miscalculations of Mozambique's preferences.

Lima (2013) further shows how the Innovative System of the Agriculture Sector program that is supported by Embrapa and ABC had difficulties thus far proving that the social impact will not be negative on small farmers in the country. She claims that Brazil's main partners in Africa, Angola and Mozambique, where most of its South–South cooperation is based on natural resources, have seen strong private sector engagement, which has the potential to be exploitative rather than beneficial for the people.

There is another side, however, to Brazil's efforts in Mozambique. Chichava et al. (2013) point out that Brazil aims to export its own development model to the Global South as an example of successful development policies. This model is guided by the principles of solidarity, non-interference and demand-driven action. Mozambique, as the top recipient of Brazilian foreign aid, receives a high rate of private investment from Brazilian companies, facilitated with credit lines from BNDES, which also guarantees Brazil access to internal processes in Mozambique; for example, Embrapa is hosted in a department of the Ministry of Agriculture. It also reflects a gradual permeation of private interests and capital into development cooperation initiatives, mainly in the agricultural sector. The critical point is how Brazilian, Japanese and Mozambican interests converge within ProSavana in order to judge the success of the project.

Ekman and Macamo (2014) call ProSavana a top-down initiative that might fail to deliver the social aspects of the program that had been promised. At the same time, the effects on the environment and small-scale farmers seem to be detrimental and underline the problems that come with Brazil's principle of non-involvement.

In the relationship with Mozambique, several issues of Brazil's ethanol diplomacy in the South–South context become clear. First, Brazil is willing to project power towards weaker partners (e.g. it would not be possible for Brazil to infiltrate US institutions in the same way), and second, private sector involvement is strong and might lead to adverse developmental effects in the recipient countries. It is unclear, however, whether Brazil is pursuing a strategy of power projection or international coalition building in the case of Mozambique.

Analytically, we can see a strong power asymmetry between Brazil and Mozambique, which in Realist terms would suggest that Brazil could either project its power and strategy on the African country and Mozambique would engage in a bandwagoning strategy or look for different partners to balance its influence. While the two countries have found a way of cooperating outside a traditional bandwagon set-up, the yields of the cooperation are not clear. This is when we need to address the internal level and see how the respective elites perceived the cooperation and what conclusions they drew from this information. It seems as though the Brazilian foreign policy complex (FPC) overestimated its own capabilities to project power and influence domestic politics in Mozambique while misjudging the true preferences of the African country.

World Trade Organization

The Doha Round of negotiations began in 2001 and broke down in 2007. Since 2011, new efforts have been made to conclude the round, and in December 2013, the Bali Declaration made it seem like progress might be made. The main negotiating groups in the area of agriculture are the United States, the European Union, G-20, G33, the Cairns Group and indirectly NAMA11 (from Non-Agricultural Market Access negotiations). The G-20 demands market access to the big developed markets but under Brazilian leadership has requested additional rights to protect their own markets. NAMA11 is a group of developing countries that demands access to markets for goods that are not covered by the agricultural agreement, which includes some agricultural products. The main target of this group is to give flexibility to developing countries in the context of any possible agreement. The Cairns Group comprises large agricultural countries, both developing and developed, that want a liberalised market. The memberships of Cairns and G-20 overlap substantially and Brazil is a member of both. At the 2003 WTO meeting in Cancun, Brazil's emphasis shifted towards the founding and leadership of G-20 reflecting its prioritisation of South–South cooperation (Ondetti and Rhodes 2010: 9). Another relevant group for the agricultural part of the negotiations is G33 and consists of developing countries that have a rather protectionist view on agricultural markets. While Cairns represents the most Liberal view on agricultural markets, G33 represents the most protectionist positions, with G-20 at an intermediary ground and overlapping partnerships. The connection between non-agricultural and agricultural topics and alliances raises the level of complexity of these negotiations (Ribeiro 2007: 24) and is covered in more detail in the chapter on Brazil's multilateral ethanol diplomacy.

In the most relevant study for Brazil's engagement in the WTO, Hopewell (2013) gives a detailed account of how the Brazilian state used resources from agro-business to advance its position in the WTO negotiations on agriculture. She further points out the conscious framing of the Doha Round from development towards agriculture and describes how Brazil developed a strong anti-North narrative to form the G-20. However, the policies that Brazil is requesting do not materially help many developing countries since at this point in time they benefit from EU import quotas but could not compete with highly efficient agro-industries, such as the Brazilian.

The other Brazilian strategy within the Doha Round is to aim for a reclassification of ethanol. Howse, van Bork and Hebebrand (2006) give a good introduction to the WTO system of agricultural regulations and lay out how the framework classifies industrial, environmental and agricultural goods. Harmer (2009) focuses on the WTO biofuel regulation in detail. Ethanol is classified as an agricultural rather than an industrial product. This means that subsidies are coherent with the WTO's AoA. I mentioned earlier that the Brazilian government has been ambiguous as to whether ethanol should be classified as an agricultural, environmental or industrial product. Their position on this issue also depends on whether the free trade or a climate change discourse is the dominant one at the given time. Thorstensen et al. (2012: 417) argue that Brazil's primary interest lies in guiding the Committee on Trade and Environment (CTE) towards classifying ethanol as an environmental good while making sure through bilateral negotiations that it will not be reclassified as an agricultural product.

Husar and Mildner (2007) see trade negotiations as a two-level game, which needs to accommodate international and domestic interests and demands. Unlike India, Brazil is not an entirely defensive actor. Brazil is offensive in opening agricultural markets and willing to bargain in the areas of telecommunications, services and industrial goods. In the area of services, in particular financial services, Brazil fears the free flow of capital and the resulting lack of sovereignty in fiscal policies. The question of financial services has a higher priority than that of agriculture and reflects the dominance of government over business. There are no formalised consultation mechanisms to include business and/or civil society in the negotiations, so the decision remains with the executive. The Brazilian government is therefore forced to seek discourse at the international level.

Unfortunately, this discourse at the international level is not always successful. In a critical assessment of Lula's foreign policy, Almeida (2010) concludes that Brazil lacks one of the most important factors for being a major power: acceptance by its neighbours. Lula's foreign policy served more of his own party's interests and his own legacy than that of the state, which led to irrational alliances on the global scene rather than fruitful relations with its neighbours. Due to diverging interests with its partners China and India, Brazil could not bring the Doha Round to conclusion. Even so, Brazil's diplomatic presence is bigger than its economic or military power would suggest.

Looking at Brazil's actions from a Realist perspective, we can see that Brazil aims to balance the influence of the traditional Northern powers within the

WTO. A Realist understanding, however, could hardly explain why Brazil chooses to stay within the WTO and is trying to reform the balance of power from within rather than creating an alternative institutional framework, possibly within the UNFCCC or within an emissions-trading scheme. In the recent past, Brazil created an alternative institutional framework with the BRICS bank as a counterweight to the World Bank. This arena switching can partially be observed as Brazil now reframes the issue of biofuels as an environmental question and pushes for quota and mandates within the climate change negotiations, but not in the trade area.

From a Liberal perspective, the Brazilian insistence on negotiating within the WTO does not seem to be a smart choice either. One can hardly believe that the interests of Brazil's international companies have been served by the lack of an agreement of the Doha Round. One could argue that the protection of the domestic market is one reason for the lack of agreement within the Doha Round, but this seems more like a political preference of the political party in power rather than of the interest groups supposedly concerned with international trade. This brings us to the Neoclassical Realist approach that looks at the inside of the FPC. In this case, the ideas of the PT as well as the assessment of the international situation by the FPC give a hint as to why Brazil remains committed to the Doha Round and why it has not been able to reach the desired general opening of the markets for ethanol and its reclassification. On the one hand, the Brazilian government values multilateralism highly and remains committed to the existing international institutions. On the other hand, the Brazilian FPC was under the impression that it could successfully shape the outcome of the Doha Round. This is due to the fact that Brazil has successfully launched two major cases within the WTO dispute settlement mechanism (the Cotton Case and the Sugar Case) and successfully built a coalition to get the Brazilian Roberto Azevêdo elected secretary general of the WTO. The Brazilian FPC, however, has not been able to transfer the success in these areas to successful negotiations, and throughout my fieldwork I will look at what obstacles the Brazilian FPC encountered and how the people involved in the process reacted to these obstacles.

At this point, we have seen an overview of the study of Brazil's international ethanol strategy. To answer the research question 'why has Brazil failed to achieve a global market for ethanol?' I rely on a Neoclassical Realist framework in a case study design with three empirical chapters, using process tracing as the central method of enquiry.

As explained in the background section, the international arena was welcoming towards increased use of biofuels during the examined period, which eliminates structural explanations as to why the global market was not created. The Liberal view cannot explain this failure either, since there is no direct participation in the negotiation process by opposing interest groups and one can suggest that a government would not enter negotiations in the first place if it was facing strong domestic opposition to such negotiations. Therefore, the Neoclassical Realist approach offers the strongest suggestion of why Brazil has failed to successfully implement its policy goal to create a global ethanol market. Generally speaking, this is caused by the role of the FPC that filters and interprets information in a way that can lead to suboptimal outputs. These include an overestimation of own capabilities, a lack of understanding the preferences of the negotiation partners and a suboptimal assessment of which arena to choose for negotiations, but also an internal lack of coordination and rivalries among agents that might be able to achieve better outcomes when working together.

In the case of Brazil–US negotiations, we can see that Brazil was overplaying its hand by not opening its market quickly and therefore discouraging the United States from making further concessions when it was possible. Similarly, Brazil reduced cooperation after the NSA scandal to a minimum, which shows how the internal political debate dominated particular interests in Brazil without actually changing the balance of power between the two countries.

In the case of Mozambique, Brazil again overestimated its own capabilities to produce results abroad. At this point, it is unclear whether Brazil also misjudged Mozambique's preferences in the negotiations and beyond or whether Brazil assumed that money and soft power could adjust them according to Brazil's needs. While the Brazilian FPC was smart to finance the ProSavana project through trilateral cooperation with Japan to avoid complaints by domestic Brazilian actors who would have rather seen investment into the domestic sugar and ethanol sectors, Brazil was not able to roll out substantial production or at least set the base for including Mozambique into the global ethanol circle through blending mandates or common standards.

The WTO case shows us that Brazil is committed to multilateralism even if it does not bear fruits in the foreseeable future. While Brazil has been successful in creating balancing coalitions within the WTO, this does not seem to greatly benefit Brazil's interests apart from the election of the Brazilian Roberto Azevêdo as secretary general – a move that merely comes with an increase in prestige and potentially soft power but has not materialised in agreements or benefits for the country. With these successes in the background, the Brazilian FPC assumed that the Doha Round could reach an equally successful outcome for the country as the two cases within the dispute settlement mechanism. The miscalculation on the part of Brazil is that because it knows how to play by the rules that it will be able to use these rules for its own benefits. In the actual Doha negotiations, however, these rules do not apply and the Brazilian

FPC has clear difficulties in orchestrating efforts to reach an agreement and in coordinating its various partners in the Southern alliances.

The literature review has shown that there are substantial gaps in the research that has been conducted thus far, and this study aims at closing these gaps, especially in terms of understanding Brazil's approach towards foreign policy implementation and its driving forces. In particular, I mean to connect the bilateral and multilateral levels of Brazilian foreign policy in one coherent structure, test hypotheses at the NPAs of the process and delve deeper into the negotiation processes and the way decisions have been made through qualitative expert interviews.

Chapter 4

THE BRAZIL–US ETHANOL RELATIONSHIP

Introduction

This chapter will analyse how Brazil and the United States reached agreements on ethanol issues in a time frame dating back to the beginning of the first Lula government (1 January 2003) to the end of the first term of President Dilma Rousseff (31 December 2014). The ethanol diplomacy between the two countries played a special role in their relationship. As was shown in the literature review in Chapter 3, the two countries have lived through ups and downs in their bilateral relationship. The early 2000s was a particularly difficult period, when Brazil was on the rise and looking towards a levelled position regarding the United States but with generally diverging interests and positions regarding questions of security, trade and South American governance. In that sense, the structural conditions for an agreement cannot be seen as particularly permissive; however, the attitudes of the leadership of the two countries that wanted and needed to show diplomatic successes added a very beneficial element. This chapter will examine whether the 2007 biofuels MoU between the United States and Brazil constitutes a new period of good relations or merely one light in a sea of darkness. It will first establish an initial account of the structural relations between the countries, the most obvious one being the structural disadvantage that Brazil has towards the United States, but also include attitudes towards each other in their respective foreign policies. This will be followed by a mapping of the actors and institutions involved in the process, which effectively means drawing out the components of the respective foreign policy complex (FPC). Finally, I will track the developments towards the 2007 MoU on biofuels, assess its outcomes and its implementation phase up to the NSA spy scandal. The process tracing will end at the end of President Dilma Rousseff's (in the following 'Dilma') first term as president of Brazil with an assessment of the rapprochement between the two countries. To conclude this chapter, I will summarise the findings and describe the mechanisms that directed the two countries' negotiation strategies and relationship in general terms and therefore the outcomes of their ethanol diplomacy. I will show that despite formal mechanisms and opportunities to engage in ethanol diplomacy, the Brazilian FPC never truly prioritised ethanol diplomacy, leading to its ultimate failure to create a global market for ethanol.

The Structural Environment

Background

Brazil's View on the United States

When looking at the state of US–Brazil relations, it becomes clear that despite the obvious gap in power and influence, Brazil aspires to be an equal partner of the United States. Even former foreign minister Celso Amorim (2015) judged it to be a fair assessment, however, that the United States has greater leverage over Brazil than vice versa. This reflects an assessment of the Brazil–US relationship as a '"core-periphery" model of international dominance' (Costa 2010: 3), which is shared by most Brazilian diplomats. While the relationship is characterised as 'central and asymmetric' (Veiga/Rios 2006: 23), there is little doubt that due to this understanding of the international system, Brazil used to pay more attention to the actions of the United States than vice versa. Former ambassador Castro Neves (2012: 4) talks about 'benign indifference' by the United States towards Brazil and a resulting 'general distrust' by Brazil towards the United States. Costa (2010: 9) even calls 'the perpetuation of the differences in power between the two countries' one of the two key factors in the bilateral relationship. The second key factor is that

> internal political processes produce additional complications. Most Brazilian diplomats understand quite well the power of US congressmen to mix parochial domestic politics with foreign policy. (2010: 10)

This is different from Itamaraty's self-perception as a prestigious institution through all of its history that only had to share its core competency – making Brazilian foreign policy – with the respective president. In practical terms, this meant that due to Brazil's economic stability in the Lula era, the country's focus switched to regional integration and new international partnerships, and the United States also became secondary in Brazil's foreign policy under Lula (Sanchez Milani 2011: 81). And while 'Brazilian officials do not ignore the United States [they] save their energy to advance their grand strategy elsewhere' (Costa 2010: 12).

Vigenvani (2011: 17), on the other hand, believes that Brazil was driven away from the United States by the 'intensification of North American unilateralism under George W. Bush'.[1] This has resulted in what Gratius (2003: 6) describes as a three-tiered Brazilian strategy on regional trade: first, Brazil under Lula tried to delay the Free Trade Agreement of the Americas (FTAA); second, higher importance was given to MercoSul; and third, Brazil was always open and eventually preferred a bilateral solution to trade questions between North and South America. In this sense, Brazil is trying to find an equilibrium between bandwagoning and balancing US power in South America and globally (Veiga/Rios 2006: 25). This can be illustrated by the fact that after the terrorist attacks of 9/11, Brazil 'instead of offering support in the global fight against terror, [...] proposed to initiate a global struggle against poverty, making clear its limited willingness' (Hirst 2013: 62) to participate in Washington's war against terror.

With the US indifference towards South America in the early 2000s and Brazil's economic rise, the Brazilian desire to be treated as an equal became more pronounced and the Bush and Lula relationship can be characterised as an ideal situation from the Brazilian viewpoint (Whitehead and Nolte 2012: 5). One could summarise the position of Brazil towards the United States with the clear power asymmetry, Brazil's desire to be treated as an equal and Brazil's struggle between balancing and bandwagoning the United States in South America and towards Brazil's neighbours.

The US View towards Brazil

Abraham Lowenthal states that Latin America has been losing importance for the United States since the end of the Cold War, given geostrategic practicalities and trade diversification. This has been more impactful for South America, where the personal and economic interdependence is not as striking as in Mexico, Central America and the Caribbean (Lowenthal 2010a: 185–89). Veiga and Rios (2006: 5) point out that after the World Trade Center attacks in 2001, the US foreign policy turned from an economic development paradigm towards a national security paradigm, while after the election of President Lula in 2002, the country's foreign policy course shifted from a Liberal trade paradigm to a national development idea. This clashed with US interests on numerous occasions, especially in the question of international agricultural regulation and trade.

In geopolitical terms, Einaudi (2011: 7) confirms that the formation of the Union of South American Nations (UNASUR) and the South American Defence Council definitely marked the end of the Monroe Doctrine, with

1. 'intensificação do unilateralismo norte-americano na administração W. Bush'.

Brazil's demand that South American defence can be dealt with in the region and without US involvement. Furthermore, Latin American countries have not been close allies in ventures on large-scale issues where the United States needs international support, such as trade and climate change (Lowenthal 2010a: 189). This is what made Brazil one of the main addressees of US foreign policy in Latin America where a strategic partnership is sought (2010a: 191). Hirst (2013: 193) describes the United States' position on Brazil as 'affirmation with a sense of opportunity'. Additionally, during Lula's second term, Brazil 'achieved a high degree of *previsibilidad*, i.e. stability of expectations about the rules of the game and about the established process by which they could be altered' (Lowenthal 2010b), and with its active participation in international fora, Brazil became a target of US foreign policy (2010a: 199).

The position of the United States towards Brazil is mainly characterised by the loss of focus after the de facto end of the Monroe Doctrine in the early 2000s. While the United States sees Brazil as a potential partner in South America, it remains difficult for the United States to assess Brazil's preferences despite its increased *previsibilidad*, and therefore, for a longer part of the period under observation, Brazil does not expect a high degree of reliability from the latter.

Why and How Do Brazil and the United States Work Together

As we saw before, the Council on Foreign Relations Brazil Task Force (CFR 2011: 7) points out that the relationship between the United States and Brazil 'has more often been characterised by distance than by close friendship, substantive collaboration has been shallow and prone to misunderstanding'. But despite these differences, the countries have a shared interest in creating a 'world market' for ethanol (Abdenur 2006) and more commonly share 'interests in improving energy efficiency, reducing carbon intensity, promoting the development of biofuels, expanding the use of natural gas, and managing offshore oil exploration and development' (CFR 2011: 31). These common interests, however, cannot distract from the omnipresent 'mutual mistrust [...] in the background of the Brazil-US relationship' (Costa 2010: 11). With the increased exchange between the two countries in the early 2000s, some authors have come to the conclusion that 'currently, relations between the United States and Brazil may be characterised as friendly' (Meyer 2010: 11). The emphasis in this assessment should lie on the word 'currently', but still this can be seen as an achievement of the work both countries put into establishing mechanisms of exchange and coordination.

At the time of Dilma's first official visit to the United States, Piccone (2012) sees the US–Brazil relationship as improving. Several issues of low strategic priority (such as education) were being worked on, and a strong convergence of interests on the global level (with the exception of Brazil's main strategic goal, a UNSC reform) was in the making. The main strategic issues, however, such as questions of regional order, have not been addressed in US–Brazil dialogues since the end of the FTAA negotiations.

One can see that at the beginning of the examined period, the two countries were neither friends nor partners. Due to an alignment of topical interests, such as renewable and later fossil energy or the desire to balance Hugo Chavez's Venezuela, from the early days of the Lula era, the two countries entered into dialogues that would eventually lead to higher levels of trust and mutual understanding. Since this interest rather than ideas guided the process, Neoclassical Realism as an explanatory approach is appropriate.

Bilateral Mechanisms in Place at the Beginning of the Lula Presidency

At the beginning of the Lula presidency in January 2003, there were two bilateral exchange mechanisms in place: the US–Brazil Bilateral Consultative Mechanism (BCM) and the Consultative Committee on Agriculture (CCA).

The BCM was established in March 2001, during the visit of President Cardoso to the United States. The aim of the BCM on trade and investment was to 'institutionalise the bilateral trade dialogue and resolve outstanding bilateral conflicts' (USITC 2002: 4–41). This mechanism, however, only convened three times during the presidency of Fernando Henrique Cardoso: once in July 2001, when multilateral trade issues (WTO and FTAA) were discussed; once in October 2001, when due to the 9/11 attacks, only political and defence questions were addressed; and finally, in November 2002, when questions about biotechnology (soy) and WTO compliance were addressed. One can say that this mechanism was little institutionalised at the beginning of the Lula era.

The CCA was established in October 2000 between the US Department of Agriculture (USDA) and the Brazilian Ministry of Agriculture (Ministério de Agricultura e do Abastecimento – MAPA). The goal was to create a high-level forum for discussion and coordination of questions related to agriculture, agricultural trade and market access, and related technological cooperation and investment (MAPA 2000). With one to two annual meetings and the agricultural questions at the centre of US–Brazil trade, this mechanism quickly achieved a high level of acceptance and institutionalisation.

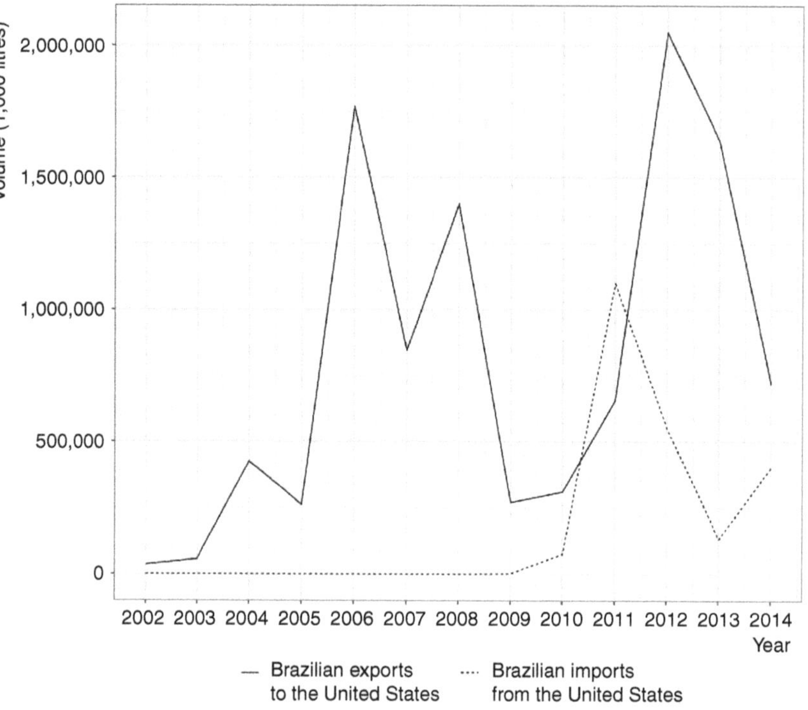

Figure 6 Brazilian sugar and ethanol production, 2003–14 (*Source*: UNICA data 2016).

Brazil–US Production of and Trade in Ethanol

Brazil and the United States are the two biggest producers, exporters and consumers of ethanol globally. It is unquestioned that it would be in both countries' interest to create a global ethanol market through the full commodification of ethanol (e.g. CEBEU 2006: 39). Between 2003 and 2014, Brazil almost doubled its annual ethanol production from 14,736 million litres to 28,480 million litres (Figure 6).[2]

Between 2004 and 2014, the United States produced on average 40 billion litres annually, but did increase its production in this time frame almost fivefold from 12 billion to 65 billion litres (Figure 7). The trade between the two

2. The Brazilian sugarcane harvest season starts on 1 April and ends on 31 March of the following year. For reasons of comparison, the Brazilian numbers used here represent the harvest output but are compared with the calendar year output of the United States . The height of the harvest is between July and December, when also the ethanol exports peak. See Santos et al. (2012), chapter 3, on planting sugarcane.

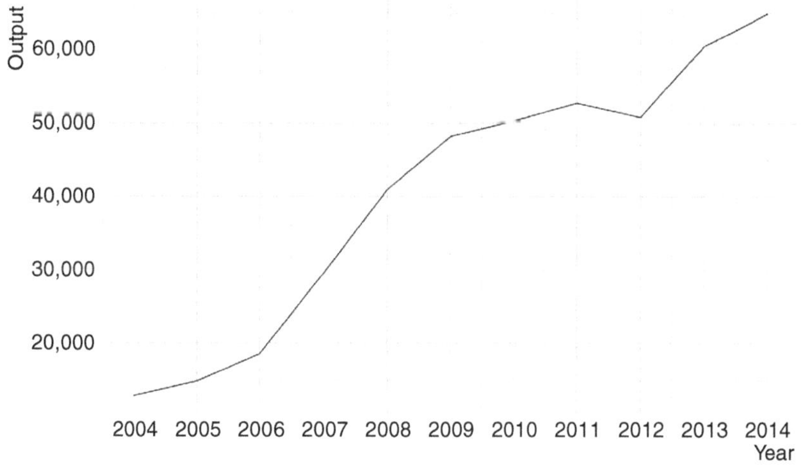

Figure 7 US fuel ethanol production in thousand litres, 2004–14 (*Sources*: US Energy Information Agency, 2004–10, http://www.eia.gov/todayinenergy/detail.cfm?id=3070; US Energy Information Agency, 2011–12, http://www.eia.gov/cfapps/ipdbproject/iedindex3.cfm?tid=79&pid=80&aid=1&cid=regions&syid=2000&eyid=2012&unit=TBPD; Renewable Fuels Association, 2013–14, http://bff.738.myftpupload.com/resources/industry/statistics/#1456770302650-ba1c280f-bad8).

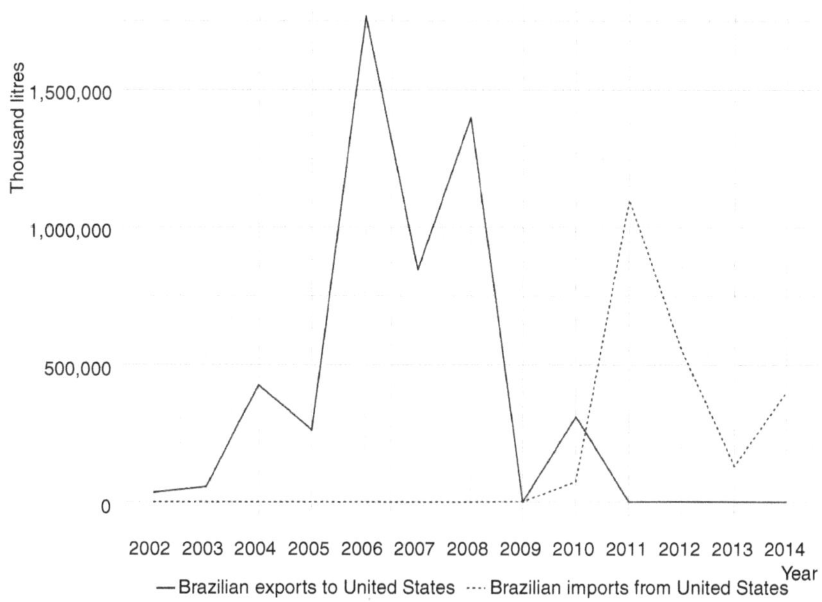

Figure 8 Ethanol trade between the United States and Brazil, 2002–14 (*Source*: MDIC – Alice Web (2016)).

countries varied substantially. While in 2003 barely any ethanol was traded, the trade peaked in summer 2006 and summer 2008 (Figure 8).

Brazil as a Strategic Proxy of the United States: Balancing Venezuela

While South America has continuously lost the attention of the United States since the late 1990s, its strategic value is still high for the country. This means that it is in the interest of the United States to make sure that South American countries generally agree with the ideals of Liberal democracy and open economies. The so-called pink tide (first used by Rohter (2005c); see also Bull (2013) and Enríquez (2013)) in Latin America in the early 2000s, when leftist parties took over governments through electoral victories, reflected a backlash against the neoliberal Washington Consensus of the 1990s and thereby also questioned Washington's dominance and influence in the region.

The main proponent of opposition towards the United States was Venezuelan President Hugo Chavez. His model of 'socialism of the 21st century' and new 'Bolivarism' proclaimed autonomy from US influence and an economic model that did not converge to the ideal that the United States pursued in the region and worldwide. Starting with Chavez's accession to the presidency in 1999, he rhetorically and politically opposed US influence in the region. Venezuela's influence continually increased with rising commodity prices – especially hydrocarbons – and gave the country a tool for political aid and building alliances. Michael Porter of the Virginia Military Institute openly talks about Venezuela under Chavez being a 'threat to US interests in South America' (Porter 2008: 2), while suggesting increased cooperation with Brazil as an alternative power in the continent. This positioned Brazil as a counterpoint towards Venezuela. Still Brazil had a leftist government with a state-driven development agenda, which was open to dialogue with the United States and committed to democracy domestically and the institutions of the Western-dominated world order internationally. Senator Lugar indicatively asked at an event at the Brookings Institution (2007) why 'Venezuela should be left with a monopoly of diplomacy' in the region and underlined the importance of finding a counterweight to Chavez's initiatives.

Burges (2007: 1343) underlines that 'officially Brazil and Venezuela are not competing for the leadership of South America. Both countries are working towards the same ends, namely the creation of an integrated South America' but are in fact competing for leadership on the continent with two different visions of integration, what he describes as the contrast between 'policy pragmatism and attempts at ideological purity'. In that sense, Brazil was important to the United States. It was the only actor in Latin America that could attract other MercoSul members away from the oil wealth that Venezuela had to offer and instead guide them towards economic openness and maintain them within the political spectrum of Liberal democracies. CFR (2011: 55) recognises that Brazil 'helped neutralise Chávez's ideological resonance in the region' and with the creation of UNASUL 'balance[d] the Venezuela-dominated Alianza Bolivariana para los Pueblos de Nuestra América (the Bolivarian Alliance for the Peoples of Our America, or ALBA)' (CFR 2011: 59). This was a tricky situation for Brazil to manage. It had to balance its own autonomy, one central goal of its foreign policy, with the benefits of cooperating with Washington but at the same time not appear as a proxy of the United States in Latin America and thereby alienate its neighbours.

With the nationalisation of Petrobras facilities in Bolivia in May 2006 – which Chavez supported – Brazil saw a breaking point in the relationship between the two countries and began to more openly criticise the Bolivarian way (Burges 2007: 1355). In this sense, Sotero (2007) sees the Brazil–US 2007 MoU on biofuels as a tool to diversify energy demand away from Venezuela and work as a countermeasure against Venezuela's 'anti-American influence across the region', while Cosh (2007) outlines the divide that ethanol created between Venezuela (against) and Cuba (in favour). The *Economist* (2007) suggests that a dependence on Brazilian ethanol would be more desirable than a dependence on Venezuelan or Iranian oil and gas for Western states.

Hence, the external pressure created by Venezuela increased Brazil's value as a moderately leftist power with influence over the future of South American integration for the United States.

When Chavez passed away while still in office in 2013, the commodity boom neared its end, and his successor, President Nicholas Maduro, does not dispose of the same rhetorical abilities or political talent as Chavez, which has decreased Brazil's importance in balancing Venezuela's influence in Latin and South America.

US FDI and Development Aid in Brazil

Brazil shows a certain dependency on the United States with regard to trade, with the latter as a destination for Brazilian products, and on foreign direct investment (FDI) (Teixeira 2011: 14). The 2008 financial crisis changed the FDI landscape and made the BRICS nations attractive destinations for FDI. Brazil was an especially good destination since it has the most open economy among the BRICS countries, with its relatively 'open investment regime with no restrictions on remission of profits and repatriation of capital' (Kapoor and Tewari 2010: 152). One can see this increasing trust in Brazil as a destination of FDI after 2008, with the 2009 two billion USD loan to Petrobras by the US Export–Import Bank to purchase drilling equipment (Langevin 2013: 14).

With Brazil's economic rise, international and especially US development aid slowed down and plays a less important role in Brazil today. As Brazil 'is considered a middle-income country [it] does not receive large amounts of US foreign assistance' (Meyer 2010: 12).

US development assistance has continuously declined in the observed period. It plays a rather symbolic and political role in today's Brazil rather than an economic one. Trilateral development projects, however, are one aspect of US assistance to Brazil that matter more as one Brazilian diplomat confirmed on the promise of anonymity. They usually entail Brazil (ABC) carrying out development projects in third countries (e.g. Mozambique) with US (USAID) funding. These types of cooperation, however, do not necessarily create dependencies that would influence the questions of trade and domestic use of ethanol.

US Attitudes towards the Use and Trade of Biofuels

Similar to Brazil, the United States in the 1970s and 1980s developed programs to incentivise the production of ethanol as a fuel to partially substitute gasoline. From the initial goal of reducing gasoline consumption, the intention switched towards improving the levels of air pollution and finally to reducing the emission of greenhouse gases (Rios et al. 2001: 51–52). Additionally, methyl tert-butyl ether (MTBE) was gradually outlawed as an octane-enhancing additive to gasoline from 2004 onwards on state levels (US EIA 2003), which opened the way 'to develop new markets for agricultural products [through] the replacement [of] MTBE by ethanol as octane enhancer' (Monteiro et al. 2012: 194).

Due to the political influence and economic importance of US corn growers, 'most [presidential candidates in 2008] are in favour of ethanol as a general proposition' (Senator Lugar at Brookings 2007), and this statement can certainly be extended to the majority of administrators and politicians on the national level. This is reflected by President Bush's signature of the US Energy Policy Act 2005 (Public Law 109–58) in August 2005, a bill that the US Congress had passed the month before with an overwhelming majority in the Senate (85–12) and a large majority in the House of Representatives (275–156). The 2005 Energy Policy Act increased the mandatory use of biofuels and laid the groundwork for the Renewable Fuel Standard (RFS) that was extended in the Energy Independence and Security Act of 2007 (Public Law 110–140). Already in the 2004 Jobs Creation Act, ethanol played a crucial role, with the strategic switch from an excise tax exemption to a blender tax credit and the extension of the ethanol tax exemption to 2010 (Tyner 2008: 647). The most relevant provision of the 2005 Energy Policy Act was the introduction of a blending mandate of renewable fuel into gasoline by volume, which would later become known as the RFS.[3] The 2007 Energy Independence and Security Act expanded on the RFS and increased the volume of mandatory biofuel blend. Under this provision, fuel producers had to blend 66.9 billion gallons (304.13 billion litres) by the year 2012, subsequently increasing annual amounts up to 36.0 billion gallons (163.66 billion litres) by the year 2022.

Tyner (2015) mentions corn ethanol's impact on food prices in the United States, which is seen critically by livestock producers and their representatives. This adds to the domestic pressure that had been created by the so-called Tortilla Crisis in Mexico 2007, when food prices rose to an extent that even middle-class people were heavily affected by it. Thomaz and Carvalho (2011) point out the discussion this caused in the United States and the pressure that was created on the government and on producers of corn and ethanol. This discussion is reflected by David Sandalow's comments at an event at the Brookings Institution (2007), when he pointed out that

> corn-based ethanol is a different product than cellulosic ethanol than sugar-based ethanol. I mean at the end they're all the same, but their impact on the environment is different. What we need to do is develop labelling systems and tracing systems so that we really give incentives to people to use the most sustainably produced biofuels.

One of these labelling systems is the 'Advanced Biofuel' certification by the US Environmental Protection Agency (EPA). Ethanol from Brazilian sugarcane has been granted this status by the EPA, which brings higher blending mandates and prioritised funding options in research and development (UNICA 2010).

In summary, the United States is very open to using ethanol as a substitute for gasoline mainly due to domestic considerations in the so-called corn belt, but also due to the strategic goal to be less dependent on oil imports. Environmental and sustainability concerns also play a role, and Brazilian ethanol as an advanced biofuel is in a strong position to fill the market gap that was created by the RFS and the phase-out of MTBE.

3. The 2005 Energy Policy Act mandated 41.8 billion gallons/190 billion litres (2006: 4.0; 2007: 4.7; 2008: 5.4; 2009: 6.1; 2010: 6.8; 2011: 7.4; 2012: 7.5) of renewable fuel to be added to standard gasoline by the year 2012.

Trade and Market Barriers

With increasing bilateral trade in the 2000s, some frictions between the two countries rose in questions of trade (CFR 2011: 68).

The main points of contention in ethanol trade between the United States and Brazil are import tariffs, domestic subsidies and the lack of common standards. I will discuss each of these issues in turn, highlighting the specific challenge they pose as a market barrier.

Import Tariffs

When Gratius (2003: 2) mentions that 'the Bush administration's foreign trade policy towards Latin America is dominated by a two-track approach to free trade that includes simultaneous multilateral and bilateral efforts', she points out how the United States tries to guide other countries towards giving up import restrictions. As mentioned before, the United States exercised a substantial import tariff on Brazilian ethanol and vice versa during the majority of the time under observation. The US import tariff on ethanol expired at the end of 2011. Until then a 54 US cents/gallon (11.89 cents/litre) was levied for ethanol imported from Brazil. This high tariff was considered one of the central causes for the lack of ethanol trade (de Gorter, Just and Tan 2009: 66).

Brazil paused its import tariff on ethanol in 2010 and extended this exemption in December 2011 until the end of 2015 (USDA-FAS 2012), possibly to entice its US counterparts to follow suit. The common external tariff for ethanol with less than 1 per cent water content is 20 per cent within MercoSul, but after pressure from the Brazilian government, it was added to the list of possible exemptions (USDA-FAS 2012). Additionally, importers had to pay a 9.25 per cent ('PIS-Cofins') on imported ethanol, which in return was credited to fully offset the initial tariff (Ewing 2015) after the domestic industry was granted a tax exemption in April 2013 (Reuters 2013). Both countries had high import tariffs at the beginning of the period under observation, which they were able to cancel at the end of peak ethanol production towards the end of this period. The cancellation of ethanol tariffs in the United States can for a substantial part be attributed to the lobbying work of UNICA (Brazilian Sugarcane Industry Association) in the United States, while Brazil's move away from import tariffs was determined by the need for higher imports (interview with one member of the Brazilian Parliament of the Frente Parlamentar pela Valorização do Setor Sucroenergético in 2014) and as a signal to open ethanol trade with the United States (Farina 2015).

Corn Subsidies

The 2002 US Farm Bill that eventually expired in 2007, with a new one to be passed in 2008, allowed the US government to subsidise US farmers at levels that made US corn based ethanol almost competitive with Brazilian ethanol (Skloven 2008: 3). In 2008, Congress overrode President Bush's veto against the Food, Conservation, and Energy Act of 2008 (2008 Farm Bill). This legislative act continued the large corn subsidies of the 2002 Farm Bill and introduced substantial state support for advanced biofuels and the development of biofuels in general.

Currently, according to Thomaz (2016: 133–34) the most important legislative drivers for the use of biofuels are the Energy Policy Act of 2005, the Energy Independence and Security Act of 2007, the California Low-Carbon Fuel Standard and the Farm Security and Rural Investment Act of 2014 (also 2014 Farm Bill). The 2014 Farm Bill was passed and signed with a delay of two years after the 2008 Farm Bill expired at the end of 2012. Thomaz (2016: 56) gives a useful overview of the central legislative acts used to subsidise corn-based ethanol in the United States.

One common thread through all these laws is the large subsidies for US corn producers. While Brazilian officials understand the difficulty of changing this regime in the United States, the question of subsidies has been contentious in bilateral meetings and is seen as a large market distortion that disfavours the cheaper Brazilian sugar-based ethanol, which is not directly subsidized by the state (Farina 2015).

Lack of Common Standards

When it comes to standards, both countries lack a common specification. This comes with high direct and indirect costs for traders on both sides of the table. The direct costs include the different standard itself, which means different operating costs and so on. The main difference between Brazil and US anhydrous ethanol specification is that US specifications require the ethanol to be free of hydrocarbons, a restriction that Brazil does not have (Trucco 2016). While this does not pose any restrictions to US exporters to Brazil, it requires an additional step of distillation for Brazilian producers.

The lack of standards also leads to a lack of financial products around ethanol. Winter (2012) points out that ethanol futures were at the time traded only on the Chicago Board of Trade and only for the US-produced corn variety, which leads to higher broker fees and the necessity to 'purchase complex forms of insurance to limit […] risks', which ultimately creates higher cost for the consumer and delays in technological development.

While the lack of common ethanol standards in Brazil and the United States does not inhibit trade from happening, it does add costs to transactions and hinders capital and investment from entering the market. In the broader picture, however, a global standard for fuel ethanol would increase trade possibilities significantly and therefore has been added to the bilateral agenda.

Actors and Institutions

This section will lay out the actors and institutions that are involved in the bilateral ethanol diplomacy. A full list of stakeholders can be found at the end of the references. It is important to note that the domestic 'ethanol complex' does not necessarily fully overlap with the decision-making FPC, but nevertheless both share significant overlap in individuals and connections.

Brazil

Several attempts have been made to map the Brazilian ethanol complex (Schlesinger 2012; Thomaz 2016; Kaup 2015), but so far only Benevides (2011) and Thomaz (2016) have tried to include its international dimension, that is, the overlap between the Brazilian FPC and the Brazilian ethanol complex. The results are mixed, and therefore, I will outline my interpretation of this important group of actors and institutions.

There are two central institutions in Brazilian foreign policy: the presidency and the Ministry of External Relations (MRE, or Itamaraty). While there is the institutional and practical prerogative of the presidency, Itamaraty sees itself as the main executor of Brazilian foreign policy. This tension can rise depending on a president's ambition, such as in the Lula years, when President Lula was actively pursuing his way of presidential travel diplomacy, or can be lower when a president such as Dilma does not make foreign policy her personal priority. Burges (2010) outlines the way Lula outshined Itamaraty with his way of representing Brazil internationally, while White (2013) gives credit to President Lula's decision to focus on Africa. This fits Beltrame's (2008: 9) characterisation of Brazilian presidential diplomacy:

> Ao conduzir pessoalmente a política externa, as ações do mandatário devem ultrapassar os atos protocolares. Interesse, capacidade, conhecimento sobre assuntos de política externa são fundamentais. Neste sentido, o presidente observa as oportunidades de inserção internacional

> e a urgência com que determinados temas devem ser tratados e assume um papel central na condução da política externa.[4]

Apart from this direct influence on foreign policy, the presidency furthermore coordinated the informal 'Council of Four', with which I became acquainted during my research interviews. It is the informal decision-making body coordinated by the presidential chief of staff in the Casa Civil which brings together the Ministry of Agriculture (Ministério da Agricultura, Pecuária e Abastecimento – MAPA), the Finance Ministry (Ministério da Fazenda – MinFaz), the Ministry of Mining and Energy (Ministério de Minas e Energia – MME) as well as the Foreign Ministry (Ministério das Relações Exteriores – MRE, or Itamaraty). In terms of agenda setting, this gives the presidency a high level of influence over the other ministries.

In Brazil, MRE, or Itamaraty, is responsible for negotiating international agreements. However, Brazil has a strong presidential system, and in the case of president Lula, presidential diplomacy was a decisive instrument of Brazil's foreign policy. Albert Fishlow (2010: 3) describes an ideological divide within Itamaraty regarding the United States; on the one hand, the ministry is oriented towards pragmatic solutions that resonate with the importance of the United States as an international power, but on the other hand, the placement of Workers' Party (PT) figures Samuel Pinheiro Guimarães as head of strategy at Itamaraty and Marco Aurelio Garcia as head of foreign policy in the presidential office gave Brazilian foreign policy a more ideological direction. Additionally, Itamaraty supervises the Brazilian Cooperation Agency (Agência Brasileira de Cooperação – ABC), which is the executing arm in Brazil's development cooperation and the technical partner of trilateral projects between the United States and Brazil.

Furthermore, the Brazilian export agency, APEX-Brasil, supports Brazilian companies in entering foreign markets by connecting the private sector of Brazil with the private sector in the receiving country and the necessary political decision-makers. It is managed jointly between Itamaraty and the Ministry for Development, Industry and Trade (Ministério do Desenvolvimento, Indústria e Comércio Exterior Brasil – MDIC).

MDIC is also involved in the US–Brazil commercial dialogue and shares oversight with Itamaraty over the influential Brazilian Chamber of Commerce

---

4. 'When conducting foreign policy in person, the actions of the agent must exceed the protocol acts. Interest, ability, knowledge about foreign policy issues are key. In this regard, the president notes the opportunities for international insertion and the urgency with which certain issues should be addressed and assumes a central role in the conduct of foreign policy' (author's translation).

(Câmara de Comércio Exterior – Camex). Within Camex, MDIC oversees the private sector advisory council (Conselho Consultivo do Setor Privado – Conex), which elaborates industry demands for Brazilian foreign trade policy.

Despite the official prerogative of Itamaraty, in the case of ethanol diplomacy, the MME and the MAPA play an influential role on the technical level as well as in bilateral dialogues. MME is very influential in the Strategic Energy Dialogue and domestically as it oversees the National Agency for Petrol, Natural Gas and Biofuels (Agência Nacional do Petróleo, Gás Natural e Biocombustíveis – ANP), which is the national fuel regulator; the national Energy Research Company (Empresa de Pesquisa Energética – EPE); and the state-controlled oil company Petróleo Brasileiro S.A. (Petrobras). Petrobras was the main producer and distributor of ethanol through its dominant and privileged position in the Brazilian fuel market.

MAPA has been at the centre of US–Brazil exchange the longest with Itamaraty since the creation of the Consultative Committee on Agriculture between the USDA and MAPA (CCA). MAPA furthermore represents Brazil internationally in sugar-related questions (e.g. in the ISO) and plays a crucial role domestically as the ministry that monitors all sugar and ethanol production. As the supervising authority over Brazil's agricultural research company Embrapa, MAPA can set the research agenda on future energy crops and international cooperation programs.

Many people interviewed for this work talked about switching arenas from trade to climate-related issues. This strategy is even adopted by UNICA, as confirmed by its president during one of my interviews (Farina 2015), which begs the question whether this will actually be successful since the Ministry of the Environment (Ministério do Meio Ambiente – MMA) is not represented in the Council of Four. With the shift in the ethanol agenda towards an environmental issue, the MMA has gained relevance in the discussion.

With all these state actors at play in US–Brazil ethanol diplomacy, one can understand how Hirst (2013: 199) comes to the conclusion that one central obstacle for effective Brazilian foreign policy is the clash between the '"statist" mark of the foreign policy conducted by Itamaraty [and] new networks of inter-ministerial interconnection'.

With only a symbolic role in foreign policy, but very influential domestically, the parliamentary sugar-alcohol caucus (Frente Parlamentar pela Valorização do Setor Sucroenergético) is a group of parliamentarians who support the sugar and ethanol industry. As people in Brazil say that nobody can be president against the will of the sugar industry, the Frente Parlamentar Sucroalcooleira represents a very powerful and financially important sector of Brazilian industry and can thereby put significant pressure on the president and co-set the foreign policy agenda in this respect.

Schlesinger's (2012) initial mapping of the actors in the Brazilian ethanol complex falls short of a systematic approach but is nevertheless helpful. He focuses on the Brazilian government but also points out that credit lines provided by the Brazilian development bank (Banco Nacional de Desenvolvimento Econômico e Social – BNDES) support private sector investments that otherwise would not be feasible. BNDES is overseen by MDIC and MinFaz.

Schlesinger (2013: 33) criticises Brazil's ethanol diplomacy for having been primarily defined by particular interest groups from the beginning and sheds light on the influence these actors have in policy making. While this suggests a rather cynical version of Liberalism, one should not forget that trade diplomacy and ethanol diplomacy in particular were central projects of the first left-wing government under president Lula and the PT that were embedded in their political strategy (Ondetti and Rhodes 2010: 6). The value of the Neoclassical Realist approach that guides this study is to inform how the international structure is interpreted by the members of Brazil's FPC.

Ferreira Capellaro et al. (2012: 10679) focus on the framework of the 'Productive Development Policy' (Política de Desenvolvimento Produtivo – PDP) within which BNDES, Itamaraty, Petrobras, APEX-BRASIL and the ANP can apply instruments for international trade promotion. While these are the primary actors in the international side of PDP, the authors also recognise that other entities, such as the UNICA, the state government of São Paulo, the biggest sugar and ethanol exporter COPERSUCAR, Petrobras and the commodities and futures exchange in São Paulo are involved in the promotion of ethanol from a non-regulatory side (2012: 10680).

It is important to understand that a wide range of domestic actors can profit from official ethanol diplomacy and therefore exert pressure towards the government to distribute funds either directly on project bases or indirectly through BNDES. One obvious representative of this group is the construction giant Odebrecht, which used to be the government's go-to contractor for infrastructure investments abroad – financed by BNDES. There are also intellectual beneficiaries of such policies, for example, the Getulio Vargas Foundation (FGV), which is the government's go-to contractor for well-paid (feasibility) studies; consultancies like Datagro, which co-organise conferences and offer information services to interested parties worldwide; and think tanks like the Institute for the Study of Trade and Negotiations (Instituto de Estudos do Comércio e Negociações – ICONE), which was an industry-funded think tank that advised the Brazilian government in international trade negotiations and subsequently opened an individual for-profit practice.

On the explicitly bilateral side, we observe two main business organisations that are dedicated to US–Brazil issues. The Brazilian Industry Coalition (BIC), which opened its Washington, DC, office in 2005 to represent the interests of the National Industry Federation (Confederação Nacional da Indústria – CNI) and the São Paulo State Industry Federation (Federação das Indústrias do Estado de São Paulo – Fiesp) mainly with regard to trade questions (Vigevani 2011: 26). The Brazil–US Business Council (Conselho Empresarial Brasil-Estados Unidos – CEBEU) was established in 1976 and describes itself as the most relevant mechanism for business dialogue between the two countries. CEBEU offers position papers and is an active lobbying force in the development of commercial policies of the two countries.

One can see that specifically on the Brazilian side, there is a wide range of actors that are involved in US–Brazil ethanol diplomacy. The representation of the government in this respect is splintered between the presidency, Itamaraty and at least five other ministries and their sub-organisations, with each claiming maximum autonomy for its respective area of expertise. The industrial representation, on the other hand, is consolidated in two organisations on the bilateral level (BIC and CEBEU), while on the domestic level, a plethora of companies, organisations and associations compete for influence and funding from the executive and through the legislative.

The United States

In the United States, the US Department of State (State) is the executing arm of civilian foreign policy. Traditionally and constitutionally, foreign policy is a stronghold of the US president. The president with authorisation by Congress established the Office of the US Trade Representative (USTR), which is part of the Executive Office of the President. According to its mission statement (USTR 2016), the USTR 'is responsible for developing and coordinating US international trade, commodity, and direct investment policy, and overseeing negotiations with other countries'. It also acts as a bottleneck for interest groups who want to influence US (presidential) trade policy. The Industry Trade Advisory Committee (ITAC) is the official link between US industry and the USTR. Foreign organisations need to directly lobby the respective experts within the USTR.

In the case of ethanol diplomacy, the Department of Energy (DoE), the Department of Commerce (Commerce) as well as the Department of Agriculture (USDA) are also involved. DoE is the US interlocutor within the Strategic Energy Dialogue and domestically important not only for standard setting but also because it houses the Office of Energy Efficiency and Renewable Energy (EERE), which is responsible for the promotion of renewable energies in the United States and has substantial agenda-setting power.

Commerce is the US interlocutor within the US–Brazil Commercial Dialogue and houses the International Trade Administration (ITA). While the ITA does not promote trade of agricultural goods, it is an important actor in technology and renewable energy questions. USDA is part of the longest standing permanent bilateral mechanism with Brazil, the CCA. Furthermore, USDA houses the Office of Energy Policy and New Uses (OEPNU), the Biomass Research and Development Initiative (BRDI) and exchanges with agricultural producers via the Agricultural Technical Advisory Committees (ATACs). The USDA also runs the Agricultural Trade Office (ATO) out of the US consulate in São Paulo. Furthermore, the EPA indirectly influences the ethanol relations between the two countries by implementing the RFS, effectively the main determinant for ethanol consumption in the United States. Therefore, EPA is a target of lobbying efforts by both US and Brazilian industry representatives.

As Whitehead and Nolte (2012: 2) point out, 'foreign policy and Latin America policy became the victims of partisan political polarisation and ideology-driven foreign policy initiatives in Congress', since the US Congress has substantial influence over foreign policy in general (here mainly the US Senate) and over fiscal decisions that influence the relationship between the two countries in the field of ethanol trade, for example, subsidies. Therefore, the US Congress is more of a target of lobbying related to ethanol trade than its Brazilian counterpart.

Thomaz (2016: 64) finds that a pro-ethanol subsidies coalition in the United States influenced the negotiations for the 2012 Farm Bill. This coalition includes: Renewable Fuels Association, American Coalition for Ethanol, Growth Energy, Biotechnology Industry Organisation (BIO), Ethanol Facts, Ethanol Promotion and Information Council, National Ethanol Vehicle Coalition, Americans for Abundant Food and Energy and National Corn Growers Association (NCGA). Interestingly, this coalition has two dimensions with regard to ethanol. On the one hand, they favour high blending mandates and producer subsidies, but on the other hand, they also favour trade barriers and restrictive market access for the Brazilian product. Hence, they partially overlap on issues with their Brazilian counterparts who are active in the United States but at the same time work against each other's preferences.

In addition to the entities mentioned above, there are many associations that represent the interests of ethanol producers politically, such as the Advanced Biofuels Association (ABFA), the Advanced Biofuels Business Council (formerly Advanced Ethanol Council), Advanced Biofuels USA and the American Coalition on Renewable Fuels (ACORE). When looking at this long list of business associations that deal with the ethanol question, it becomes clear how much bigger the US stakeholder list is on the business side. One can add a significant amount of companies and lobbying agencies that try to influence Congress on their behalf. The aforementioned BIC is very active in representing the interests of the Brazilian industry in Washington, DC, and has established itself as an authoritative voice about issues pertaining to Brazil.

These business organisations are complemented by an abundance of non-governmental organisations (NGOs) and think tanks that play the game from a more ideological angle. One NGO, particularly noteworthy in this context, is the Environmental Working Group (EWG), which supplies government and industry with data on environmental impacts of legislation.

Not only the private sector interests in the United States are fragmented and at times unclear, but the executive branch is also multi-layered. One should not forget another set of actors in the executive, the state governments. The State of California has implemented strong incentives for the use of biofuels and thereby created a strong demand for Brazilian ethanol.

On the business level, several actors play key roles in the bilateral relations on ethanol. A special role has been taken by the Brazil–US Business Council (Conselho Empresarial Brasil-Estados Unidos – CEBEU) due to its long-standing tradition as one of the first bilateral business organisations. The US–Brazil CEO Forum was established in 2007 as part of the Commercial Dialogue and is chaired by government officials from both countries. Its recommendations are therefore highly regarded by both governments and usually find their way into legislation. In terms of public diplomacy, the US Chamber of Commerce (AmCham) in São Paulo serves as a vehicle to transport US business interests into Brazil. Vigevani (2011: 27) sees in it a 'structure to articulate North American business interests',[5] but at the same time, this organisation serves as a space to exchange opinions and create joint agendas with the Brazilian business community.

Moniz Bandeira (2009: 50) assesses with a bitter tone that American foreign policy traditionally tries to 'promover interesses privados específicos, interesses empresariais, com ênfase na promoção de mercados abertos, livre iniciativa e boas vindas aos investimentos estrangeiros',[6] which might in fact be a correct statement. This indeed is the explicit mission of Commerce, and during my interviews there, this was confirmed without doubt.

What is interesting, however, is to see how the United States can project influence through professional trade diplomacy abroad despite a fragmented business sector. Compared to Brazil, it seems like competencies are clearly assigned in the US administration and the exchange of information guaranteed.

---

5. 'estrutura para articular os interesses empresariais norte-americanos'.
6. 'promote specific private interests, business interests, with an emphasis on the promotion of open markets, free initiative and welcoming foreign investments' (author's translation).

Furthermore, rather than working towards various institutionally different goals, each segment of the US ethanol FPC seems to follow Bandeira's imperative to serve the advancement of US interests abroad.

From the Strategic Energy Dialogue to the 2007 MoU on Biofuels

Establishing Bilateral Mechanisms

In 2003, when Lula came into power, the United States was focused on the war on terror in the Middle East and, as a result, Latin America was somewhat sidelined. One strategic goal of the Bush presidency was to reduce and minimise the dependency on Middle Eastern oil and also to balance Venezuela's influence in Latin America. An overarching goal was to initiate free trade agreements in the post–Washington Consensus era. In Latin America, the post–Washington Consensus era was manifesting in what some authors call the 'pink tide' – the election of leftist governments who did not agree with the neoliberal stance of the Washington Consensus. Since the Lula government 'inherited an anti-American predisposition already installed in different circles of Brazilian society' (Hirst 2013: 229), it was even more important to create a solid and unambiguous relationship with Washington.

Lula's vision when he came into power was a neo-developmental agenda (CEBEU 2006: 9), which means that the state finances development through exports that in return create internal demand and therefore foster prosperity. At the beginning of the Lula administration, the Brazilian government was very concerned that the United States would view the election of a leftist president as a threat to their regional interests. Therefore, in the first two years, we witness a transition period where the Lula administration tried to show the United States that the new Brazilian government in fact represented a social democratic and not socialist or even communist agenda, or to aim to demonstrate 'the unsoundness of the alarm generated by the rise of a leftist leader' (Hirst 2013: 63).

In order to build trust between the two governments, Lula travelled five times to the United States in his first two years in office. Initially, ethanol was not high on the agenda. The objective was to initiate general and strategic channels of exchange and subsequently work on the technical issues. The groundwork for the strategic dialogue between Brazil and the United States began with President Lula's first visit to Washington, DC, in the first year of his presidency (19 to 20 June 2003) with the establishment of working (consultative) groups on energy, agriculture and economic growth (Abdenur 2006). These included a 'modest Memorandum of Understanding' (Langevin 2013: 15) between then minister of MME Dilma Rousseff and secretary of energy Spencer Abraham to initiate talks about certain topics, among them carbon credits and biofuels.

In terms of trade, Brazil and the United States had different priorities (Veiga/Rios 2006: 15). In practical terms, one could witness this during the first meeting of the CCA in September 2004, when the Brazilian delegation offered very concrete demands to abandon technical non-tariff trade barriers, whereas the United States was working towards general trade questions and demanding greater openness from Brazil in terms of trade. Trade was also at the centre of State Secretary Rice's visit to Brasilia in April 2005. She and Foreign Minister Amorim mainly discussed the progress of FTAA and WTO, but with no clear agreement in sight.

The different perspectives on trade became even clearer during the 2005 Summit of the Americas in Mar del Plata, Argentina, when the members of MercoSul, under Brazilian leadership, rejected the US proposal for an FTAA. Brazil was considered the key facilitator during these negotiations and the driving force behind them (Gratius 2003: 1).

Directly following the 2005 Summit of the Americas, US President Bush visited Brazil. It was clear to the Brazilian FPC that this was the time to pick up some of the broken glass from Mar del Plata and suggest further bilateral cooperation with the United States. It was time for Brazil to offer something to President Bush that he could display as a success upon his return to the United States. Ethanol was a fairly uncontroversial issue since both countries are the biggest producers and consumers of the fuel, and it yielded potentially strategic value for the United States and tactical value for Brazil. This is when the idea of ethanol as a uniting element between the two countries took off. For President Bush, ethanol offered a chance to diversify domestic energy supply and therefore work towards his administration's goal to decrease dependency on Middle Eastern oil, on the one hand, and led to a clear US–Brazil connection that could be useful to balance Venezuela's influence in Latin America, on the other hand.

For President Lula, ethanol was of tactical value. In Brazil, the domestic sugar and ethanol industry is a very influential political actor and therefore needs to receive political acknowledgement on a regular basis. By putting ethanol on the foreign policy agenda, President Lula was able to appease this rather conservative and therefore critical domestic actor at a lower cost than domestic market intervention would have created. This way, big business was integrated into the policy-making and decision-making process and therefore less likely to openly support the opposition in Brazil. On the international strategic level, President Lula offered the biofuels MoU to the United States to make up for blocking the FTAA and therefore securing the support of the United States for Brazil as a potential regional power.

Rapprochement after Mar del Plata

During President Bush's visit to Brazil in 2005, the two presidents also initiated a commercial consultation mechanism between the US Department of Commerce and the MDIC in addition to the trade mechanism that had existed between the USTR and Itamaraty since 2001. During the second meeting of agricultural consultation committee (Comitê Consultivo Agrícola) in Washington, DC, on 29 September 2005, ethanol was only a fringe topic that was discussed off the official agenda. The meeting had been postponed after it had been scheduled for May of the same year due to disagreements about the agenda.

During his visits to Washington in May and July 2006, Silas Rondeau (MME) discussed the question of renewable energy as a central topic at the meeting with Secretary of Energy Samuel W. Bodman (CEBEU 2006: 36). Both meetings were characterised as productive and certainly advanced the idea of a joint ethanol agreement.

In June 2006, the US secretary of commerce, Carlos Gutierrez, visited Brazil and officially established the US–Brazil Commercial Dialogue with the Brazilian minister of trade and development, Luiz Fernando Furlan. The letter of intent did not include any concrete issues; however, it was a step towards regular exchange between the two ministries that committed to support the already existing bilateral mechanisms. During his four-day trip to Brazil, the US secretary of commerce focused on areas where a 'win-win situation for both Brazil and the United States' was achievable (US International Trade Administration 2006). Therefore, difficult topics were avoided, and the focus was on uncontroversial questions with ethanol being one of those.

In September 2006, CEBEU (2006: 21–36) suggested to move forward from the FTAA failure with a bilateral agenda that focused on trade and win-win situations with business facilitation and energy as the main two topics that seemed promising. In concrete terms, CEBEU (2006: 31) demanded the full commodification of ethanol in order to create an international market, with the central problem to find common standards. Many of the demands will later be manifested in the 2007 MoU on biofuels.

These were the first rounds of negotiations to take place. On the US side, this was being coordinated between the USTR and State, and on the Brazilian side by the five organisations that are involved in the negotiations: Casa Civil, Itamaraty, the MAPA, the MME and MDIC. While the negotiations did not move forward quickly and did not yield any quick results in the first term of the Lula administration, there was a constant exchange of opinions and experts. What contributed to the slow progress was that there were political campaigns in Brazil in 2006 (when President Lula was re-elected in October of the same year), which explicitly focused on Brazil's standing in the international arena and its international initiatives, including ethanol. This probably secured President Lula the domestic support of the sugar industry that was necessary to win the elections.

The Beginning of Lula's Second Term

Once Lula was re-elected, one of the main foreign policy objectives in the second Lula term was the further improvement of US–Brazil relations (Davilha 2006), which finally led to the signature of the MoU on biofuels in the third month of President Lula's second term.

And ethanol offered the easiest win as President Bush mentioned ethanol and renewable fuels as a central aspect of his energy strategy in the 2007 State of the Union speech. On a multilateral level, both countries were instrumental to the establishment of the UN International Biofuels Forum (IBF) on 2 March 2007, which offered a space for discussion and coordination for the advancement of the shared interests of both countries. On the fringes of this occasion, bilateral meetings between the Brazilian ambassador to the United States (and later foreign minister) Antonio Patriota and the Brazilian representative to the United Nations Ronaldo Sardenberg took place with officials from the United States to integrate the work of the IBF into the MoU.

The biofuels MoU was finalised during Condoleezza Rice's visit to Brazil to prepare President Bush's visit on 8 to 9 March 2007. The two foreign ministers signed the MoU under the auspices of the two presidents in São Paulo on 9 March 2007. Another outcome of the meeting with Amorim was the establishment of the Economic Partnership Dialogue (EPD), created to provide a forum for the United States and Brazil to discuss how to promote economic growth between both countries.

Hirst (2013: 235) attributes this quick success to a 'pragmatic emphasis [...] [on] the treatment of the economic-commercial agenda, with the attribution of special importance to coincidences with regard to renewable energy sources.'

The 2007 MoU on Biofuels

The Components of the MoU

The 2007 MoU contained three main components: support for domestic producers, investment in research and development, and standardisation. While the support for domestic producers as well as investment in research and development are uncontroversial issues, the question of standardisation is a bit more complicated. The 2007 MoU aimed to implement these three components within three pillars, one each on bilateral cooperation, global cooperation and trilateral cooperation (Seelke and Yacobucci 2007: 1). Especially in the area of trilateral cooperation, the outcomes were quick and noticeable.

The Council on Foreign Relations Brazil Task Force praises the 2008 expansion of trilateral biofuel cooperation to predominantly Central American and Caribbean countries (including Guatemala, Honduras, Jamaica, Guinea-Bissau and Senegal) for domestic use and, in 2009, the expansion of scientific cooperation to El Salvador, Haiti, the Dominican Republic and St. Kitts and Nevis (CFR 2011: 72). The Central American and Caribbean countries have preferential access to the US market through the Caribbean Basin Initiative, which means that they not only benefit from potentially lower energy dependence and investments in research but also have a perspective of biofuel production for export in the future.

According to Seelke and Yacobucci (2007: 21), one central aspect of the MoU was the symbolic, political attempt to 'improve the US image in Latin America and diminish the influence of President Chávez in the region'. This includes the promotion of biofuels within Latin America by Brazil.

Direct Outcomes and Issues

The most important outcomes of the 2007 MoU in the longer term have been the 2011 addendum on biofuels in aviation on the bilateral level, the founding of the Global Bioenergy Partnership (GBEP) on the global level and several feasibility studies carried out in third countries on where and how to implement ethanol policies. The latter were supported by the Inter-American Development Bank (IDB) and the Organisation of American States (OAS) and carried out mainly in Central America and the Caribbean as well as in sub-Saharan Africa.

But the central problem of the 2007 MoU was that the three main ethanol markets at that time, the United States, Brazil, and the European Union, each had, and still has, different standards for anhydrous ethanol, and their harmonisation is key to creating an international market for fuel ethanol. While Brazil and the United States have lower purity standard for anhydrous/dehydrated fuel ethanol (99.3 per cent ethanol content in Brazil and 99.5 per cent in the United States), the European Union applies a significantly higher standard with 99.5 per cent ethanol at a lower temperature, which cannot be achieved by distillation processes, but rather with further chemical cleansing of the product (specifications from Murtagh and Associates 2016). This contributes significantly to the cost of production, which leads to a loss in price advantage of the Brazilian product over the European product, a non-tariff trade barrier (Rodrigues 2016).

One point that was excluded from the 2007 MoU was the question of tariffs on ethanol imports. Langevin (2013: 24) sees this as a central flaw of the MoU and as emblematic for Brazilian foreign policy to not be able to resolve the burning issues, but instead establish mechanisms for coordination with questionable success. Joerißen and Steinhilber (2009: 5) agree on the failure to include the tariff questions, as all substantial cooperation would be doomed to fail unless this issue is resolved. Other authors, however, claim that up to 75 per cent of the duties on ethanol could be avoided via other loopholes, for example, channelling imports through third countries (Seelke and Yacobucci 2007: 15).

While this was certainly a market barrier that needed to be addressed politically, the formal cooperation on biofuels between the two countries encouraged Brazilian industry representatives to engage stronger in the US market and political arena (Meirelles 2016). UNICA was one of the first and strongest ethanol-lobbying groups that set up shop in Washington, DC, in 2007.

Secondary Effects in the US Legislature

These industrial efforts paid off, as shown by Thomaz (2016) in her work on Brazilian ethanol lobbying in the United States, with the final abandonment of US import tariffs on Brazilian ethanol at the beginning of 2012. In June 2009, US representative John Shadegg (Republican from Arizona) introduced a bill to the House Committee on Ways and Means to eliminate the ethanol import tariff, while in July 2009, US representatives Joseph Crowley (Democrat from New York) and Mary Bono Mack (Republican from California) introduced the Affordable Food and Fuel for America Act (H.R. 3187) to the same committee. These were the first steps to phase out the Volumetric Ethanol Excise Tax Credit (VEETC), a subsidy for ethanol producers, and the tariff on imported biofuels. In June 2011, the US Senate passed a bill that was introduced by Senators Coburn (Republican from Oklahoma) and Feinstein (Democrat from California), and a week later, a similar bill introduced by Representatives Wally Herger (Republican from California) and Joseph Crowley (Democrat from New York) passed the House of Representatives.

While these later outcomes were not outright visible at the time of the signature of the MoU, Seelke and Yacobucci (2007: 23) expected the first and third pillars of the agreement to likely result in quick successes, but the second pillar, the internationalisation of ethanol, would face more difficulties that are out of the control of the United States and Brazil. At an event at the Woodrow Wilson International Center for Scholars (WWC) in 2008 (WWC 2008: 5), former DoE official Sam Hornbeck expressed his low expectations of the US–Brazil ethanol cooperation but at the same time emphasised on the importance of keeping 'the lines of communications open'.

Nolte and Stolte (2007) assess that the MoU served two more pragmatic than idealist purposes from a US perspective: the diversification of US energy supply and strategically balancing the influence of Venezuela in South America, while Sanchez Milani (2011: 78) sees the biofuels MoU as the only successful bilateral cooperation between Brazil and the United States in the Lula era.

Diverging Perspectives on the MoU

In terms of Brazil's long-term goal to create a global ethanol market, the 2007 MoU was a necessary step to include the biggest ethanol consumer and producer (the United States) in its efforts. Furthermore, the 2007 MoU set the stage to expand the producer and consumer base of ethanol through trilateral programs with the United States to new regions, such as Central America and sub-Saharan Africa. For President Lula, it also offered some relief of strategic pressures, internationally from US suspicion of his leftist ideology, but also to counter Venezuela's increasingly hostile rhetoric. Domestically, Lula was able to offer a rather cheap measure to the sugar and ethanol lobby that did not translate into high government spending. For the United States, the MoU offered a vehicle to present itself as partner of Latin America and to overcome the embarrassment after the FTAA failure. Globally, the United States could now show that it did indeed care about climate change and could be an agent of responsible environmental governance. The 2007 MoU was also the start of increased exchange between the United States and Brazil, which subsequently had spill-over effects to other policy areas. And finally, it did at least rhetorically offer a way to diversify the US energy supply. In conclusion, one can say that the 2007 MoU on biofuels was a success, perhaps not as large as was hoped for or would have been required to truly implement a global ethanol market.

The Implementation of the 2007 MoU until the NSA Spy Scandal

The Lula/Bush Years

The relationship between the Lula government and the US government had moved to a trustful partnership that exceeded the diplomatic superficiality of high-level summitry as well as the technical level of biofuels. When Under-Secretary Nicholas Burns and then assistant secretary Thomas Shannon travelled through Chile, Uruguay and Brazil from 9 to 13 July 2007, they confirmed that the bilateral agenda had expanded to 'regional and world security, environment protection, energy and trade' with 'cooperation in biofuels' at the centre of it (US Department of State 2007). Biofuels were on the agenda when US secretary of the reasury Henry Paulson met with Lula at the same time to discuss questions related to the WTO and Lula brought forward complaints about the US tariffs on ethanol (Globo 2007).

High-Level Diplomacy Versus Continuous Mechanisms

While ethanol remained a topic in this form of high-level diplomacy, it was no longer included in the primary diplomatic and economic consultation mechanisms, such as the EPD that met four times between the first EPD in Brasilia in December 2007 and when Obama entered the White House in 2009. Ethanol was talked about only on the fringes and indirectly, for example, when talking about food security, cooperation in third countries and the tariff classification of Cachaça in the United States. The same accounts for the third meeting of the CCA that, after being postponed twice, took place in Brasília on 19 and 20 May 2008 and did not cover issues directly related to ethanol, but instead focused on phyto-sanitary questions between the two countries.

Within the framework of the Commercial Dialogue that met four times before Obama became president, a working group on standards (along with four other working groups) was created and charged with elaborating a way forward in the biofuels question. By the end of 2008, the results were not actionable.

Since its inception in October 2007, the US–Brazil CEO forum met once in Washington, DC (April 2008) and once in São Paulo (October 2008), a session that was co-chaired by Secretary of Commerce Gutierrez and Dan Price, the assistant to the president for international economic affairs. The CEO forum issued a list of recommendations after each meeting. While these recommendations were very detailed in terms of tax policies and suggestions to tariff reductions, the question of ethanol was raised in more general terms. This might be a reflection of the lack of representatives of the sugar and ethanol industry in the forum, which consists of 20 (from 2009, 24) CEOs from both countries. The half-hearted push for ethanol support might have come from the representatives of commodity trading companies such as Cargil or ADM. The aviation industry, however, is well represented in the forum, which later would become a strong supporter of the 2011 MoU on aviation biofuels. The sugar and ethanol industry is represented in the private sector advisory group of the MoU on biofuels. Their biannual meetings did not proceed quickly enough for the private sector (US Embassy Cables

07BRASILIA1826 and 08BRASILIA1366), and the cables show that the Brazilian side used templates by UNICA for policy development. Participants noticed progress on all three pillars of the MoU, while results were noticeable only in the area of third country participation.

During this time in the United States, legislation was passed that advanced the purpose of ethanol with the December 2007 US Energy Independence Act, which implemented the new RFS, and the 2008 Farm Bill – officially the Food, Conservation and Energy Act (FCEA). The 2008 farm bill extended the 0.54 USD per gallon tariff on ethanol imports until 2010 and the tax credit for ethanol blending (Monteiro et al. 2012: 195).

In any case, progress was slow, not only on the legislative side in the United States but also on the bilateral agenda. During the review of the MoU in Brasilia in March 2008, US secretary of state Condoleezza Rice acknowledged that 'of course, we have more work to do there' (Joint Remarks 2008).

The Obama/Lula Years

When Barack Obama entered the White House in 2009, the implementation of the 2007 MoU was progressing slowly, but gained momentum with the new administration. Despite Obama's support for domestic corn-based ethanol subsidies and his support for the import tariff extension through the 2008 farm bill (Rother 2008), his new multilateralism in general and his focus on (or at least acceptance of) climate change as an international issue brought new momentum to these issues. At the same time, at the 7th WTO Ministerial Meeting in Geneva in late 2009, it became clear that the WTO trade negotiations would be stalled for the foreseeable future and the question of ethanol as an alternative fuel gained traction in the upcoming climate debate. This brought the Brazilian Ministry of the Environment into the picture. Still, with regard to ethanol, Obama was initially viewed sceptically since he had in the past supported the US ethanol subsidies and was expected to continue these policies that he inherited from the previous administration (Macias and Zissis 2008).

The debate, however, took a turn in Brazil with the discovery of the so-called pre-salt oil fields off Brazil's coast in 2006. This led to the Santos pre-salt development plan in 2008 and the beginning of extended well tests (EWTs) in the Santos Basin Pre-Salt Cluster (SBPSC) in 2009, with the initial operation of the first definitive production system in late 2010. Institutionally, this resulted in the creation of the Pré-Sal Petróleo S.A. (PPSA) through law 12.304/2010 and decree 8.063/2013 and a public company connected to the MME that manages the exploitation of pre-salt resources.

Pre-Salt and the Brazilian Oil Bonanza

The focus of the Brazilian FPC thus shifted from ethanol and climate diplomacy to public rhetoric of an oil bonanza that would increase Brazil's domestic welfare and international power, as 'Lula's top priority for 2010 is legislative approval of a new regulatory framework that will increase the state's role in the exploitation of Brazil's considerable offshore oil reserves' (Meyer 2010: 3).

Brazil then paused its import tariff on US ethanol from 2010 to 2012, and there are two reasons for this effort. On the one hand, Brazil's sugarcane industry suffered poor harvests in the 2009/10 season and therefore could not fulfil the domestic demand for ethanol, and on the other hand, the FPC thought that this move could pressure US legislators to finally lift the import tariff on Brazilian ethanol. This resulted in net imports of US ethanol to Brazil from 2010 to 2013. During Lula's welcome visit to Obama in March 2009, he raised the question of biofuels and the tariffs in their meeting. In their press conference, Obama recognised that 'the issue of Brazilian ethanol coming into the United States has been a source of tension between the two countries [and is] not going to change overnight', while Lula emphasised the climate benefits of ethanol (Obama and Lula 2009).

The Executive (US) Push Forward

After this meeting, the bilateral agenda moved forward quickly with climate change at the centre of attention. When Todd Stern, US special envoy for climate change, visited Brazil in August 2009, he gave Brazil equal credit for its ethanol program and the reduction in deforestation after a meeting with Foreign Minister Amorim and Chief of Staff Rousseff in preparation for the upcoming climate talks in Copenhagen (Benson 2009). While the Copenhagen preparations ended fruitless, the two countries proceeded already before it had ended with the 4th session of the EPD in Washington, DC, in December 2009, which coincided with a meeting of the Steering Group of the US–Brazil biofuels MoU. In the area of outreach, the EPD discussed trilateral projects in Mozambique, and at the Steering Group, State's Coordinator for International Energy Affairs David Goldwyn and Under-Secretary General for Energy and High Technology André Amado invited partner institutions like OAS, IDB or the UN Foundation, as well as technical consultants working in third countries to develop local biofuels production to speak. The EPD resulted in demands for quick, but at that time officially unspecified steps ahead.

The decision by the EPA to favour Brazilian ethanol for the updated RFS-2 might have contributed to a friendly climate for the background negotiations

(Vigevani 2011: 12), and during US secretary of state Clinton's visit to Brazil in March 2010, the two countries started the Global Partnership Dialogue (GPD), signed a MoU on climate change and a MoU on technical cooperation in third countries, all three with the potential to be beneficial for creating a global ethanol market. According to Clinton, the agreements aimed at 'redoubling our commitment to our bilateral partnership in renewable energy, energy efficiency, and other climate and energy issues' (Clinton 2010).

In July 2010, the Energy Ministers Márcio Zimmermann and Steven Chu established a joint working group on energy with a concrete joint action plan (Langevin 2013: 15). Since climate change had gained importance on the general agenda, ethanol was no longer the central renewable energy resource, but instead competed with solar and others. Nevertheless, the Joint Action Plan (2010) suggested a 15 per cent blending mandate for ethanol.

While some authors praised the Lula/Bush years, the two-year overlap between Obama and Lula produced quick results and concrete, actionable guidance towards achieving the establishment of the global ethanol market in terms of widening the producer base and creating higher demand in both countries and beyond, despite the diplomatic disagreements over Honduras in 2009 and Brazil's Iran intervention in 2010.

The Dilma/Obama Years

In January 2011, Dilma Rousseff was inaugurated as Brazil's first female president. As her foreign minister, she nominated Antonio Patriota (who served in this position until August 2013), an experienced diplomat who served as ambassador to the United States from 2007 until 2009. This is representative of the importance that Brazil assigned to the United States during this period, and even though Dilma has a reputation of being a far less pragmatic politician than Lula, the bilateral exchange between the two countries thrived during the first years of her presidency. Dilma made two official visits to the United States, and Obama made a trip to Brazil in this period (Neto and Albres 2012: 79). During this time, ethanol initially remained on the agenda. Langevin (2013: 15) expects and ultimately sees continuity in the energy diplomacy towards the US while Einaudi (2011: 13) recognises 'the enormous challenge of institutionalizing [her predecessors'] success' in the area of energy cooperation.

When Dilma took over the presidency, the discourse of the government changed substantially. First, President Rousseff placed less emphasis on foreign policy than her predecessor. Secondly, coming from MME and Petrobras, her focus in the field of energy was on national self-reliance and oil exploitation. Ethanol diplomacy became the 'step child' from the Lula era.

A New Start

Following US treasury secretary Tim Geithner's visit to Brazil in February 2011, Cárdenas (2011) sees the potential for a new start in the relationship given Dilma's directive to Itamaraty to re-evaluate Brazilian foreign policy towards the United States and the common dissatisfaction over Chinese treatment of FDI and its currency. This session of the EPD set the stage for the upcoming state visit of Obama, symbolised by Assistant Secretary for Economic, Energy and Business Affairs Jose W. Fernandez, who attended several business conferences that addressed questions like investment opportunities in Brazil and Brazil's growing energy infrastructure needs. At the preparatory meeting at the end of February, Hillary Clinton promised that the two countries would continue to cooperate 'closely [...] on issues and global challenges, including food security and human rights and clean energy and global inequality' (Clinton 2011a).

Obama's state visit in March 2011 ended with the signing of 10 bilateral agreements, 'a signal that both countries are willing to forge closer ties on bilateral, regional, and global issues' (CFR 2011: 64). There are two agreements that are particularly relevant for the issue at hand: the MoU on the aviation partnership that mentions the aim to develop biofuels for aviation and the proclamation of the Strategic Energy Dialogue.

While representatives of the ethanol industry were openly excited about these agreements, for example, UNICA's Leticia Phillips (2011), who declared a 'new chapter for US-Brazil Energy Partnership', Hillary Clinton (2011b) made the switch in priorities away from ethanol clear at the 41st Washington Conference on the Americas in May 2011 when pointing out the 'work plan for energy that will help us collaborate on advancing sustainable technologies such as hydropower, smart grids, and energy efficient housing' and the promotion of 'inclusive growth and sustainable energy security' without explicit or exclusive focus on ethanol and biofuels.

The New Mechanisms

According to Langevin (2013: 24), the Strategic Energy Dialogue adds a list of mechanisms to systematically address mainly issues of energy security and safety in the realms of deep-water drilling and nuclear energy, instead of discussing questions of market liberalisation for biofuels, which makes it less strategic than technical in nature. It further lacks the participation of important stakeholders which would be necessary to clarify practical terms and a time line with specific points of evaluation.

This was slightly adjusted at the GPD/EPD meeting in Washington, DC, in June 2011, when ethanol was high on the agenda with a strong emphasis on trilateral cooperation and the recent aviation biofuels MoU, which was also a central topic at the meeting of the Steering Committee of the MoU on biofuels.

While this was happening in Washington, DC, the sugarcane harvest in Brazil was poor due to bad weather conditions. This forced Brazil to reduce its ethanol blend from 25 per cent to 20 per cent in October 2011.

Help from US Congress

At the end of 2011, the US Congress led deadlines pass to extend both the VEETC and the import tariff on ethanol, which meant that from 2012, both countries could trade ethanol without tariff restrictions. This was a great success for the Brazilian sugar lobby in the United States but has also been attributed to the lobbying work of the US livestock industry, which sought cheaper feed (Gallagher 2007: 9). Winter (2012) applauds the end of the import tariff and points out that the only noteworthy success of the 2007 MoU was in Central America because 'diplomats and other officials often spent time hashing out disputes instead of finding ways to work together'.

In the short term, the end of the US tariff on ethanol did not lead to exports to the United States but rather from the United States to Brazil due to the bad harvest in 2011.

This shifted the debate about ethanol further away from the energy security discourse towards a question of climate change and the inclusion of third counties. Deputy Secretary of State William Burns's (2012) speech at the American Chamber of Commerce in Rio de Janeiro connected the Strategic Energy Dialogue with pre-salt but clean energy and biofuels with sustainable development and trilateral cooperation ('we are finding new ways to work together in Africa, like our agricultural biotechnology collaboration in Mozambique').

Dilma Diplomacy

In April 2012, Dilma conducted her first official state visit to the United States, and Roberta S. Jacobson, acting assistant secretary, put high hopes into the Strategic Energy Dialogue, including biofuels, calling them a 'prime area of engagement between our two countries' (Jacobson 2012). But during Dilma's visit the pragmatic approach and technical talks prevailed over the ceremonial part, which reflected the different attitude Dilma presented as opposed to her predecessor. Neto and Albres (2012: 82) discover in their discourse analysis, though, that in terms of summitry, the joint statements of Dilma and Obama focused more on convergent, soft topics, like the similarities of the two countries in terms of being large democracies, of having elected a president from a disadvantaged group for the first time and the common commitment to human rights, democracy and global (economic) justice and climate change mitigation globally, as well as the two countries' open government initiative. Analysts like Diana Negroponte (2012) have a reserved view of the outcome of this visit, which resulted in a disappointingly 'standard series of agreements' that could not deflect the disagreements over strategic questions like a permanent seat at the UNSC for Brazil, defence deals or the Iran nuclear negotiations. It is clear that ethanol diplomacy does not play in the same league as those strategic questions; however, this working visit was 'only possible after' (Negroponte 2012) the lifting of US ethanol tariffs and served as one of 'small confidence building measures' that would eventually allow talks on bigger issues such as UN reform or the future of the WTO.

Furthermore, the two presidents seem to understand Brazilian energy security in different ways. While Obama pointed out Brazil's role in the development of a low-carbon economy and its achievements in renewable fuels, it is clear that during their first three meetings, Dilma and Obama had a strong focus on pre-salt exploration and an understanding of energy security that was heavily based on fossil fuels (Neto and Albres 2012: 85).

The Mechanisms Continue

After the lifting of the tariffs and Dilma's technocratic visit to Washington, the next GPD meeting in April 2012 saw the signing of a MoU on cooperation in third countries, including in development and food security. As before, the 2007 MoU proceeds in the way that the outreach pillar and the research pillar are further expanded – the latter with a loan from the IDB to develop bio-jetfuel – but the standardisation issues remain unresolved (Clinton 2012). In terms of the creation of a global ethanol market, the two countries cannot take advantage of the Rio +20 Summit in June 2012 either, since the discourse regarding biofuels at the summit is dominated by the food versus fuel debate. While Rio +20 is seen as a success, it remains unclear how the result would translate into a coherent or successful ethanol strategy.

Despite this lack of a new strategy for ethanol, the implementation of the GPD went well, exemplified by the Joint Statement (2012) issued by Secretary of State Hillary Clinton and Foreign Minister Antonio Patriota during his visit to Washington, DC, in October 2012. The statement underlined the excellent working cooperation between the two countries regarding the SDG agenda, mentioning the US–Brazilian work in Mozambique, regarding the Rio +20 process and the successful Strategic Energy Dialogue. The statement even went so far to acknowledge Brazil's claim to reform the UN Security Council, a large concession – even if just lip service by the United States – to the South American country. Ethanol cooperation, however, did not appear in the statement, and that might be caused by Brazil's slow reaction to the lifting of US tariffs in 2009. This might also be due to the lower importance that ethanol played in the strategic realm of energy geo-politics at the time. US shale gas started taking pressure off the US market from 2010 and the food versus fuel debate had outmanoeuvred ethanol in the climate negotiations, especially from the European and African side.

The Grand Finale

All these hurdles did not stop Foreign Minister Patriota from putting the question of sustainable energy and the Rio +20 agenda at the centre of his first meeting with Secretary of State John Kerry in May 2013 (Patriota 2013). The meeting in Washington was also the preparatory meeting for Vice President Joe Biden's trip to Brazil later the same month, which was announced to 'mark in 2013 the start of a new era of US-Brazilian relations' (Biden 2013) with biofuels as an integral part of the relationship and in the background nearing a solution to the standards issues (Kloss 2015). Despite some differences, Neto and Albres (2012: 86) assess the rapprochement between Brazil and the United States as underway and the relationship as gradually improving during summer 2012 and possibly thereafter. The cooperation in biofuels, while still on the agenda, did lose importance (2012: 87).

In the summer of 2013, the whistle-blower Edward Snowden released evidence that US intelligence agencies spied on Brazilian President Rousseff.

Broken Relations due to the NSA Spy Scandal

The Snowden revelations led President Rousseff to cancel a planned visit to the United States and to freeze all high-level negotiations. While work continued on a technical level, the lack of leverage and importance that comes with high-level endorsements also stalled progress on these lower levels (Kloss 2015). That meant that by the end of President Rousseff's first term in office in late 2014, there had been no substantial steps towards increasing the trade volumes of ethanol between the United States and Brazil nor had there been successful attempts at international standardisation. The abrupt pause of the bilateral mechanisms reflects a low level of institutionalisation and the fragility of the relationship between Brazil and the United States.

Final Remarks

In the relationship with the United States over the period analysed, Brazil was punching above its weight. Expanding the ethanol market between the two countries was important to Brazil, and at the same time, it did not receive the attention that such an important economic issue would have deserved. Strategically, the United States managed to maintain ties to Brazil and limit its ambitions to counter US approaches in Latin America by offering a strategic dialogue that gave the Brazilian FPC the impression it was negotiating with an equal partner. However, organisationally, Brazil could not follow suit with the strongly structured US State Department and had five different government entities involved in the negotiation on biofuels at any given point in time. The southern partner failed to develop one coherent strategy with one focal point for the northern interlocutors. This shows that already during Lula's presidency ethanol was not of highest priority for Brazil in their US relations and even less so after the discovery and exploration of the pre-salt oil fields. The importance of ethanol in foreign policy further declined during the first Dilma presidency. Energy and ethanol in particular were not considered of higher strategic priority by 2010, as a report by the Stanley Foundation (2010) shows, which only mentions Brazil's strategic ambitions to become a producer of nuclear fuel in the energy realm in addition to questions of UN reform and financial questions.

While there were promising approaches such as the MoU on biofuels in aviation, they did not have the desired effects. This is partly due to the bad harvests that hampered the ability of Brazil's industry to deliver the necessary output to keep exports as a viable option. This difficult financial situation was further thwarted by President Rousseff's focus on the domestic oil industry and subsidies for gasoline consumption in order to curb inflation. This measure depleted the Brazilian ethanol industry of its competitive advantage over gasoline and resulted in significantly lower sales of hydrous ethanol and hence cut off finance supply, which in turn lowered the yields in the following years. The industry therefore prioritised focusing on domestic market support over international expansion and at the same time started to break with the government, which thereby lost expertise in the exchange with the United States. Hirst (2013: 250) finds that 'bilateral relations came to encompass a more challenging picture of trade negotiations, since bilateral commercial understandings are enmeshed with disputes that are dealt with in multilateral forums and difficult regional negotiations'.

In conclusion, the Brazilian FPC never considered ethanol of high priority in the bilateral relations with the United States; the efforts therefore lacked a coherent strategy with a streamlined process. This was weakened by Dilma's focus on domestic issues and oil, leading to an end of Brazil–US ethanol diplomacy at the latest after the spy scandal.

Within the broader context of the relationship between Brazil and the United States, this chapter shows another oscillation towards good relations and back to low points as prescribed by Hirst (2005). Brazil was able to maintain its autonomy but failed to be recognized as equal partner of the United States. While the structural environment was not particularly permissive to Brazil's rise in status, the intervening variables of the leadership of both countries lead to hope for success. Nevertheless, the institutional set-up, particularly in Brazil, spoiled the success at the stage of implementation in the end.

Chapter 5

THE BRAZIL–MOZAMBIQUE ETHANOL RELATIONSHIP

Introduction

Mozambique is one of Brazil's closest partners in Africa. The two countries have had diplomatic relations since 1975, right after the African country's independence from Portugal, with a Brazilian embassy opening in 1976. In 1998, Mozambique opened its embassy in Brasilia, and regular political and diplomatic exchange between the two countries started to take place. 'Under Lula's leadership, Brazil conferred considerable weight to prioritising Brazil's Africa relations' (CFR 2011: 60), with Lusophone countries, and particularly Mozambique, at the centre of Brazilian diplomatic attention. As a general diplomatic strategy, 'Brazil's leadership is proactively seeking wider and all-inclusive relations' (Costa 2010: 2). According to Rossi (2015: 26), 'Mozambique is the best canvas to display Brazil's arrival in Africa' because it is the biggest partner of Brazilian cooperation, where between 2003 and 2013, over 30 Brazilian institutions were active (2015: 178). Brazil's total investment in Mozambique was 10 billion USD, which made Mozambique Brazil's most important investment partner worldwide (Frey 2016).

This chapter begins, according to the Neoclassical Realist approach, with an overview of the structural environment that determines the framework in which Brazil's foreign policy with Mozambique takes place. As a second step, I analyse the actors and institutions involved in the policy implementation before shedding light on two micro-cases that represent necessary points of analysis. These cases are the 2007 Brazil and Mozambique biofuels memorandum of understanding (MoU) and the ProSavana project, a trinational development project between Brazil, Mozambique and Japan. The chapter concludes with an assessment of Brazil's ethanol diplomacy through a Neoclassical Realist lens.

What is particularly challenging in the realm of Brazilian–Mozambican relations is 'the way in which many programme officials use the current point of inquiry to talk about the past [...], especially since the 're-writing of history' is already apparent among many official ProSavana actors' (Funada-Classen 2013b: 5). Throughout this chapter, I rely primarily on my interviews with representatives of the Brazilian FPC but am able to triangulate their statements with published literature on the topic.

Background

Mozambique and Brazil have a very close relationship; the Brazilian embassy in Maputo opened immediately after the establishment of diplomatic relations, which was not the case in many other countries as opening embassies is associated with high costs, and that is something Brazil tried to save money on throughout 20th century. As a consequence, President Lula on his first trips to Africa opened over 20 new Brazilian embassies within the first years of his presidency.

Another indicator of the importance of the Brazilian–Mozambican relationship is the number of high-level state visits between the two countries, which happen on almost a regular biannual schedule. Given that Mozambique is such a small country, it is quite remarkable that it actually tops the list of state visits, with more visits to Mozambique than to a very important partner, like the United States, for example. This close diplomatic relationship has been the foundation for exchange and cooperation in other areas, such as development, trade and cooperation in international organisations, like the WTO or the Community of Lusophone Countries (Comunidade dos Países de Língua Portuguesa – CPLP).

Trade

While trade between the two countries is small in absolute terms (with a peak at 148 million USD in 2013), it has been increasing from 2000 to 2013 (see Figure 9). The majority of the Brazilian imports from Mozambique consists of coal, while exports to Mozambique are mainly wheat and poultry (MRE 2013: 23). Sugar and ethanol do not make up a significant amount of trade between the two countries, which can be seen as an indicator that Brazil's ethanol diplomacy towards Mozambique was not as successful as hoped.

The nature of the structural environment between the two countries can also be understood by looking at their respective GDP. By this metric, Brazil outstrips Mozambique by 10 times, and in terms of GDP per capita, Brazil is even 15 times larger than Mozambique (see Figure 10). In terms of trade interdependence, in 2012 Mozambique was ranked 100 among Brazil's trading partners (MRE 2013: 18). Brazil, on the other hand, in 2016, was Mozambique's 55th export destination and 21st import country – from 34

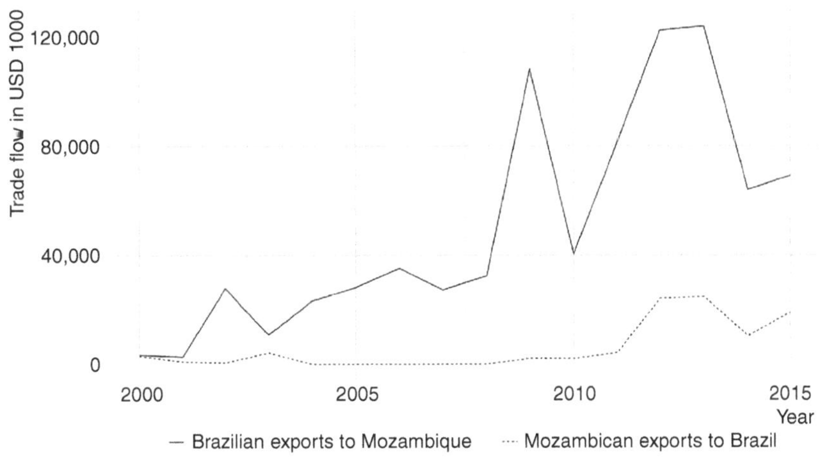

Figure 9 Trade flows between Brazil and Mozambique, 2000–15 (*Source*: MDIC (2016)).

and 19 in 2013, respectively (UN Comtrade 2017). The asymmetry of the relationship can hardly be clearer. Brazil is in a stronger position in every aspect. This pronounced power asymmetry means that we cannot speak of a 'levelled partnership'. The idea of South–South cooperation aims at working in levelled partnership, which raises the question whether Brazil is practising South–South cooperation as portrayed in its rhetoric or whether Brazil might be replicating dependency patterns of traditional development assistance.

The previously mentioned trade statistics show that the main connection between the two countries consists of primary goods exchange. This means that both countries are primary goods exporters and they trade in them, with Brazil having a positive trade balance over Mozambique. Mozambique's main exports to Brazil are minerals, while Brazil mainly exports agricultural products to Mozambique. It is commonly thought that the Brazilian investment in and trade with African countries have different motivations than accessing natural resources and raw materials (e.g. Romero 2012). The reality, however, shows that the main traded goods are raw materials, particularly coal. Brazil's motivation might be different from, for example, China's drive to secure access to energy resources, as the country does not require this access for its own energy security. It might instead be a way for Brazilian companies to improve their position in global markets by outbidding competitors and to create markets for the sale of manufactured Brazilian goods. In the case of Mozambique, China has been considerably successful while Brazil seems to have failed.

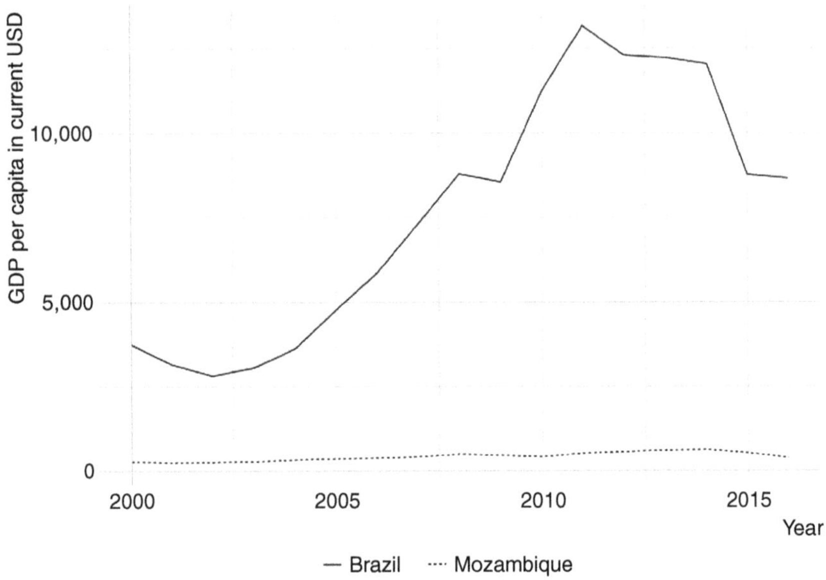

Figure 10 Brazilian and Mozambican GDP per capita, 2000–16 (*Source*: World Bank (2017)).

Rossi (2015: 25) makes the point that trade between Brazil and Mozambique is a function of their political relationship when saying that due to the presidency of Dilma Rousseff, trade between the two countries declined despite the fact that the number of state visits remained constant. While this argument is debatable, it certainly shows how fragile the relationship in terms of trade is, and might as well hint towards a politics-guided relationship, rather than a bottom-up relationship determined by (business or civil society) interests. The assumption that the relationship is politics guided raises the question whether Brazilian development aid would also be allocated to countries where Brazilian business does not have a considerable stake as destination for Brazilian goods or capital exports. In order to further explore this point, I will first provide an overview of the political actors and institutions involved in Brazilian-Mozambican relations with a specific focus on the ethanol sector.

Actors and Institutions

This section will analyse the FPC involved in Brazil's ethanol diplomacy towards Mozambique and give an overview of the actors and institutions that have shaped the process.

The Executive Level in Brazil

Brazilian President Lula was a strong force behind Brazil's drive for Africa, especially in the commercial sense. One interviewee who is familiar with Brazil's activities in Africa described Lula as a 'traveling salesman'. Rossi (2015: 59) confirms that the president first checked in with Brazilian business before presenting ideas to African governments and finally connecting the two parties to promote Brazilian solutions.

His successor, Dilma Rousseff, travelled to Mozambique, Angola and South Africa during the first two years of her mandate and created Grupo África, 'an inter-ministerial group, with private sector representatives, focusing on Brazil's relations with Africa' (Cabral et al. 2013: 15). While President Lula followed a political approach to Africa, President Rousseff applied a more pragmatic approach that was guided by economic interests. But in both administrations, South–South cooperation was primarily the responsibility of the presidency – with a lower priority under President Rousseff. Boschi (2016: 164) explains this presidential diplomacy with the powers gained by the presidency through the introduction of provisional measures in the 1988 constitution and the president's de facto control of Banco do Brasil, BNDES and Petrobras plus other smaller government enterprises.

On the executive level, it is very important to see that Brazil disposes of a large and professional civil service. The foreign ministry (MRE, or Itamaraty), for example, is very strong, with a high level of institutional establishment that is not necessarily always in line with the president. Although MRE generally sets and implements foreign policy, the influence of the Chamber of Commerce (CAMEX) and the export credit agency under the presidency (COMACE) 'on issues related to trade and investments is significant and has, at times, generated tensions between commercial and development cooperation objectives' (Cabral and Shankland 2013: 7). Within Itamaraty, the question whether Brazil's Africa policy should be guided by ideology or interests is contested (Vieira 2011: 5).

In both countries, the Ministry of Agriculture is highly involved in this particular relationship. Zanella and Milhorance (2015: 5–11) make a strong point for the dualistic character of Brazilian agricultural politics, with two ministries that work on agricultural policies: the Ministry of Agriculture and Livestock (MAPA) and the Ministry for Rural Development (MDA), the former more a representative of agro-industry, the latter more a representative of rural peasant populations and smallholder farmers. In the context of Mozambique, MDA's positions and policies certainly informed documents and language; however, decisions were made by MAPA. Cabral et al. (2016: 47) point out the complementarity of agribusiness and family farming in Brazilian agriculture – or at least in the official discourse about it – while Nogueira and Ollinaho (2013: 14) emphasise a more conflictual relationship, including the refusal of parts of MDA to participate in ProSavana due to ideological conflicts.

Brazilian State Agencies

In the wider FPC, the community of foreign policy makers, who shape Brazilian foreign policy, consists, on the one hand, of state agencies, including the Brazilian development agency (ABC), the federal agricultural research agency (Embrapa), the National Development Bank (BNDES), the federal export agency (Apex-Brasil) and the Brazilian Chamber of Commerce.

ABC implements Brazil's so-called horizontal cooperation, mainly through facilitating exchange and knowledge transfer, but more generally by displaying 'political and social loyalties with other developing countries' (Hirst 2013: 215). ABC has a low institutional position within the Brazilian FPC, being a fourth-level unit of Itamaraty and thereby lacking political and budgetary autonomy. Because of this position and due to a lack of legislation, ABC cannot permanently settle or spend money abroad and therefore has to channel its funds through the United Nations Development Programme (UNDP), which charges a 5 per cent administration fee (Rossi 2015: 199–200). This slows down ABC's work and increases the cost of Brazilian support significantly. Mozambique is the only country where ABC has a permanent agriculture cooperation officer who is based in the embassy in Maputo as opposed to the other handful of representatives who have been short-term contractors (Cabral and Shankland 2013: 15).

Embrapa is the most visible part of Brazil's cooperation with Mozambique. Embrapa is a fairly autonomous organisation, with its own international cooperation division that manages and coordinates technical cooperation (Cabral and Shankland 2013: 12). The Embrapa office in Maputo was established in late 2009, and field trials in the Nacala corridor (the area where ProSavana is taking place) began around the same time. Embrapa is closely linked with Brazilian agricultural development but also carries the image of being close to agribusiness (Scoones et al. 2016: 6).

BNDES grants long-term credit for 'acquisition or export of machinery and equipment, construction of new plants, or infrastructure projects' and has risen to be one of the largest development banks and the biggest holder of long-term investment in Brazil due to the country's little developed financial market (Torres and Zeidan 2016: 101). BNDES has become a vehicle for Brazilian development cooperation by financing large projects of Brazilian companies in developing countries, because of a general 'consensus that BNDES is part of a developmental strategy' (2016: 102). Through its Administrative Council, the bank is directly controlled by the Brazilian government. BNDES can lend only to businesses that are based in Brazil. It then channels the majority of Brazil's funds for development or technical cooperation through Brazilian companies, which in turn ask for guarantees from the governments where investments are realised.

Apex-Brasil was founded by President Lula through decree 4584 in February 2003, and while it is organisationally independent from the government, its supervisory board consists of representatives of export-relevant ministries as well as industry organisations. It can therefore be understood as a state agency dedicated to implement business interests. The main lines of work of Apex-Brasil are research into potential Brazilian exports, research of potential markets and the organisation of events that facilitate knowledge exchange between potential exporters, the Brazilian government and representatives of export markets (Pianto and Chang 2006: 101). Apex-Brasil co-organised many events in Brazil and Mozambique that focused on Brazilian foreign direct investment (FDI) into the Mozambican agricultural sector, for example, a trade mission in 2009 that encompassed 93 Brazilian companies (Stolte 2015: 100).

Business interests in the bilateral area are represented through the Chamber of Commerce, which in Brazil is directly linked to the Ministry of Commerce, and thereby assumes a sort of policy-making function.

Brazilian State Corporations

Apart from these official foreign policy actors, two big energy corporations, Vale and Petrobras, played a decisive role in Brazil's ethanol diplomacy towards Mozambique. Petrobras, the national oil company, which also invested in biofuels and ethanol in particular, can be seen as a state actor. Through the direct ownership of 54 per cent of shares by the Brazilian government plus 10 per cent held by BNDES, the government has de facto control over the company, its strategy and investments. With its expertise in the entire value chain of ethanol, Petrobras representatives were part of trade delegations to Mozambique and Petrobras was one of the first companies to commit to investing in ethanol production sites in Mozambique.

The other main driver for Brazil's interest in Africa that needs to be mentioned is the national mining company Vale, which was the first big Brazilian company to set foot on the African continent. Rossi (2015: 139) calls Vale 'Brazil's anchor in Mozambique'. Vale is a publicly traded company, but the ownership structure leaves 12 golden shares to the Brazilian government with which it can veto and in practice direct important strategic decisions of the company (SEC 2014). Despite a different ownership structure, Vale can be seen as a state actor like Petrobras in this particular case. One interviewee familiar with Brazil's Africa engagement said with respect to Guinea that it is more useful to ask the local Vale representative than the embassy about Brazilian foreign policy updates, as they are closer to the decision-makers in Brazil. Rossi (2015: 33) critically assesses that Vale with its annual revenue of approximately 30 billion USD (as of 2016) has a bigger budget and therefore more power than most countries in the Southern African Development Community (SADC) with Mozambique's budget not even reaching 15 billion USD in 2015. Therefore, negotiations between such a company and a poor government are unequal and the support of the Brazilian government reinforces this unbalanced relationship.

Particularly after the budget cuts to MRE that were imposed by President Rousseff, one interviewee mentioned that Brazilian foreign policy is practically implemented by Vale rather than local embassy staff in small African countries. While this is not a clear-cut case in Mozambique, the practical implications of Vale's engagement in the country are significant, particularly as a node in Brazilian business networks that attracted interest in investment in Africa. Through this network, Vale initially brought FGV Projetos, the consultancy of the Brazilian think tank Getulio Vargas Foundation (FGV) to Mozambique (Rossi 2015: 35). Vale, 'motivated by its interests in the region [...] sponsored' (Nogueira and Ollinaho 2013: 8) initial land-use and biofuels feasibility studies for Mozambique, Senegal, Zambia, Liberia, Guinea Bissau and Guinea (Unica 2014). Vale's direct involvement in financing such studies ultimately led to issues with EU cooperation partners as they identified potential conflicts of interest (Afionis et al. 2016: 138).

Smaller Brazilian Actors

The FGV was charged with planning projects that practically influenced the foreign policy between the two countries. FGV Projetos can be hired by third parties to run projects, and this unit was highly active in Mozambique.

FGV was responsible for developing initial feasibility studies for ethanol production in Mozambique and later on developed the so-called ProSavana Master Plan, a document that outlined the future of the Nacala corridor, an area in the tropical north-east of Mozambique, roughly the size of Germany. Finally, FGV also realised an investment fund, the Fundo Nacala, that aimed at raising funds for industrial agro-investment in the area that would be developed within the ProSavana framework. Due to the lack of success in project implementation, the Brazilian government through BNDES decided in 2012/13 to hire different consultancies for future studies and ultimately did so with Bain & Company for the 2013 biofuels in West Africa feasibility study (Afionis et al. 2016: 134).

Besides these major actors in Brazilian-Mozambican ethanol relations, there is a plethora of smaller businesses, private investors and NGOs involved, particularly within the context of ProSavana. These actors do not exercise significant influence over the process on an individual level, but channel the representation of their interests through a selection of the above-mentioned primary actors.

The Executive Level in Mozambique

On the other side, the political system in Mozambique is smaller and less fragmented than in Brazil, which makes the wider FPC easier to map out.

In Mozambique, presidential diplomacy is at the centre of decision-making. The foreign service is small and highly dependent on the presidency. In the time period under investigation, the presidency of Mozambique was held by Mozambique's second and long-term president, Joaquim Alberto Chissano, and then from 2005 to 2015, by Armando Guebuza, who promised a 'green revolution' (Shankland and Gonçalves 2016: 37) when he assumed power – a claim that fit well with Brazil's interests in the region. He was also referred to as 'Mr. Guebusiness' due to his wide network of business connections and interests in the country (Nhachote 2012). It is fair to say that the foreign service of Mozambique facilitates and organises dialogue but actually does not implement policy, whereas presidential and business interests guide the cooperation with Brazil, as several Mozambican diplomats confirmed during my interviews.

In Mozambique, the Ministry of Agriculture (MINAG) coordinates the Centre for Promotion of Commercial Agriculture (Centro de Promoção da Agricultura – CEPAGRI), an organisation with the aim of attracting FDI into Mozambican agriculture, as well as the national agricultural research institute (Instituto de Investigações Agrárias de Moçambique – IIAM), which hosts Embrapa in Mozambique.

Cepagri provides a platform for the exchange between policy makers and agribusiness, including multinational consortia. Cepagri was established by presidential decree 20/2006 with the aim of enabling an agro-industrial sector in Mozambique (MINAG 2013b). Cepagri's director, Abdul Cesar Mussuale, is quoted by Rossi (2015: 257) as advertising Mozambican land as 'the cheapest land on the planet'. It is noteworthy that in Mozambique, all land is owned by the state and can only be leased at a nominal charge plus a land-use tax (DUAT). These costs, however, are indeed very low and a sign of how agro-industrial interests have influenced decision-making in the Ministry of Agriculture. Cepagri's role is widely criticised by NGOs and farmers' unions (foodtank 2016).

Civil Society Actors in Mozambique

The most vocal actor in the resistance against industrialisation of Mozambican agriculture is the smallholder farmers' association, União Nacional de Camponeses (UNAC), which was very active in resisting the policies that resulted from Brazilian ethanol diplomacy in Mozambique, with ProSavana in particular. UNAC is an umbrella organisation that unites about 2,200 local associations and cooperatives, representing almost 86,000 members (UNAC 2017). UNAC also cooperates with NGOs from Europe and Brazil to collect and publish data on land use and ownership change in Mozambique. NGOs like Friends of the Earth, Human Rights Watch and the Brazilian Federation of Organs for Social and Educational Assistance (Federação de Órgãos para Assistência Social e Educacional – FASE) support UNAC's work through funding, research and publication of alternative narratives to the one that is presented by official Brazilian and Mozambican sources. UNAC has been successful in preventing the eviction of farmers from lands that were acquired by international investors or in one case where 'hundreds of protesters [...] blocked the entrance to a Brazilian coal mine in a row over a compensation deal agreed after they were [...] resettled on arid lands and had suffered food shortages' (BBC 2013).

In cases that do not involve state-controlled businesses like Vale or Petrobras, such inter- or multinational investors usually form consortia with local businesspeople who have ties to political decision-makers. The most prominent multinational consortium in this context is Agromoz (Agribusiness de Moçambique SA), a joint venture between the Américo Amorim group (Portugal), Intelec (Mozambique) and Pinesso (Brazil). There are many similar consortia, but Agromoz is – according to Nogueira et al. (2016: 14) – the only 'agribusiness group [...] with Brazilian presence [...] consolidated [...] in this region permanently' and therefore often featured in the literature on ProSavana. It is also the target of many protests by smallholder farmers and activists.

Political Mechanisms

Finally, there are bilateral mechanisms of institutional exchange between Brazil and Mozambique. It is noteworthy that these bilateral mechanisms are not highly institutionalised. They happen on an irregular timeline – only every couple of years – on short-notice basis. In the US case, such mechanisms have a higher level of institutionalisation with meetings being held on a more regular basis – approximately every six months.

One area which has been a focus of the bilateral mechanisms is debt forgiveness. Already in the last year of the Cardoso government, Vale's Africa approach was laid out and debt forgiveness for target countries of Vale's African expansion was put on the agenda (Rossi 2015: 90). These countries, including Mozambique, were later invited to enter in regular exchange with Brazilian officials.

During President Chissano's state visit to Brasilia in 2004, Brazil officially offered a 90 per cent debt forgiveness to Mozambique and the two countries aimed for a higher level of institutionalisation of their cooperation. The promises of debt forgiveness and a higher formality in technical cooperation were part of Brazil's effort to further institutionalise bilateral mechanisms. In the time period that is covered in this study, three sessions of the joint committee meeting took place, which will be examined more closely later in this study.

Another form of bilateral exchange takes place within the framework of the Community of Portuguese Speaking ('Lusophone') Countries (CPLP) which can be interpreted as a vehicle for Brazil's international power projection. While this assumption of power projection can be contested, CPLP certainly is one coordination mechanism in which both countries engage. One example of this mechanism at work is Mozambique's request to put in place a CPLP framework for cooperation with Brazilian biofuels projects (Timossi and Assunção 2012: 17).

Under President Dilma, the agenda towards Mozambique changed. The focus was put more on trade as opposed to political interests, which is represented by the influence that CAMEX gained in terms of policy formulation towards Mozambique (Rossi 2015: 317).

The Mozambican Agriculture Sector and Policy Initiatives

Mozambican agriculture is characterised by smallholder family subsistence farming. The Food and Agriculture Organization (FAO) (2017) states that these are 'the vast majority [...] with some 3.2 million smallholder farmers accounting for 95 per cent of the country's agricultural production [while] roughly 400 commercial farmers produce the remaining 5 per cent'.

In the time frame under consideration, the Land Law of 1997 (Lei de Terras 19/97), the Green Revolution Strategy from 2007 that focuses on food security, the Strategic Plan for Agrarian Development (PEDSA) for 2008–19, the National Action Plan for Food Production and the Strategy and Action Plan for Food and Nutritional Security were the governing legislative frameworks in Mozambican agriculture (Amanor and Chichava 2016: 19). While the language of these programmes acknowledges family subsistence farming as a reality, Mozambican politicians aimed for large-scale investments, with high-ranking officials continuously reaffirming their commitment to create spaces for investors to prosper (2016: 51).

The 1997 Land Law established that all land in Mozambique belongs to the state, and while individuals (or companies) are not allowed to own land, they can lease concessions, so-called Land Use and Benefit Titles (Direitos de Uso e Aproveito de Terra – DUATs), that are granted for 50 years, can be renewed and are taxable at a very low rate (1 USD/ha as of summer 2015) (Clements and Fernandes 2013: 52).

On 17 May 2009, the Mozambican government passed the National Strategy for Biofuels (Resolução 22/2009), which is a result of Brazil's efforts to influence Mozambique towards biofuel production and consumption. The exchange between Brazil and Mozambique led to a transfer of legislation from the Brazilian experience into Mozambican law, which will be discussed in the section on the biofuels MoU. PEDSA was updated with the introduction of the National Agricultural Investment Plan (PNISA) in May 2011 and from that point consisted of four pillars: (1) the increase in agricultural productivity, (2) infrastructure for market access, (3) sustainable use of resources and (4) strong agricultural institutions (MINAG 2013a). None of these pillars explicitly addresses traditional Mozambican farming structures and instead focus on agro-industry and FDI. UNAC and GRAIN (2015a: 4) see this as a consequence of the international pressure on Mozambique to open its agricultural land to international investors.

Looking at the legislative framework in Mozambique, the preference of the Mozambican government for an agricultural transformation towards large-scale agro-industrial production becomes clear. At the same time, when comparing Mozambican political efforts to attract investors and incentivise the production and use of biofuels, one can draw parallels to Brazil's efforts in this respect. The exchange between the two countries facilitated this policy learning.

Reconstructing Brazil's Ethanol Diplomacy towards Mozambique

This section will reconstruct and analyse Brazil's efforts to guide Mozambique towards the production and use of biofuels. The first part will focus on the 2007 MoU on biofuels, its aftermath and consequences. The second part will focus on the trilateral cooperation project ProSavana, which received extensive press coverage and public criticism but has also been a representative case study for Brazil's practical efforts to implement South–South cooperation.

The Biofuels MoU

> Brazil is a pivotal actor in the expansion of biofuels initiatives in Africa. Synergy has been notable between the Brazilian private sector and development agencies like BNDES and ABC in promoting biofuels and technology development in Africa. (CFR 2011: 61)

The Path towards the 2007 Biofuels MoU

The biofuels MoU between Brazil and Mozambique can best be traced by following the joint committee meetings. It was first put on the agenda during Brazilian foreign minister Amorim's first Africa trip in early May 2003. Mozambique was his first stop, where he met with political prominence in Maputo (Rossi 2015: 91–92). During this trip, Amorim was accompanied by the then president of BNDES, Carlos Lessa, who was seen as a guarantor of Brazil's intentions to financially support Mozambique, primarily in return for granting mining concessions to Vale (2015: 94). Lessa also presented the experience of BNDES in financing the value chain of ethanol, from agricultural investment over refineries to the distribution networks (Agência Brasil 2003) and thereby introduced this possible role of BNDES to the Mozambican audience. The visit was also used to prepare the first meeting of Presidents Lula and Chissano.

President Chissano's state visit to Brasília took place in early September 2004 and covered three main topics: Brazilian debt relief for Mozambique; Vale's aspirations to mine coal in the Moatize mine, including the attached infrastructure investment; and biofuels. While debt forgiveness was portrayed by Brazil as not guided by political or business interests and as an act of South–South solidarity, a critical view of this is appropriate. For example, Brazilian debt relief was necessary to clear new lines of credit for Brazilian business in Mozambique that otherwise would have suffered from damagingly high interest rates or would not have been possible at all (Rossi 2015: 27). Former diplomat P. Almeida (2009: 176) says clearly that debt cancellation and technical cooperation came with expectations for support in Brazil's quest for a permanent seat in the UN Security Council (UNSC). Another example for this self-interestedness is the Nacala airport, which was financed by BNDES and built by the Brazilian construction company Odebrecht – a project that would not have been possible without the debt forgiveness (Rossi 2015: 47). P. Almeida (2009: 171) writes that 'Lula talked about a 'diplomacy of generosity' […] [but] direct financing by BNDES did not materialise, and only the engineering projects of Brazilian companies […] were approved'.

Another limitation to the South–South generosity model is that Brazil portrays its development assistance as 'demand driven', which means that countries need to request relatively concrete measures. The debt relief made it difficult for Mozambique to diversify their development interests away from Brazil and in the end led to demands that ultimately matched well with Brazil's interests in the African continent in general and in Mozambique in particular. The promise of a debt relief therefore can be understood as a practical example of soft power at play, where Brazil actively created pull factors that attracted the Mozambican FPC towards Brazil.

Another idea that was further developed at the initial joint committee meeting during President Chissano's state visit to Brasilia in 2004 was to establish a biofuels MoU. Although this process was initiated during the first presidential meeting, formal negotiations were started only during the third session of the joint committee meeting in 2005.

Due to the change and restructuring of the Mozambican administration in 2005, when Armando Guebuza became president, as well as the streamlining of energy-related processes in MRE through the creation of the renewable energy department, the negotiations for a biofuels MoU did not make the desired quick progress. The time frame between 2005 and 2007 can be called two 'lost years' in Brazilian–Mozambican ethanol diplomacy, as Mozambique's 'new president spent most of the year trying to gain control over the state machine, as resistance to change proved much fiercer than expected' (Hanlon 2015: 15).

Signing and Implementing the 2007 Biofuels MoU

Coinciding with the first state visit by Mozambican president Guebuza to Brazil in September 2007 was another joint committee meeting where the MoU was finalised and then subsequently signed by Brazilian foreign minister Amorim, Brazilian energy minister Hubner, Mozambican business minister Alcindia Antonio de Abreu and Mozambican energy minister Salvador Namburete. The language of the 2007 MoU shows a clear imbalance. While Brazil's commitments can be summed up in five lines, the commitments of the Mozambican side fill half a page. The goals are clear and openly named: to replicate the Brazilian development and biofuels model and produce ethanol.

It is an MoU on biofuels in general, but the focus lies on ethanol for international markets instead of creating sustainable energy security for Mozambique. This is a result of Brazil leveraging its power over Mozambique. The MoU potentially opened the Mozambican market for Brazilian companies and for Brazilian investment. This intervention came at a very low political cost for Brazil.

One explicit part of implementing the MoU were exploratory missions from Brazil, which included Brazilian officials as well as Brazilian industry representatives, to Mozambique. This exchange in Mozambique facilitated the commission of a biofuels feasibility study by the Mozambican Ministries of Agriculture and Energy, funded by the Embassy of Italy and the World Bank. The study finds that Mozambique is suitable for a variety of biofuel feedstocks and suggests domestic demand creation by first introducing a mandatory blend of biofuels into gasoline and diesel (Hoyt 2008). It furthermore shows that biofuels based on sugarcane would not reach the level of competitiveness of their Brazilian counterparts but could still offer cost benefits over production in the European Union (2008: 440). The suggested strategy therefore is to first create small- and mid-scale production sites with a low investment bar and scale up later (2008: 441), which fits well in Brazil's overall strategy.

The missions and initial studies showed quick successes, such as spinoff projects like ProSavana, AgroMoz and ProCana (a dedicated sugarcane project). ProSavana will be discussed in detail later in this chapter. AgroMoz was an operation that combined the Mozambican investment company Intelec, the Portuguese company Américo Amorim and the Brazilian company Grupo Pinesso (JornalDomingo 2012). Intelec Holding is one vehicle of President Guebuza to facilitate business deals and be involved in the economic life of Mozambique (Carmona 2007; Nhachote 2012). ProCana started already in December 2007, with the aim of developing sugarcane plantations to supply an ethanol plant with a daily output of 480,000 litres (Hanlon 2015: 51). It received much criticism due to its water use from the Massingir Dam that potentially competed with rice plantations, as described by Franco et al. (2010: 687). It underwent significant restructuring and de facto failed by 2014. Nhantumbo and Salomão (2010: 15) offer a comprehensive overview of the first 10 ethanol projects that were submitted to the Mozambican government by 2010, while Schut et al. (2010) give detailed analyses of each of those projects.

Based on the promises of the first feasibility studies and the initial run for Mozambique by Brazilian investors, Brazil and the European Union signed an agreement to support biofuels production in Africa and Mozambique during the fourth Brazil–European Union Summit in July 2010, with the aim of securing the European Union's increasing need for biofuels and facilitating Brazil's goal of expanding global biofuel production. Such a design would allow Brazilian agro-industrial investors to produce in Mozambique and export to the European Union, thereby avoiding high tariffs that are to be paid for Brazilian ethanol imports to the European Union (Reuters 2010). Civil society pressure in Europe and perceived conflicts of interest between Brazilian state and private entities led the European Union to reduce its engagement in Mozambican–Brazilian biofuels cooperation to a bare minimum (Afionis et al. 2016: 138). Therefore, Cabral (2014: 22) calls the EU-Brazil trilateral development cooperation in Mozambique (and beyond) 'at best, a lukewarm affair'.

Despite having the main legislative framework in place to allow for successful biofuels production in Mozambique by 2009, progress was slow and incremental. To speed up the implementation of the MoU and to start a significant biofuels production in Mozambique, Brazil had to adapt its strategy. During the 2010 Brazil–Africa Dialogue on Food Security, Brazil 'introduced the adaptation of Brazilian agricultural policies into the technical cooperation portfolio' (Cabral and Shankland 2013: 16). This streamlining of the political process with technical knowledge transfer should lead to the desired success as Brazil's experience and success was supposed to be replicated in Mozambique.

In preparation of President Dilma's 2011 state visit to Mozambique, another joint committee meeting took place in late 2010, where biofuels were prominently featured on the agenda. During the routine update on the progress of projects within the realm of biofuels cooperation, the Brazilian business side openly expressed dissatisfaction with the state of policy implementation, as the interviewed institutional relations coordinator at UNICA confirmed.

During this committee meeting – and potentially before – both sides entered into non-public negotiations. While formal documentation of this exchange is not publicly accessible, interview partners told me that Brazilian business asked the Brazilian political negotiators to encourage Mozambique to request Brazilian experts to be sent to Mozambique. The aim was that these experts would join the respective ministries to help Mozambique improve the implementation of the MoU on the ground. By that point, only two biofuels projects had been formally approved, ProCana and a project by UK-based investment group Principle Energy (Locke 2009). Only in 2009, Principle Energy had received DUATs for 18,000 ha for sugarcane production with the goal of building a sugar-refining plant by 2013 (Hanlon 2015: 81). Principle Energy had started raising funds in late 2007 and initiated the DUAT process in 2008 (Reuters 2008). The NGO Environmental Justice Atlas (2013) reports that 'construction was to start in 2010 and conclude by 2013, but by 2011 sugar cane production had not yet reached a level to warrant the start of construction'. Mozambique recognised the need for speedier implementation and requested Brazilian expertise, which led to direct domestic action in Mozambique. By the end of 2010, the Mozambican parliament approved a law to introduce a 10 per cent ethanol blend into gasoline, which illustrates how Brazil's pressure to make policy happen actually succeeded – a late success for the Brazilian FPC.

Results of the Biofuels MoU

As a direct consequence, the committee meeting in 2010 led to the introduction of the mandatory ethanol blend and the commitment to invest in an ethanol plant by Petrobras and Guarani, a Brazilian-French ethanol production company. The latter is seen as an incentive by the Brazilian government for the Mozambican government to introduce the former (MacauHub 2011). In this process, Brazil demonstrated practical power politics through financial incentives for political action.

The 2011 law led to a blending mandate of 10 per cent ethanol into gasoline and 3 per cent biodiesel into diesel by 2012, which can be explained by the rapid expansion of sugar production and difficulties to expand the production of Jatropha[1] for biodiesel (Hanlon 2015: 110). Sugar production in Mozambique increased significantly during this period, almost doubling between 2009 and 2014, with still low yields compared to Brazil. In Brazil, the yield per hectare is about double the yield of Mozambique, which shows that while it was easy to expand the cultivation area, the technology transfer from Brazil to Mozambique, that is, improving the yield per hectare, did not happen significantly until at least 2014. Comparing the results of the Jathropa expansion with the sugarcane expansion, the influence of Brazil's technical cooperation is obvious and should not be overlooked.

Nevertheless, Brazil wanted to open the Mozambican market for its corporations, and the Mozambican government had little options to fundamentally object to Brazil's advances. As a consequence, Brazil exported to a certain extent its economic model of the 1970s, which consists of going from smallholder farmers to large-scale production with the aim of producing for an international export market. This model came with some potentially bad practices, including the displacement of local populations and corruption allegations.

While no explicit corruption allegations have been brought forward with regard to ProSavana or ethanol projects in Mozambique, the country has seen another case, where funds for the Moamba dam project were temporarily suspended by Brazilian authorities, due to 'suspicions of over-invoicing and of favouritism' (Hanlon 2016) within the Lava-Jato investigation. This has sparked debate in Mozambique about the possibility of a similar investigation into the presidency of Guebuza, something opposition parties demand but many observers see critically due to a possible implosion of the ruling party and thereby the Mozambican state (Chichava 2017: 2).

1. *Jatropha curcas* is a tropical plant with a high oil content that can be used for biofuels.

In conclusion, the unsatisfactory outcomes of the MoU can to a large extent be attributed to miscalculations of the Brazilian FPC. Brazilian foreign policy makers did not really understand the situation between smallholder farmers and land ownership in Mozambique. Furthermore, Brazilian investors and experts were not prepared to work effectively in Mozambique as they did not realise the lack of infrastructure and education – including technical experience – in Mozambique.

In the beginning, problems managing the political system in Mozambique were added to this equation. This is why in 2010, the Brazilian FPC increased the pressure, yielding quick legislative results and indicating Brazil's willingness to exercise practical power over Mozambique. As in Brazil, the discovery of large deposits of fossil fuels off the Mozambican coast decreased excitement about biofuels significantly (Afionis et al. 2016: 134–35) and gave the Mozambican government a higher degree of autonomy after 2011. This exacerbated the trend towards dissatisfactory implementation and unsatisfactory outcomes of the MoU.

The ProSavana Project

The ProSavana project is a program of triangular cooperation between Brazil, Mozambique and Japan. It was officially started in 2009 to develop land for agricultural production and attract private investment. ProSavana is the first time that Brazilian development aid was openly and officially intertwined with private business interests (Rossi 2015: 46). Despite its prominent character in Brazil, Mozambique and Japan, the project has not been the subject of much research (Funada-Classen 2013b: 9), and most of my research is based on the four academic texts written on the project as well as official statistics. This chapter tests Brazil's interests against the material outcomes of ProSavana and puts them in an international relations context.

Project Inception and Implementation

The idea behind ProSavana is that Mozambique (recipient country from the Global South) receives technical assistance, while Brazil (donor country from the Global South) offers technology and knowledge. A traditional donor country from the Global North, in this case Japan, offers the funding and a potential export market. That is the basic idea of triangular development cooperation. Japan had already supported Brazil in the development of its Cerrado region in the 1970s through the bilateral PRODECER programme, which inspired ProSavana (Rossi 2015: 234).

The Nacala corridor of Mozambique is at the same latitude as the Brazilian Cerrado, one of the regions in Brazil that display the success of Embrapa's agro-engineering. In the 1980s, the Brazilian Cerrado region was deemed unfit for agricultural use, but through soil management and the introduction of GMOs, Embrapa was able to transform the region by the late 1990s into Brazil's biggest agricultural region and into one of the biggest agricultural production areas worldwide. The purpose of ProSavana was to replicate this Brazilian model in the Nacala corridor in Mozambique.

The idea was originally born in 2007, and while Brazil's (and Japan's) development cooperation is supposedly demand driven, Rossi (2015: 181) shows how Brazil and Japan first sketched out the project and later decided to implement it in Mozambique. Funada-Classen (2013b: 15) goes even further and accuses the Japanese government of actively 're-writing' history in this respect. Nogueira and Ollinaho (2013: 10) clearly trace the process from the 2000 'Japan-Brazil Partnership Program' (JBPP) to the high-level political approval between Japan and Brazil in the absence of Mozambique in July 2009. They identify and examine the discussions towards and signature of the agreement to 'develop tropical savannahs in Africa' (Rossi 2015: 247) in April 2009, the 'roadshow visit to the Brazilian Cerrado' (Nogueira and Ollinaho 2013: 10) as well as the joint mission to Mozambique in June 2009 as important intermediate steps. Funada-Classen (2013a: 3) offers a convenient overview of Brazilian-Japanese consultations from 2000–10 that led to ProSavana and eventually included the Mozambican government.

The agreement with Mozambique was signed only in September 2009. Interestingly, this April agreement cannot be found in the official and public record of the Brazilian Foreign Ministry, but interviewees continuously hinted at the possibility that ProSavana was primarily influenced by Japanese interests through their cooperation agency. Embrapa (2011) outlines a timeline that attributes the signature of a first agreement between ABC, MINAG and JICA (Japan International Cooperation Agency) to the first half of 2010 and the signing of the ProSavana implementation document to November 2010. In 2011, the planning process and implementation phase began under the oversight of FGV.

When talking to people about the nature of the ProSavana project, it is difficult to find one common definition. Rossi (2015: 247) sees three projects in ProSavana: 'Pesquisa e Investigação' (research and field trials) run by Embrapa, the 'Plano Diretor' (Master Plan) run by FGV and the 'Projeto de Extensão e Modelos' (expansion and modelling project) run by ASBRAER and SENAR, two agencies that are connected to MAPA through the Brazilian agriculture and livestock association (Confederação da Agricultura e Pecuária – CAN). While this is an elegant way of depicting the fault lines of ProSavana, the truth is that these projects all form part of the overarching operation and are closely intertwined. A similar stance, however, has been developed by ABC, whose representatives in my interviews tried to distance themselves particularly from the Master Plan project, which is seen to have injected corporate interests into the development project.

The research component of the project seems fairly uncontroversial. Here, Embrapa installed a research operation to find the most suitable crop varieties for the Mozambican savannah and the Nacala region in particular. Embrapa is hosted by and housed in the offices of the national agricultural research institute (Instituto de Investigações Agrárias de Moçambique – IIAM) (Rossi 2015: 252). The IIAM is part of the Mozambican Ministry of Agriculture and informs decision-makers based on their own and compound research activities. Through this route, according to one interviewee, Brazilian agricultural interests found their way into Mozambican decision-making.

Once the implementation progress started, protests by smallholder farmers and environmental organisations broke out in Mozambique mainly because of a lack of transparency during the planning phase. These smallholder farmers felt uninformed (Rossi 2015: 231), which created anxieties that were channelled into political action by umbrella organisations based in Maputo, like UNAC, that helped inform and organise the rural population against the project. ProSavana's planning phase did not include citizen consultations – according to Rossi (2015: 242), only 0.025 per cent of the population in the affected regions was able to give some input into the process – at a lower level than would be expected from a project of this scale and required by law in Brazil. This put Brazil's rhetoric of South–South solidarity in question and additionally took a toll on Brazil's reputation in Mozambique. ProSavana's success rate in terms of biofuels was low at the first review in 2013. At that point, only 3,500 tons of ethanol were produced in Mozambique, which was less than 1 per cent of the projected amount (Atanassov 2013: 13). A review of the process was scheduled for the year 2021 but never materialised. After President Dilma's oust from power in 2016, the project lost the attention of the Brazilian FPC, while the economic crisis in Brazil made the Brazilian agricultural industry focus on domestic issues rather than international expansion. ProSavana became a de facto bilateral undertaking between the governments of Japan and Mozambique (Funada-Classen 2019: 28–33). After several court rulings, public controversy and social uprisings, the Mozambican government finally pulled the plug on the project in the summer of 2020 (DW 2020).

In 2011, the Brazilian partners of ProSavana organised a series of events in São Paulo and Brasília titled 'Agronegocio em Moçambique – oportunidades de investimento'. At these events, ABC, Embrapa and JICA brought together potential Brazilian investors with policy makers from Mozambique and promoted the idea of attracting investment by creating confidence between investors and Mozambican political decision-makers (Embrapa 2011). During this time period, FGV Projetos was hired by Vale to produce another feasibility study on biofuels in Africa ('Estudo de Viabilidade de Produção de Biocombustíveis em Países da Africa'), with one chapter focusing on Mozambique.

The Master Plan

The Master Plan is a detailed document that outlines Mozambique's geography and climate, the political situation, infrastructure and possible types of crop for large-scale agriculture. It furthermore develops propositions for agricultural zoning and special economic zones for the export of crops. The Master Plan is a document that is continuously reviewed, and new chapters like community engagement and 'theories of change' are being included in the review reports.

During the first review in 2013, the ProSavana Master Plan ('Plano Diretor') was leaked to the press and taken up by NGOs.[2] This leak confirmed the fears of smallholder farmers that the vision for their land was to enable big agricultural corporations to invest in this area and install Brazil-style agricultural production. Previously, UNDP was chosen by ABC to run a public tender for the elaboration of the Master Plan, which resulted in a decision in favour of FGV to develop this part of the project. Rossi (2015: 252) remarks that FGV won the tender only by offering a below-cost price but was aiming to make up for this investment by creating a 2 billion USD investment fund, the African Opportunity Fund, or 'Fundo Nacala'.

Generally speaking, the Master Plan suffered from a lack of transparency and lack of public involvement, with public consultations being carried out in 2012 in only five cities and in 2013 with a survey aimed at a thousand farmers (Rossi 2015: 254). The original document still has not been made public, and it is questionable that working documents would have been published as is common now, if the leaks had not happened. After the leaks, ProSavana management published a 'Draft Zero' (ProSavana 2015) in March 2015. This second document is less specific than the leaked reports and leaves more room for interpretation, especially regarding the rights of rural populations and questions of water access of different crops. It is reasonable to believe that the working document is actually different from the published one for which the government explicitly invites citizen and civil society commentary.

---

2. The leaked 2013 progress reports of the Master Plan can be found online (GRAIN 2013).

The FGV Master Plan also faced problems regarding accuracy. Rossi (2015: 267) reports that despite the official estimate of a three-month process for individual investors to receive approval and DUATs, Brazilian farmers had to wait for over 30 months for such paperwork. This highlights how the Master Plan's insights and overly optimistic view of the project geared the Brazilian FPC and thereby ProSavana towards failure.

The Investment Vehicle

One of the goals of ProSavana was to attract investment for Mozambican agriculture. Funada-Classen (2013b: 33) shows how the ProSavana Development Initiative Fund (PDIF) was successfully used to channel Portuguese-Brazilian investment into the Nacala corridor to establish mid-size industrial farming operations. Many of the investments that went through Mozambican channels remained small and under the radar, but one investment vehicle gained particular prominence in the criticism of ProSavana: the Nacala Fund (Fundo Nacala).

In July 2012, FGV Projetos presented its latest venture in Brasília, the Nacala Fund. The Nacala Fund is 'a privately managed and Luxembourg regulated SICAR fund [...], a 10-year private equity fund, that provides private equity funding for the development of sustainable, agribusiness operations in the tropical savannah of the Nacala Corridor' and 'will widely follow the objectives established in the Master Plan of the "ProSavana" initiative' (FGV Projetos 2012: 25). FGV advertised the Nacala Fund in its own publication, 'Agroanalysis', to be run by Brazilian investment firm 4I.Green with minimum investments of 1,000,000 USD (Agroanalysis 2012: 10). 4I.Green is a subsidiary of the Brazilian private equity firm Vigna Brasil, which focuses on large-scale agricultural investments (FASE 2015: 6). The prospectus of the fund with an organisation chart of the fund structure, the types of investments it offers and the promise of a 12 per cent return on capital (FGV Projetos 2012: 35) can still be found online. Civil society organisations saw this fund as the manifestation of capital interests taking over the agricultural development of Mozambique and organised a campaign against the fund.

The resulting negative image of the Nacala Fund made ABC distance itself from the project (Rossi 2015: 264). While my interview partners at ABC did not explicitly mention the investment fund, they expressed their dissatisfaction with the commercial part of the ProSavana project that had taken over the technical cooperation part in public opinion and was worthy of criticism. By mid-2014, the Nacala fund was on a trajectory to fail due to lack of strategic coherence between the partners, lack of clarity between the investment goals and the ProSavana development goals, and societal pressure that made investments in Mozambique unattractive (FASE 2015: 12).

Nevertheless, in 2014, FGV founded a company called 'Mozil' to administer the investments of the fund in Mozambique (Rossi 2015: 268) and to transfer it into a Mozambican legal entity. The company was planned to have three areas of activity: '1) inputs (seeds/agrochemicals/fertilisers), 2) primary agriculture and 3) logistics and trade' (Agrix 2014: 58). This company, however, does not seem to be operative by Spring 2017, which raises the question whether the Nacala Fund is actually operative.

Resistance to the Project

Already in 2011, resistance to ProSavana started to materialise. At the centre of the criticism of ProSavana is the allegation of 'land grabbing', which refers to the practice of governments and investors taking land from smallholder farmers in rural societies where people do not have formalised ownership titles of land that they cultivate and where land was traditionally passed down through generations. The lack of official titles makes it relatively easy for the government, and by proxy big investors, to buy vast areas of land, receive an official title and evict the smallholder farmers from their land. In a less-extreme form, farmers receive official land titles but are later pressured into selling those to investors at very low compensation rates.

A debate about land grabbing shook the Mozambican public and political sphere after the Brazilian newspaper *Folha de São Paulo* quoted that Mozambican agriculture minister José Pacheco during his April 2011 visit to Brazil as saying that Mozambique 'had offered 6m ha of land, without environmental restrictions, free to Brazilian farmers' (Hanlon 2015: 106). This led to protests by smallholder farmer groups and a response from the government that reassured the importance of traditional land use and environmental regulations.

However, in May 2013, civil society groups from Mozambique published an open letter to the presidents of Brazil, Japan and Mozambique that outlined their criticism towards the project (UNAC et al. 2013). They found that

> there are many discrepancies and contradictions in the sparse information and documents available, which are indications and evidence to confirm the existence of defects in the programme design; irregularities in the alleged process of public consultation and participation; serious and imminent threat of usurpation of rural populations' lands and forced removal of communities from areas that they currently occupy.

They explicitly criticise the 'importation into Mozambique of the built-in contradictions of the development model of Brazilian agriculture' (2013). The resistance to the project was voiced to the Brazilian, Japanese and European governments through NGOs from the respective countries that are active in Mozambique. This pressure succeeded in the sense that the management of ProSavana opened up its planning process to a certain extent and that the foreign governments made sure that at least lip service was paid to smallholder farmers' and indigenous communities' rights and environmental concerns. The ongoing protests in the field remain widely uncovered in the media but seem to have significantly slowed down the progress of ProSavana.

Outcomes of ProSavana

The target of the whole project was to develop up to 35 million hectares of land, roughly the size of Germany, and make it the largest land acquisition project in Africa. Some opponents of this project called it 'the biggest land grab in history' (e.g. Wise 2014; Shankland 2016). NGOs report that 'since 2006 the Mozambican government has signed at least 35 long-term land leases covering more than 535,000 hectares, [...] that thousands of smallholder farmers were displaced to make way for these agricultural investments which have often focused on crops for export' (UNAC and GRAIN 2015b). It is obvious and explicit that land development at such scale was not mainly geared towards the traditional smallholder farmers but rather to attract large-scale international agricultural investors. Many of these investors might come from the Global North; however, the proximity to government institutions and their domestic experience also attracted a number of Brazilian investors.

In this sense and to assess the diplomatic efforts, the results can be seen as somewhat successful with the concrete outputs of developing some land and attracting some Brazilian investors. The Embrapa part of the project was to a certain extent successful in including smallholder farmers in the agro-industrial production chain by popularising 'certified seeds' that result in higher and more reliable yields but also cost up to 15 times as much as traditional seeds and potentially create dependencies on multinational seed companies. One insightful account as to how this value chain is jointly created between international development agencies and international biotech multinationals shows how a local farmer in northern Mozambique turned into a seed dealer for the South African company Pannar (DAI 2017). While this is a success story for all participants involved, the loss of traditional knowledge about sustainable farming as well as the potentially problematic dependency on seed supply remain unmentioned.

The ProSavana Master Plan was translated into Mozambican agriculture and zoning laws, including special economic zones with free ports to export agricultural produce tax free. Furthermore, ProSavana generated spin-offs like the ProCana project, to implement a similar idea with an exclusive focus on sugar and ethanol, but which as of 2017 had ultimately failed.

Reception of ProSavana

ProSavana has become a subject of intense study and debate within the community of researchers who focus on the Brazilian-Mozambican relationship in particular and more broadly on South–South cooperation and the question of rural and economic development. One of the tensions that this project made clear is the balance between pursuing a business-oriented agro-development strategy versus preserving traditional farming structures.

The academic debate on ProSavana reached its peak in 2013 with a contribution by Fingermann (2013) that received broad attention and pushback from the development/NGO community and a widely cited article by Funada-Classen (2013b). Fingermann (2013) argues that there are three myths that hurt ProSavana's reputation. The first is that ProSavana is a replica of ProCeder, the Japanese programme that helped Brazil develop its Cerrado region. While she acknowledges that ProSavana is based on ProCeder, she points out the procedural differences and the fact that in today's communication age, the population cannot be ignored in the same way it happened in Brazil. Secondly, she rejects the position that ProSavana is geared towards the introduction of large-scale industrial agriculture. Her argument is that only the third pillar of the project (expansion and modelling) focuses on industrial agriculture and thereby faces the same issues as her argument that the Fundo Nacala does not have anything to do with ProSavana. These arguments are formally accurate but do not stand the test of practical implications. Her third argument, that land conflicts between local smallholder farmers and industrial-scale agriculture operations seem unlikely due to the protection offered by Mozambican law, is naïve at best.

Funada-Classen (2013b) rejects Fingermann's position in a detailed and evidenced way. Shankland and Gonçalves (2016: 36) argue that one outcome of ProSavana was the increased organisation of civil society groups that had not happened before in Mozambique. This was clearly an unintended consequence of Brazil's involvement in Mozambique.

ProSavana also fell short of expectations. The desired production levels of ethanol (and other crops) were never achieved. This is not only due to the resistance of the local population and the political hurdles in Mozambique but also because investment could not be attracted at necessary levels, especially after 2012, to build sugar and ethanol refineries. Luis Sitoe, economic adviser to the Mozambican minister of agriculture, states: 'ProSavana failed' (Wise 2014).

Summary and Final Remarks

To answer the questions of what Brazil's ethanol diplomacy towards Mozambique looked like and why it ultimately did not fulfil expectations, this chapter focused on two particular events: the 2007 MoU on biofuels and the ProSavana project.

2007 MoU

Out of 37 biofuel-related projects that applied for licenses between 2008 and 2014, only five were operational in 2015 and most of them pilot projects (Tomei et al. 2016).

The Brazilian–Mozambican ethanol partnership was overshadowed by the display of corporate interests. Brazil's strong rhetoric of South–South solidarity, particularly of the Lula government, does not hold true. Based on Rossi (2015), it is clear that this was the strategy of the Brazilian FPC from the beginning. Corporate interests were not, however, reflected in the rhetoric of solidarity that many Brazilian political leaders chose to use. The ethanol partnership also failed with regard to the goal to significantly enlarge the consumer or producer base of ethanol. While a 10 per cent ethanol blend was introduced in Mozambique, this policy did not have a significant impact as the quantities used in Mozambique are very small compared to those in industrialised countries. Additionally, Argüelles et al. (2014: 93) raise the concern that the competition between food, feed, fibre and fuels has been introduced to Mozambique through the introduction of investment vehicles for agro-industry.

ProSavana

The unofficial nature of the connection of Vale's projects and the Fundo Nacala with ProSavana (Nogueira 2013: 4) casts a shadow of doubt on commitments to transparency and lack of commercial interests of the project. ProSavana is definitely a model trilateral cooperation project. It created spin-off projects and raised a considerable amount of Brazilian and international investment, even if this was less than initially hoped, which may partially be attributed to the commodities crunch after 2012. But the project also met considerable resistance in Mozambique, and overall, the expectations were not fulfilled.

The failure of the ProSavana project can be attributed to a high degree to the Brazilian FPC's miscalculation of Mozambican preferences and the lack of deep understanding of the domestic structure mainly with respect to the efficiency of the local administration but also the organising strength of the smallholder farmers. Particularly, the uncertain and customary land laws in Mozambique led to delays in and resistance against the projects (Afionis et al. 2016: 138). Additionally, lack of transparency sparked protests that might have been avoidable with proper community engagement (Rossi 2015: 243).

The Brazilian Narrative

As Afionis et al. (2016: 131) state, there are two conflicting narratives of Brazilian engagement in Africa: the official discourse of South–South solidarity and a more critical one about a Brazilian form of neocolonialism. The argument that Brazilian development cooperation is purely demand driven has been widely disregarded in the literature. Stolte (2015: 111) understands it as 'actively promoted, contrary to official wording', Funada-Classen (2013b: 2) states that ProSavana 'clearly did not emerge from nor was it accompanied by the discussions or aspirations of Mozambican society' and Fontaine (2016: 408) questions whether 'there are no conditions attached to Brazilian donor activity, […] [but rather] political and economic interests played an important role in the allocation of development aid'.

The FPC in Brazil is strongly influenced, if not also determined by private sector engagement in this particular case. Mozambique did not seem to be high on the political agenda, but it is important to remember that politics followed investment, which followed politics for more substantial investment in the case of Mozambique. As Rossi (2015: 36) points out, there were barely any Brazilian business interests in Mozambique at the beginning of the Lula administration, with the exception of Vale, and those private interests were supported by the state either institutionally or through credit lines. Once politics secured the status of Mozambique, more investment followed. Hirst (2013: 217) states: 'in the end, from the point of view of the configuration of the Brazilian presence in Africa, it becomes difficult not to find a correlation between foreign policy, business interests, trade flows and technical assistance'.

In other countries of Southern Africa, Brazil has a mixed record with its approach of South–South cooperation as well (Mukwereza 2015). Rossi (2015: 150) points to the example of Odebrecht's biofuels plant in Angola, which was managed poorly but had constant political support due to continuing bribery. With Brazil's public–private investment in Africa (Vale: 8.2 billion USD; BNDES: 3 billion USD; Banco do Brasil: 1.3 billion USD), it is hard to think of the engagement as interest free, in the financial and political sense (2015: 52).

If it is true that President Lula's 'diplomatic Africa offensive' lacked a legal framework and was thereby understaffed and underfunded (Stolte 2015: 150), it is more understandable that 'President Rousseff is revealing a more pragmatic attitude' (Cabral et al. 2013: 14) and switched Brazil's Africa strategy from political to economic interests (Stolte 2015: 159). Thereby, she might be taking away the strongest argument in favour of Brazil's engagement in Mozambique: the understanding of the Brazilian FPC that despite its economic and political size, Mozambique offers opportunities by welcoming Brazilian engagement.

ProSavana in the South–South Context

Brazil's strategy of South–South cooperation claimed to help other developing countries progress without interest. It was conceptualised in contrast to traditional development models from the Global North that raised suspicion of neocolonial practices. Brazil nevertheless consciously benefitted from these relations, incidentally as the official narrative proclaimed but actually very consciously, as Amorim (2015) expressed in an interview for this study. At the time, Brazil was aiming for autonomy through diversification and autonomy through participation (Vigevani and Cepaluni 2007), which in Realist terms can be understood as a form of balancing by finding new allies for its initiatives in the global structure, particularly within multilateral bodies. As such, ProSavana can be understood as an effort to sway a potential ally through direct support but also by means of politics of prestige. Brazil aimed to present itself as a problem solver. This is particularly true for the wider context of new trilateral cooperation projects where finance was provided by the Global North, while expertise was provided by Brazil, which presented itself as an equal partner to the recipient of these projects. This shows how Brazil wanted to differentiate itself in two ways from the traditional donors and former colonialist powers. The goal was clearly to not appear as a new version of the old and to not openly express interests that could be misinterpreted. The failure of ProSavana shows, however, how Brazil's South–South initiative collapsed. While the structural environment was very permissive to successfully implementing those projects and thereby building a coalition/alliance to promote Brazil's interests at higher levels of global governance, Brazil's strategic culture as well as its institutional set-up prevented the projects and thereby the overall South–South strategy from succeeding. Brazil's effective departure from the project following President Dilma's oust from power in 2016 only left a veneer of South–South cooperation to ProSavana. The formal abandonment of the project by the Mozambican government in the summer of 2020 finally put an end to a project that had been on life support for its latter half.

Brazil as a Realist Actor

If Stolte's (2015: 8) assessment is true that Brazil wanted to contribute to problem solving to increase its position in the international hierarchy instead of using hard power, that is, a strategy of prestige as defined by Morgenthau (1978), then the results are mixed, as very few problems have actually been solved in Mozambique. Scoones et al. (2016: 9) describe Brazil's engagement in Mozambique, and more broadly in Africa, as a 'complex mix of aid, investment, trade, and diplomacy', which makes it more difficult to disentangle the interests of states and business and whether a policy reflects tactic or strategy. But this does correlate with Ferrando's (2015: 355) assessment that 'Brasilia exercises a peculiar soft power, a form of control associated to hegemony rather than imperialism' and thereby follows a Realist strategy that has been adapted to Brazil's means and situation in the 21st century.

On the analytical level, we can see that Brazil is willing to project power towards weaker partners. These cases display that within a Realist framework, Brazil combines a path of individual power projection with coalition building to achieve global public goods. President Lula saw strategic value in African countries as a counterpoint to Global Northern dominance (Rossi 2015: 65).

On a case level, it is clear that Brazil was able to dictate the terms and conditions of the biofuels MoU. These actions can be explained with Classical Realist theory. The influence over Mozambique was large enough that the Brazilian FPC was able to recalibrate and influence Mozambican politics in the short term when initial progress was lacking, which led to Brazilian in-house support for the Mozambican administration. Brazil is 'by standing at arm's length of local politics [...] reproducing the double standard historically deployed by [donors from the Global North], who have selectively engaged with, and sometimes plainly ignored, principles and rules of their own creation' (Cesarino 2016: 388). But pure Realist or Liberal approaches cannot fully explain the nature of Brazil's engagement in Mozambique.

Before returning to the cases that have been elaborated earlier, it is worth noting that the biggest humanitarian project that Brazil has thus undertaken was the construction of a factory overseen by FIOCRUZ to produce anti-retroviral drugs in Mozambique (Rossi 2015: 207). This project, however, was mainly financed by Vale (2015: 212), which is one example of how Brazilian foreign aid and foreign policy are intertwined with big Brazilian business. From a strategic point of view, this and other Brazilian engagement in Mozambique (and in the wider Lusophone community) has secured support and votes in international organisations for Brazilian causes. There is the obvious difficulty of proving causality between the two issues, but it is worth asking why Mozambique has continuously voted along Brazilian lines in the WTO and in the FAO even if it did not match their obvious preferences, as a German diplomat pointed out during my interviews. Several Brazilian diplomats confirmed that Mozambique was a reliable partner in these two organisations.

Brazil was able to draw on support from Mozambique and other African countries to secure the election of two Brazilians at the top positions in the FAO and WTO. The interest taken in Africa, and particularly in Mozambique, which ultimately led to African support for the Brazilian nominations for FAO and WTO leadership, was unusual. Brazil lobbied with its agro-industrial experience and implicit promises to African governments for its FAO leadership (Rossi 2015: 228) and successfully brought its agenda to the organisation, including the trademark 'Zero Hunger' programme of the Lula administration and the focus on South–South cooperation (Haddad 2011). According to Amanor and Chichava (2016: 21), the FAO 'mediated' Brazilian initiatives in Mozambique, which included official aid and private investment with the aim of increased food security. The campaign for the WTO candidacy was even more extravagant with the candidate Roberto Azevêdo going on a road show through Africa on a Brazilian air force plane accompanied by representatives from ABC and Embrapa (Rossi 2015: 230).

The main strategic goal of Brazil, a permanent seat in the UNSC, has not been reached at this point, even though Brazil lobbied African recipients of development aid and investment in this direction (Rossi 2015: 51). Based on internal documents from Itamaraty, Rossi (2015: 96) comes to the conclusion that the three main tasks for the Brazilian ambassador to Mozambique, Leda Lúcia Camargo (2004–08; followed by Antonio de Souza e Silva, 2008–12; followed by Lígia Scherer, 2012–15) – and therefore Brazil's strategic interests in Mozambique – were (1) Vale, (2) the construction of a FIOCRUZ production site for HIV drugs and (3) gaining support for a Brazilian permanent seat in the UNSC.

While I do not share Rossi's (2015: 219) assessment that the G-4 initiative to gain permanent UNSC seats for Brazil, Germany, Japan and India was the main driver behind Brazil's engagement in Africa, ethanol diplomacy in Africa certainly needs to be seen before the backdrop of this strategic factor that has the highest priority in Brazilian foreign policy. It is questionable, however, whether Brazil was able to permanently 'strengthen its position as global player and peruse its international goals as gaining support for a permanent seat in the United Nations Security Council' as Fontaine and Seifert (2009: 15) suggest.

Instead, Brazil was able to engage in Africa in general and in Mozambique in particular without stepping on any great power's feet (Stolte 2015: 139). In a certain sense, Brazil competed with China over access to resources, but Brazil's mining experience, its position as a counter-balance to Chinese influence and Brazil's overt interest in Africa as a market rather than just a point of extraction helped consolidate its presence (2015: 139–42). In this game of emerging powers, Mozambique applied a bandwagoning strategy rather than a balancing strategy. The Mozambican government decided to react to Brazil's power projection by going along and trying to reap benefits from Brazil's engagement. This was the preferred strategy over building or joining a coalition against Brazil by bandwagoning with China, for example.

The question of causality remains as to whether private interest sparked government action or vice versa. The sequencing is clear: Vale's engagement in Mozambique was followed by political action, which was followed by smaller investments by a wider range of investors. From a Liberal point of view, one might argue that Brazil's government action in Mozambique was merely a function of these private interests. However, given the strategic importance of access to mineral resources in Africa, particularly in competition with China, and given the quasi-state character of Vale, one might consider turning to a Neoclassical Realist perspective for more insights. In this view, Vale forms part of Brazil's FPC and bases its decisions not only on business opportunity but also on strategic considerations of the Brazilian state. The action to invest in and project power towards Mozambique becomes a function of structural pressures from the international system and Brazil's willingness to change the status quo.

Another reason for the failure of Brazil's ethanol diplomacy towards Mozambique can be identified in the limited political interest in ethanol after the discovery of fossil fuel reserves in Brazil and Mozambique combined with the commodities crunch. That is a theme present throughout this study. Ethanol was a prominent project that was highly talked about, but only little political investment was made. Even between Brazil and Mozambique, if one would merely focus on energy security, energy trade is mainly limited to fossil fuels. This raises the question whether ethanol diplomacy during the Lula administration was just a means to the end of another strategic goal, for example, garnering international support in international organisations.

In this chapter, I presented the case of Brazilian–Mozambican relations to assess whether Brazilian ethanol diplomacy succeeded in building a global market for biofuels. I outlined what policies Brazil implemented towards Mozambique and how Brazil's FPC was able to exercise power over Mozambique. In the political arena, Brazil was able to secure Mozambique's support in international organisations but did not achieve a significant impact on a technical level. This can be attributed to the deficiencies of the Mozambican political system, its lack of technical experience and, most importantly, the Brazilian FPC's lack of understanding of this predictable situation. A Realist view of this problem fails to explain Brazil's lack of problem-solving power, while a Liberal perspective is not able to account for Brazil's top-down approach towards Mozambique. By opening up the black box of the FPC, as suggested by the Neoclassical Realist Approach, one can trace how each actor understood the Brazilian–Mozambican ethanol partnership differently, which resulted in inconsistent agendas at different levels. As this analysis shows, despite intensive diplomacy and attempts at business investments in Mozambique over the past decade, the 2007 MoU and ProSavana were unsuccessful in establishing a new partner for a global ethanol market.

Chapter 6

BRAZIL'S MULTILATERAL ETHANOL DIPLOMACY

Introduction

Since the 1990s, Brazil has been a proponent of multilateral organisations. Despite its traditional focus on autonomy, Brazil understood that multilateral organisations and global governance arrangements could leverage its power resources vis-à-vis the countries of the Global North and at the same time limit the extent of their reach, especially that of the United States. With its strategy of autonomy through participation, Brazil aimed at shaping the global governance framework, and thereby the international structure, to its benefit. Brazil's multilateral ethanol diplomacy is one example where the country aimed for a substantial structural adjustment in its favour by displaying expertise, exerting power over smaller partners and balancing against the United States and the European Union.

As outlined by Kloss (2012), Brazil aimed at promoting ethanol as an alternative fuel on the multilateral level, particularly within the World Trade Organization (WTO). The WTO was founded in 1995 as a result of the General Agreement on Trade and Tariffs (GATT) negotiations in order to reduce tariffs and, more generally, obstacles to international trade. Brazil is a founding member of both the WTO and GATT.

The main issue Brazil faces regarding its multilateral ethanol diplomacy is that apart from nuclear energy, there is currently no global energy governance system in place. Therefore, ethanol is traded according to WTO rules of agricultural products, which means that ethanol made from sugarcane can be subjected to tariffs and trade is subject to bilateral rules and commitments.

Brazil therefore aimed to include ethanol into a general governance regime that would free ethanol from such restrictions and enable a global free market, which would discriminate less against ethanol as compared to fossil fuels. The WTO Doha Round seemed an appropriate venue for this undertaking with its focus on sustainable development.

Ethanol, however, faced other issues as well, mainly questions regarding standards of quality and sustainability. Brazil sought venues outside the WTO to address these questions, in particular the United Nations–supported International Biofuels Forum (IBF) and the OECD- and G8-supported Global Bioenergy Partnership (GBEP). Both fora were also used to run outreach and information campaigns for third-party countries – mainly from the Global South – to convince them of the introduction of an ethanol economy.

This chapter will analyse the question how Brazil applied its ethanol diplomacy to multilateral organisations and then identify reasons why Brazil's ethanol diplomacy had little results regarding the improvement of global ethanol governance during the Lula and Dilma governments.

The chapter begins with an analysis of the power structures and actors involved according to the Neoclassical Realist approach, which outlines the structural environment with a focus on the workings of the WTO, its actors and institutions, and particularly the new alliances that Brazil helped create within that system and Brazil's successes within the WTO system. In a second step, I will analyse Brazil's role in the WTO negotiations towards the 2013 Bali ministerial meeting and Brazil's initiative to introduce ethanol into an environmental goods agreement. After this, Brazil's forum shopping, its engagement in fora such as the IBF and GBEP as well as climate negotiations will be outlined.

The chapter closes with a summary and analysis of Brazil's multilateral ethanol diplomacy.

Background

Brazil openly favoured a multilateral and global solution to the question of biofuels not only because of the general multilateral approach of the Lula government (Amorim 2015b) but also due to the pragmatic reason of including European and Asian markets into a global biofuels trade regime (Joerißen and Steinhilber 2009: 5). Brazil furthermore attempted to create pressure on the United States by influencing the WTO system according to Brazil's preferences (Meyer 2010: 16). This shows how the bi- and multilateral approaches of Brazil's trade policy intertwined. Brazil did not necessarily need to reach an absolutely favourable solution within the WTO – even though that would have been preferable – but it was useful as a mechanism to put pressure on other bilateral trading partners, in particular the United States and the European Union, to underscore their need to move towards Brazil's position in bilateral negotiations. It is important to understand the complexity of the international trade system to see how Brazil could exert pressure on stronger trading partners through the possibility of an outcome of the WTO negotiations that would be less favourable to the bilateral partners.

The next paragraphs will therefore outline the structural environment and elaborate on the difference between the WTO as an established organisation and the WTO as an evolving system with its framework of trade negotiation rounds.

The Structural Environment

Global trade has – with the exception of the onset of the global financial crisis in 2008/09 – been on the rise since 2001 (World Bank 2017) and almost doubled between 2000 and 2012. Brazil at that time was one of the emerging markets whose world trade participation increased significantly. Therefore, the country was interested in shaping the global rules and norms that govern trade. In particular, this was reflected in Brazil's focus on South–South diplomacy and WTO presence (Fishlow 2010: 7). 'Anarchy is what states make of it', Andrew Moravscik (1992) famously claimed. The WTO as an institutional space allows for countries to organise through alliances and coalitions. Hopewell (2015: 315) points out how important it is for a state to 'attract followers and mobilise other states into effective coalitions' to increase its individual leverage in negotiations.

Within the multilateral realm of the WTO, anarchy is organised within interest coalitions. These can reflect regional trade blocks like the European Union or MercoSul. In the realm of agriculture, the groups have traditionally been organised along the lines of industrialised countries (G-4, G-10), developing countries (G-33, G-90, ACP, LDC), agricultural producers (Cairns) and agricultural importers (G-10); however, the WTO is a complex web of negotiations that exceeds agriculture, with manufactured goods (non-agricultural goods) as a second pole of negotiations. While bargains may be struck within one area, it is also possible that concessions in one area are weighed as bargaining chip in the other area. In the Doha Development Round, Brazil has been member of the following groups relevant for this study: MercoSul (regional trade block), Cairns (agricultural producers/exporters), G-20[1] (developing countries, mainly agriculture but also NAMA) and NAMA-11 (developing countries seeking to limit industrial market opening).

WTO Organisation Versus WTO Trade Negotiations

The WTO can conceptually be understood as an organisation with a legislative function (main tool: trade negotiations) and a supervising function (main tool: dispute settlement).

1. It is important not to confuse the G-20 group of developing economies in the WTO with the G-20 group of major economies (in the following: 'G-20 (FIN)').

The central principle of the WTO is the 'most favoured nation treatment' (Blustein 2009: 19). This means that member states have to treat every other nation as they treat the 'most favoured nation' in terms of trade, thereby not discriminating against individual countries. There are two exceptions to this rule: the possibility of creating regional trade blocks and preferred market access for least developed countries (WTO 2017a). If a member state deems itself discriminated by another member, it can bring cases forward to the WTO Dispute Settlement Body.

The WTO's dispute settle mechanism was protected by a so-called peace clause until 2003, which meant that a case could be brought forward only if a country exceeded the total allocated rate of subsidies or had introduced new subsidies after 1992 – a framework that effectively stopped developing countries from challenging developed countries' subsidies (Josling 2015: 239). From the early 2000s, when the end of the peace clause was nearing, several high-profile cases were brought forward by developing countries.

Brazil sees this mechanism as a chance to contest policies of developed countries and, also due to its successes in the mechanism, regards it as a highly trusted instrument in norm-based international policy making (Amorim 2011: 153). Two relevant cases, the cotton case against the United States and the sugar case against the European Union, will be subject to closer review later in this chapter.

On the other hand, the WTO system encourages further trade liberalisation through its legislative function. Here, new agreements are being negotiated on a permanent working level culminating in the biannual ministerial conferences ('ministerial'). The current round of negotiations is the so-called Doha Development Agenda that was initiated in 2001. The majority of this chapter will focus on Brazil's attempts to promote ethanol within this framework. The Doha Round has not been concluded so far due to the mechanisms in place, which lead to a 'no [as] the easiest answer when in doubt' (Monheim 2015: 182).

How Negotiations and Ministerials Work

The WTO trade negotiations are mainly visible through the biannual meetings at ministerial levels that aim to push forward the global trade agenda with new agreements. These ministerial meetings receive wide press coverage and public attention and are hosted by a member country. In the alternating year, a mini-ministerial or preparatory meeting is held in Geneva in order to advance the agenda such that a draft agreement can be produced by the WTO director general secretariat and that the main points of contention can be clearly addressed. These Geneva meetings are usually attended by a smaller group of negotiators, especially the ambassadors to the WTO. The WTO director general and the General Council chair are the two key organisers who are responsible for arranging the modalities of the negotiations, but outside of Geneva, the respective host minister chairs the conference which can be a wild card (Monheim 2015: 185).

Until the 2003 breakdown in Cancun, it was a practice that the chairs of technical topics would collect position papers from the member states (or negotiating groups) and subsequently elaborate a draft version of the final document of a ministerial (Amorim 2015: 421). A structural issue at preparatory negotiations is that countries' specialist representatives and ambassadors do not have the mandate to 'cross red lines' in the negotiations, which only ministers or elected officials can do (Monheim 2015: 181). This leads to delays and perceived failures of negotiations. After Cancun, this mode was replaced by top-level diplomatic meetings that worked on the draft versions of such documents. After the failure of the 2007 Potsdam meeting, the Doha Round returned to this previous practice (Amorim 2015: 421).

It is noteworthy that the WTO language and negotiations are highly complex constructs and the issues at hand highly technical and difficult to fully grasp. Amorim (2015: 370) shows how this can lead to misunderstandings that in turn pose significant hurdles to quick progress, especially on the executive level. A new director general of the WTO usually needs four years to get acquainted with all the modalities of the system and begin successfully implementing their agenda (Monheim 2015: 194). As decisions in the negotiations need to be made consensually, Brazil sees itself at a privileged position to mediate interests between the different factions (Amorim 2011: 152) and was able to score successes. In the Doha Round, two modes of negotiations, the green room and small-group transparency, can be observed (Monheim 2015: 179). The green room refers to an exclusive, invite-only, pre-negotiation between the biggest partners, whereas small-group transparency means that the negotiation chair divides the parties into small groups and attempts at coordinating their preferences in a more transparent way. At the beginning of the Doha Round, the traditional way of doing things was to prepare decisions within 'the Quad', the biggest trading nations (the United States, the European Union, Canada and Japan) in the green room, who would then impose their compromise on other member states (Hopewell 2013: 2), but post-Cancun, Brazil, India and China were included to a new core group at the expense of Canada and Japan (2013: 9). This core group is not fixed. For example, in June 2007, the G-4 group (the United States, the European Union, Brazil and India) met in Potsdam to informally discuss critical points.

It is important to remember that the negotiations are a mix of technical compromises and political bargaining. The European Union and the

United States are two central players that shape the system, and Brazil was able to secure its spot on this negotiating table.

Biofuels and the WTO

What's the role of the WTO in bio-ethanol regulation?

In order to understand the regulation of biofuels in general, and ethanol in particular, under the WTO regime, one must recognise the difference in treatment between agricultural and industrial goods within the WTO and the Doha Development Round of trade negotiations (Motaal 2008: 76). This is relevant to understand the different actors involved in the negotiations on the Brazilian side and the different pressure groups that influence the decision-making processes in the Brazilian Ministry of Foreign Affairs (MRE) department for energy, which deals with ethanol and biodiesel in one strategy.

As Harmer (2009: 5) points out, there is no 'WTO jurisprudence dealing specifically with biofuels', which means that the WTO lacks a specific regime or agreement on biofuels leading to a different treatment of ethanol and biodiesel. The central difference is that ethanol is classified as an agricultural product, since it comes from agricultural feedstock, whereas biodiesel is classified as a chemical and therefore falls under the industrial goods regulations (Weiß 2011: 169). In this study, the focus will be only on ethanol, which means that the WTO Agreement on Agriculture (AoA) is the main governing regulation.[2] Harmer (2009: 5) points out that

> agricultural goods are subject to both the WTO Agreement on Subsidies and Countervailing Measures (SCM) and to the specific provisions of WTO AoA. As a result, it is possible that there could be subsidies for ethanol that are permissible under the AoA.

The classification leads, therefore, to the need for 'tariffication of particular quantitative restrictions, and special rules on subsidies apply deviating from the SCM' (Weiß 2011: 172). While the 'WTO subsidy disciplines do not prohibit all subsidies or support to biofuels' (Harmer 2009: 15), the question for Brazil is to clarify through litigation or negotiation which subsidies are permissible or should be banned, respectively.

2. Ethanol is categorised under chapter 22 on beverages, spirits and vinegar in the Harmonised Standard (HS) system under code 2207, covering un-denatured (220710) and denatured (220720) alcohol.

Within the AoA, there are three forms, or 'pillars', of support: export competition, market access and domestic support, whereby market access is increasingly relevant for ethanol, but the main focus lies on domestic support (see Harmer 2009: 7), as the question of export subsidies has been litigated within the sugar case and subsequently banned under the 2005 Hong Kong ministerial. The WTO classifies domestic support in three boxes – amber, blue and green – depending on how they affect (distort) trade. To understand whether a specific biofuels policy complies with WTO rules, one must look at the box to which it is attributed (2009: 7). The blue box covers measures to reduce production, which is not relevant for the topic of ethanol at this point. The green box covers measures that have little impact on trade, do not count to the aggregate measure of support (AMS) and do not need to be reduced. Green-box subsidies are closely defined and therefore a constant point of contention; that is, complaints in trade disputes will try to argue that green box–reported subsidies might actually be amber-box subsidies.

> That said, however, an examination of the green box provisions of the AoA shows that this is not a broad and expansive category for subsidies that have some environmental, energy or rural development objective or outcome. (2009: 10)

The amber box covers highly priced distorting measures, and members report the amount of such support measures to the WTO as AMS that member states agreed to reduce. Exceeding the reported AMS opens the member state to trade disputes (2009: 7). The question whether a specific subsidy complied with WTO rules is difficult to answer. Harmer (2009: 8–12) makes an attempt to categorise the most common forms of subsidies for biofuels and only sets out a general approximation. In that sense, she finds that tax credits and reductions might be admissible if they are within an 'appropriate benchmark' (2009: 9), which poses the problem of defining such. Output-linked payments appear to conform with WTO regulations, as long as they do not 'have adverse effects on the interests of another WTO Member' (2009: 9). Blending mandates appear to fully conform with WTO standards, as long as they do not contain explicit local content requirements. Direct loans and loan guarantees need to be proven by the plaintive to be favourable to those available on the market (2009: 10). Feedstock subsidies, on the other hand, seem to be easier to prove in dispute settings and therefore have been the issue of several WTO cases (Brazil and Canada vs. US corn subsidies, Brazil vs. Thai sugar regime), as 'payments to agricultural producers that grow biofuel feedstocks, such as corn or sugar, which are basic agricultural products, clearly fall within the AMS definition' (2009: 11). In the future, it will become of great interest to develop a mechanism to categorise feedstock for second- or third-generation biofuels, such as algae or waste (2009: 5).

In summary, ethanol is categorised as an agricultural product within the WTO system and can therefore be subsidised under certain circumstances. Brazil can either pursue the litigation route of challenging other members' subsidies as they did in the EU sugar case, where the European Union subsidised the export production of Brazil's main ethanol feedstock, sugar. This route requires certain legal and diplomatic capabilities from Brazil, one aspect of soft power that might attract other countries to follow suit in the litigation efforts. Brazil can also work towards favourable results in the WTO trade negotiations either by further liberalising agricultural markets or by allowing for special support for biofuels.

The negotiating positions

According to former foreign minister Amorim, the WTO is the most important organisation in economic terms as the Doha Round aims at making international trade more just, thereby offering Brazil a compelling narrative for its newly adopted prominence in the international system (2011: 79). The WTO is also the only way for Brazil to force other countries – mainly the United States and the European Union – to effectively reduce their subsidies for agricultural products (2011: 128–29).

Within the WTO, Brazil is in an interesting position – particularly in the agricultural negotiations – as it has several overlapping and contradicting positions, which leads to a variety of different coalition options. On the one hand, Brazil relies on the United States to put pressure on the European Union to open its agricultural market, while it equally shares an interest with the European Union in making the United States reduce its trade-distorting subsidies (Amorim 2011: 511). On the other hand, Brazil's power base in the WTO stems from its leadership of the G-20, which is a diverse coalition that not necessarily shares Brazil's positions on agricultural liberalisation or industrial protection. The former is seen as tactical coalitions, while the latter is understood as its strategic underpinning (Amorim 2015: 297).

In terms of ethanol, Brazil's well-established and competitive ethanol sector is keen on open markets, whereas the United States seeks to protect its young ethanol industry for the sake of energy security, and the European Union tries to protect its small, yet environmentally oriented biofuels industry (Motaal 2008: 64). China, India and Thailand subject their local ethanol sectors to their respective agricultural preferences (2008: 66).

According to Amorim (2015: 309), agriculture would be seen as the locomotive of progress in the Doha Round for the Brazilian government. One might add that agriculture is the major roadblock of negotiations if industrialised countries protect their agricultural markets with the same zeal that developing countries protect their industrial markets.[3] Brazil realised this and spread its investment between opening agricultural markets and introducing the category of environmental goods, which might have offered a second avenue within the WTO framework for increased biofuel trade. Nogueira (2009: 3–4) gives a concise overview of Brazil's main positions in the Doha Round.

In summary, Brazil's negotiation position regarding ethanol is complex; on the one hand, it strives for agricultural market liberalisation, with a disregard for non-tariff trade barriers (like ecological labelling); on the other hand, it pursues the approach of including ethanol as a biofuel into a possible agreement on environmental goods that would allow for special and differential treatment for ethanol based on factors like eco-labelling. Brazil's third approach in the multilateral sphere is to seek conversion of industrial standards, while a distant and less strongly pursued fourth strategy is to raise the profile of ethanol in international climate negotiations.

Actors and Institutions

This complex negotiation position is reflected in a complex web of actors and institutions involved in Brazil's multilateral ethanol diplomacy.

Brazilian Actors and Institutions

The successful conclusion of the Doha Round was an explicit foreign policy goal of the Lula government and MRE in particular (Hopewell 2013: 7). It was seen as a project of internal prestige for Itamaraty to take the lead in the Doha negotiations and to be in the driver's seat internally in spite of or maybe because of the many powerful Brazilian actors that are interested in global trade. In the Brazilian foreign policy complex (FPC), CAMEX, consisting of representatives of the Ministry of Finance; Brazilian Ministry of Agriculture, Livestock and Supply (MAPA); MRE and Ministério da Indústria, Comércio Exterior e Serviços – Ministry of Development (MDIC), is the main decision-making body for trade policy next to the presidency. This group coordinates the positions of the different ministries and gives direction to Itamaraty, as both civil servants from MAPA and Brazilian diplomats confirmed. Particularly under Lula, the WTO was also a project of presidential diplomacy as many of the issues of the Doha Round were topics of non-WTO meetings as well.

3. This leads to a very interesting position in terms of biodiesel, which is an industrial product for which Brazil wants bigger market access while at the same time trying to protect the markets for other industrial products.

Amorim (2015) on many occasions underlines the close and trustful relationship that he and President Lula had in terms of their Doha commitment.

According to Hopewell (2013: 1), however, the main driver behind Brazil's forceful WTO engagement was 'its export-oriented agribusiness sector'. This assessment certainly leaves out other big industrial parts of the Brazilian economy; it is true though that Brazilian agribusiness has a particularly strong interest in agricultural market liberalisation, as expressed in many of the actions taken by the Brazilian Rural Society (Sociedade Rural Brasileira – SRB), 'the country's oldest and most prestigious agricultural lobby group' (Goldberg et al. 2006: 237). This group not only prepares political positions but also helped finance Brazil's litigation efforts and, very importantly, organised support in the conservative factions of the Brazilian Congress for Brazil's and Lula's multilateral engagement on behalf of its agricultural and ethanol industry.

The two lobby groups, Abrapa (for cotton) and UNICA, financed consultancies that prepared the WTO dispute cases on behalf of the Brazilian state (Hopewell 2013: 7), and the industry-funded research institute ICONE had 'a central role in formulating Brazil's negotiating position in the Doha Round' (2013: 10), with its representatives presenting at meetings in Geneva on behalf of Brazil (WTO 2008: 223) and officially attending the 2005 Hong Kong Ministerial (WTO 2005b). Amorim (2015: 314) attributes an important role to Brazilian NGOs that were included in a routine dialogue in the WTO but also in the Brazilian representation. This civil society interaction is more relevant for international climate change mitigation efforts than for the highly technical WTO negotiations.

International Actors and Institutions of Influence

The WTO director general (DG) is the most visible and central actor in the WTO trade negotiations. He prepares and coordinates positions and selects the negotiation mode. It sometimes depends on the diplomatic skills and grit of the WTO DG to keep negotiators at the table and to bring negotiations to a successful conclusion. According to the trade consultants interviewed for this study, possibly the main reason for DG Supachai Panitchpakdi's replacement by Pascal Lamy was that he did not handle the Cancun crisis well.

The dominant members of the WTO are the United States and the European Union. They are involved in all decisive closed-circle negotiations and represent the biggest trading blocks. It is therefore important to understand the involvement of their respective representatives.

In the United States Congress periodically concedes trade authority to the US president. As part of the executive office, the US Trade Representative

(USTR) is the main negotiator on behalf of the United States in the WTO. The USTR represents the United States at the WTO ministerials and works directly under the president, not as an autonomous member of the Cabinet. The US president is involved in WTO diplomacy indirectly through informal meetings mainly at the fringe of G8 and bilateral meetings.

The commissioner of trade is the main representative of the European Union at the WTO. While all EU members are individual members of the WTO, they have delegated their negotiating position to the European Union as one trade block. That makes the EU trade commissioner one of the most important figures in WTO negotiations. It should be noted that EU heads of government can formally influence the EU trade commissioner's policy through the Council of the European Union and informally through their regular exchange within the European Union and formats such as the G8.

New Alliances at Cancun

The 2003 Cancun ministerial was a crucial point in the formation of new alliances in the WTO. Pre-Cancun, the Quad was the leading group in the WTO, followed by the United States and the European Union as individual actors, and opposed by regional groupings and issue coalitions; during and after Cancun, developing countries formed several new coalitions, such as the Core Group of Developing Countries on Trade Facilitation, the Cotton-4, NAMA-11 and the G-20 (Finger 2009: 98; Hopewell 2015: 319). Brazil was instrumental in creating NAMA-11 and G-20, while being supportive of the Core Group, the Cotton-4, and a mediator in many of the other new coalitions (Hopewell 2015: 324). The most influential and visible group to emerge during this process was the G-20, which will be subject to further enquiry later in this chapter. As the NAMA-11 focus lies on non-agricultural market access, it is not central to the question of Brazilian ethanol diplomacy and therefore will not be subject to further enquiry in this section. Before focusing on the G-20, it is useful to look at one group that is not an official part of the WTO negotiations but was Brazil's first international strategic undertaking of the Lula administration, the cooperation with India and South Africa within the IBSA framework.

IBSA

The Dialogue Forum India, Brazil, South Africa (IBSA) was established in June 2003. The basic document of IBSA is the 'Brasília Declaration' that was signed by the foreign ministers of the three countries. The declaration encompasses strategic topics for Brazil, including UNSC reform, new threats to security and global development, but also points out concrete areas of cooperation such as cooperation within the Doha Round and in the fields of biotechnology and alternative energies (IBSA 2003). IBSA encourages cooperation through its dialogues and does not have a permanent organisational structure (Arkhangelskaya 2010: 1). Alden and Vieira (2005: 1089) understand IBSA primarily as an instrument of the foreign ministers of the three countries to 'instigate and shape' processes like 'the intensification of IBSA's political articulation within the G-20 framework'. This is understandable as the trilateral commission of foreign ministers was the highest coordination mechanism of IBSA until the first IBSA summit in 2006. Brazil intended to take advantage of the 'mutually reinforcing' nature of its cooperation within IBSA, G-20, BRICS and possible agreements between regional blocks (Hirst 2013: 212). The first IBSA summit therefore produced an assertive declaration that included a plethora of strategic and current topics, including the Doha Round, UNSC reform and questions of sustainable development (IBSA 2006a).

The summit furthermore produced an MoU on biofuels that outlines an agenda that follows Brazil's interests very closely and explicitly mentions the promotion of ethanol and the creation of a global market for the biofuel (IBSA 2006b). According to Barreto (2012: 516), IBSA was established as a coordination mechanism for Brazil, South Africa and India to underline their respective regional leadership and translate it into action on the multilateral level, in particular at the United Nations and the WTO. The declarations from the IBSA (2007 and 2008) summits contain calls for UNSC reform, a commitment to WTO/Doha success, and explicitly mention biofuels. One can observe that the section of biofuels has vanished from the IBSA (2010) declaration of the fourth summit, while remarks on the WTO are limited to one short paragraph, leading to the conclusion that IBSA was primarily seen as a coordination mechanism for the Doha Round. As trade among the three countries remained low, they attempted to improve this by reaffirming their commitment to build a joint group with the focus on development in trade during the second IBSA summit in 2007 (Raja 2007). This commitment to development was coined by several analysts as a priority to maintain agricultural subsidies and industrial protectionism (e.g. Barreto 2012: 519), a combination that was not uncontested as Brazil generally does not support agricultural subsidies.

At a preparatory meeting for the 2008 IBSA summit in New Delhi, Brazil tried to convince India to take a more open position in terms of agriculture (Amorim 2015: 425) but ultimately failed to achieve the goal to elaborate a common IBSA position by the time of the summit. During the IBSA summit in 2008, the group formally remained committed to representing the interests of developing countries in the Doha Round (Barreto 2012: 521), although the group had collectively failed to achieve this central purpose. This 'breakdown in IBSA solidarity' (Brands 2011: 40) shows the difficulties Brazil faced and still faces regarding the coordination and alignment of its interests with other rising powers in an environment that is fundamentally anarchic and self-interested.

Analysts and academic commentators had higher hopes for IBSA than for Brazil's other global groupings, as the three participating countries share core characteristics, for example, size and multicultural democracies from the Global South (Brands 2010: 46). Diverging interests in trade and limited resources to successfully implement projects, however, remain challenges for IBSA (Arkhangelskaya 2010: 4). Nevertheless, IBSA had its role as a preparatory mechanism in the creation of the G-20 and thereby the reshuffle of WTO power dynamics.

G-20

The formation of IBSA in the early summer of 2003 led to an increased interest by Brazil to lead a bigger group in the WTO negotiations (Barreto 2012: 517). Creating a coalition like the G-20 was a tactical idea that had been brewing since the previous administration in Itamaraty but was brought to fruition under the leadership of Celso Amorim and his permanent representative at the WTO, Luiz Felipe de Seixas Corrêa (Ricupero 2010: 31). Hopewell (2015: 325) calls Brazil's push for the implementation of this idea 'the real game changer at the WTO', and while the Doha Round has not been concluded thus far, it is worth exploring its origins before critically assessing its role in trade negotiations.

In February 2003, the chairman of the WTO committee on agriculture presented a first draft on agricultural modalities for the Doha Round – the 'Harbison Paper' – which reflected a divide between the European Union and Japan, who wanted to protect their markets, and the United States and the Cairns group (of which Brazil is part) that wanted further agricultural trade liberalisation (da Motta Veiga 2006: 19). The subsequent haggling over domestic support, market access and export subsidies within the Quad while leaving out developing countries led to a backlash and the creation of the G-20 (Schott 2004). Brazil saw its interests bypassed and mobilised with its IBSA partners and a group of 20 developing countries[4] that in August 2003 presented a joint counter-proposal on agriculture to the compromise between the European Union and the United States (Barreto 2012: 565). This proposal

4. Argentina, Bolivia, Brazil, Chile, China, Colombia, Costa Rica, Cuba, Ecuador, El Salvador, Guatemala, India, Mexico, Pakistan, Paraguay, Peru, Philippines, South Africa, Thailand and Venezuela.

was introduced as a negotiation position at the Cancun ministerial (WTO 2003) and is seen as the founding document of the G-20.

One major issue at the first G-20 summit in Cancun in 2003 was that though there was a unified position on the opening of agricultural markets, there were no provisions for poor countries who would be hit by highly advanced agro-industrial competition from countries like Brazil and Argentina (Bourne 2008: 163). The Cancun ministerial ultimately failed and led then WTO DG to not run for the position again. Despite the official reason – the 'Singapore issues'[5] – agriculture was crucial to the breakdown of the Cancun negotiations as the G-20 was created to oppose the joint US–EU proposal on agriculture (Goldberg et al. 2004: 252). Hopewell (2013: 2) goes further and argues that the formation of the G-20 was successfully aimed at destabilising the cohesion of the Quad.

The G-20 has lost and gained members over time, but it was in Brazil's interest to secure leadership over this group to direct a possible conclusion of the Doha Round in its desired direction (Hirst 2013: 198). This is reflected in Brazil's efforts to organise G-20 ministerial meetings in Brasília in December 2003 and in São Paulo in June 2004 (Hugueney 2004: 2). Therefore, Hopewell (2013: 14) suggests being critical of the G-20 and to 'question this purported concurrence of interests and how well the G-20 truly represents the interests of developing countries' since 'these notions also served to disguise whose commercial interests were truly at play'. It can surely be argued that Brazil's agribusiness sector was the dominant force behind Brazil pushing towards agricultural liberalisation, but this ignores another important aspect of the G-20. The formation of the G-20 should at the same time be understood as a vehicle for and result of Brazil's global leadership aspirations. Such an understanding of the group can explain why the lack of coherence in its interests was not of primary importance to Brazil and why the country 'did the "heavy lifting" for the group' (2013: 9). Brazil displayed practical soft power by solving problems for its allies and was thereby aiming for increased prestige to manifest its following by this group. Defraigne (2012) cites former Brazilian agricultural minister and later head of UNICA, Roberto Rodrigues, comparing the G-20 to 'friends setting off for a trip to the cinema [and] everyone wants to see the first movie, Export Subsidies, [...] about a fifth go home before the second one, Domestic Subsidies [and] by the final movie, Market Access, only about 40 per cent are left'.

Despite the 2008 break between Brazil and India, and the lack of a successful conclusion of the Doha Round, the G-20 has achieved gradual

5. 'Investment, Competition Policy, Transparency in Government Procurement and Trade Facilitation' (ICTSD 2003).

successes. Hopewell (2015: 320) points out the tiered formula for the reduction in domestic support, the elimination of export subsidies, a 'tiered formula for reducing tariffs, rather than the blended formula sought by the US and EU' as well as the successful resistance to the extension of the peace clause. The latter served Brazil's interests well by opening markets and ending subsidies through litigation.

The G-20 therefore extended Brazil's latitude in the WTO in terms of forming a veto coalition in the negotiations and also in terms of prestige and being accepted to the exclusive circle of key negotiation parties. This should have enabled Brazil to successfully implement its ethanol diplomacy as the formation of the G-20 had an effect beyond the WTO.

G77/G33/G90

Brazil's initiative to create a new grouping within the WTO agricultural negotiations did not remain unnoticed in the developing world. The oldest group of developing countries, the G77, dates back to the first UNCTAD in 1964, which can be understood as a group that applies 'a collection of "norm governed" strategies which have sought to work within the existing framework of multilateralism' (Alden and Vieira 2005: 1091). Through this non-disruptive approach, G77 had maintained a low profile and was not seen as an influential stakeholder in the GATT and WTO negotiations (Fogarty 2013: 131–32). However, with its technical expertise, Brazil was able to create a following of developing countries that in turn were influenced by Brazil's preferences (Hopewell 2013: 11), which led to the G77 issuing increasingly assertive statements during WTO ministerials, while not formally being a part of it, and Brazil taking advantage of its membership in this group that had seemingly been dormant for decades.

The G33 is a group of developing countries that advocate flexibility for developing countries in agricultural market opening and support. The group is also called 'Friends of Special Products' and is formally led by Indonesia, but dominated by India, and certainly inspired by Brazil's push for influence in the WTO. It is seen as a counter-coalition to Cairns. Since the Cancun ministerial, G33 has put forward several impactful proposals in the agriculture negotiations (Bellmann et al. 2013: 2–3). Brazil is not a member of G33, but other countries' membership overlaps with that of the G-20 and even Cairns. G33 can be considered a protectionist group in terms of their own market opening (WTO 2017b).

The creation of the G90 was inspired by the success of the G-20 and encouraged and supported by Brazil. During the Cancun conference, the groups of least developed countries (LDCs), the African Group and the African, Caribbean and Pacific Group of States (ACP) formed the G90

(Soares 2005). The LDCs and ACP benefit from preferential treatment that gives them certain benefits in terms of access to the EU and US market. With a potential new agreement on the horizon that would liberalise market access to the European Union, the G90 faced potential competition in agriculture from the more developed agro-industry of countries like Brazil. The main interest of the G90, therefore, is to fight preference erosion (Chomthongdi 2005). While Brazil is not a member of this group, it keeps close contact with the group and attends their meetings on a regular basis as an observer in the spirit of South–South solidarity (Amorim 2015b). Hopewell (2013: 3) criticises that the 'North-South divide is being mobilised strategically as a tool to advance the interests of business actors'. Nevertheless, smaller countries are bandwagoning, and Brazil uses this to its advantage to increase its leverage in the negotiations and subsequently be recognised as a leader and accordingly get invited to the decision-making table. With diplomatic finesse, Brazil was able to secure support of and ease fears by developing countries by teaming up with India and thereby acquiring the necessary credibility, by accepting trade-offs in terms of market access for developing markets in order to target the European Union and the United States, and by keeping controversial issues off the table (2013: 12).

Through smart coalition building and its expertise in trade questions, Brazil was able to disrupt the way negotiations were managed in the WTO until Cancun. Brazil's attraction towards smaller, developing countries was based in its economic rise but also in its bold approach towards and success within the WTO system.

Brazil's Successes within the WTO System

Brazil has shown several times that it can manage the system of the WTO well. This includes two major trade disputes, one on cotton and one on sugar, as well as the election of Brazilian diplomat Roberto Azevêdo to the WTO's highest position, the director general. Additionally, Brazil's successes in the WTO also include its successful resistance against the Agreement on Trade-Related Aspects of Intellectual Property Rights (TRIPS) regarding intellectual property rights of medicines to fight HIV/AIDS.

Goldberg et al. (2004: 238–45) show how under deputy minister of agriculture Camargo, Brazil developed its strategy of 'negotiation through litigation'. This means effectively bringing cases forward to WTO trade dispute panels and thereby leveraging its own position in the negotiations on concrete terms. While the rules on trade were initially not in Brazil's favour, Amorim (2011: 82) recognises that Brazil knows that it can achieve its goals through the rules and norms-based system. Through a 'rare example' of coordination within the Brazilian FPC, the two most famous trade disputes were brought forward and subsequently decided in Brazil's favour (Ricupero 2010: 31). Additionally, Brazil used its newly gained leverage to position itself as a trustworthy power broker that negotiates rather than takes advantage of its right to retaliate. In this way, the United States and Brazil agreed on changes in the agricultural markets in the developed countries that were desirable for Brazil (Abdenur 2006). Brazil's dispute settlement successes offered it a new, stronger position in the Doha Round – now being invited to the exclusive green-room meetings (Goldberg et al. 2004: 256), thereby letting Brazil present itself as a leader from the Global South and leverage its position significantly.

The Cotton Case

On 18 June 2004, a WTO dispute panel decided in Brazil's favour against US cotton subsidies. Then deputy agricultural minister Pedro de Camargo Neto had filed the complaint (dispute number DS267) in person on 27 September 2002 and positioned Brazil 'as an undisputed leader at the WTO and earned the respect and support of his peers in all corners of the globe' by successfully challenging developed countries' agricultural subsidies for the first time (Goldberg et al. 2004: 236).

In 2002, at a cotton conference of the International Cotton Advisory Committee (ICAC), Brazil started forming its political coalition of cotton-producing countries, in particular attracting the support of India and West African states (Goldberg et al. 2004: 242). MAPA initially aimed for building a case against US soy subsidies, but since cotton and soy can be used as rotational crops and MRE was blocking the effort against the soy case, Camargo redirected towards cotton (2004: 241). MRE initially blocked the case due to strategic and protocol considerations until finance minister Pedro Malan convinced them otherwise (2004: 245). In the meantime, Camargo had been building informal coalitions and disseminating information to possible co-complainants, whom he was not supposed to contact as it is MRE's prerogative to interact with foreign governments (2004: 244).

After filing the complaint, it became clear that Brazil could not convince other countries to come forward as co-complainants because of fear of possible US retaliations; however, Benin and Chad as well as Argentina, Australia, Canada, China, India, New Zealand, Pakistan, Paraguay and Venezuela signed as third-party signatories (Goldberg et al. 2004: 248). Brazil's leadership encouraged African nations to bring forward their own cotton proposal to the Cancun ministerial in 2003, a step that was seen as unconventional and surely would not have happened without Brazil's initiative (2004: 250).

The United States appealed against the 2004 decision but on 3 March 2005, the dispute settlement understanding (DSU) Appellate Body confirmed the previous ruling and on 15 July 2005 referred the case to an arbitration panel that agreed to suspend its work due to a settlement between the United States and Brazil (Goldberg et al. 2004: 258).

The two main results were that the direct payments to US farmers as warranted by the US Farm Bill were classified as amber-box rather than green-box subsidies, which meant that the United States had exceeded their allocated subsidies, while the second result clarified the distinction between price-based and non-price-based forms of subsidies (Goldberg et al. 2004: 255). This laid the ground for future cases before the WTO dispute settlement mechanism (DSM). The decision in the cotton case was described as the 'litmus test' (CTA 2013a: 4), as to whether or not the WTO would take development seriously in the Doha Round. The two most significant takeaways are that subsidy programmes are accepted as harmful to other WTO members and that the WTO is able and willing to hold even the most powerful members accountable (Skloven 2008: 10).

Brazil opted not to retaliate (or in official WTO language 'withdraw concessions') against US cotton subsidies in order to extend its hand for further negotiations and to find a solution to the Doha Round; however, in 2008, this seemed to no longer be an option (Wheatley 2008). In 2009, Brazil finally opted to break US pharmaceutical patents as a retaliatory measure against US agricultural subsidies (Wheatley 2009).

Brazil had won more than a 'bargaining chip' (Goldberg et al. 2006: 266), as this victory raised Brazil's profile as a leader of the Global South. It had stepped up for a disadvantaged group, displayed its expertise in trade through successfully litigating the case and established itself as a worthy partner of the developed countries by withholding retaliatory measures. The cotton case was the first battle in a fight against developed countries' agriculture subsidies, and while the case itself did not have high economic value for Brazil, it was a piece in a much bigger puzzle.

The Sugar Case

Brazil's second major victory at the WTO, the sugar case, has a similar symbolic value in terms of its leadership claims and its soft power projection through its display of trade expertise. In the WTO literature, it comes second to the cotton case mainly due to the fact that it was chronologically not the first case brought forward and won by a developing country against a developed country. Brazil 'picked product areas [...] of economic significance and [...] chose appropriate allies', which led to the economically and symbolically big win against the EU sugar regime in 2005, when Brazil partnered with Australia and Thailand (Bourne 2008: 174).

Australia and Brazil submitted their complaints in September 2002 (DS265 and DS266), while Thailand submitted its complaint (DS283) in March 2003. Two main points were at the centre of the case: whether EU sugar produced for export was indirectly subsidised through sugar subsidies for the internal market and whether the preferential treatment for sugar from ACP states under the Cotonou Agreement was receiving indirect subsidies through a mechanism that allowed the import of ACP sugar at EU internal prices while being exported at world market prices (Josling 2009: 273).

Given the strong cases presented by the plaintiffs, the European Union already in the summer of 2004 made moves in its negotiation position, which analysts attribute to the anticipated ruling against the EU position in the sugar case (Goldberg et al. 2004: 256). In October 2004, the panel report was circulated and appealed, and by April 2005 the Appellate Body report was published. Brazil and its partners had won three out of the four points brought forward, including the most important ones mentioned above (WTO 2017c). While this win like the cotton case came with significant economic benefits and increased Brazil's prestige, it also carried negative consequences for the LDCs and ACP, who would lose part of their export markets through the privileged access to the European sugar market after its liberalisation. The change in the EU sugar regime led to a price decline for ACP raw cane sugar in the EU internal market by roughly 100 €/tonne and increased the share of sugar from Brazil and other countries, thereby putting the ACP suppliers under stiffer competition (CTA 2013b: 8).

While the verdict in the sugar case is clear, its political outcome is complex. Winning the sugar case did carry significant financial benefit for Brazil's sugar and ethanol producers as competition from the European Union who cannot produce competitively without subsidies. The decision also led to the gradual opening of the EU sugar and ethanol market and thereby potentially opened new markets for Brazilian producers. In that sense, the WTO sugar case can be seen as a successful campaign within Brazil's overall ethanol strategy. Brazil's move to question the EU sugar regime, however, had mixed effects. On the one hand, it underscored Brazil's potential as a leader in the WTO and gave Brazil a bargaining chip for its bilateral negotiations with the European Union. On the other hand, many members of the G90 were adversely affected by the ruling as they had certain privileges in terms of exporting to the European Union before the case. Their loss underscored lost confidence in Brazil's ability to lead a Southern coalition in a way that is beneficial for developing and poor countries, which had to be restored at a significant cost, as can be seen in the electoral races for leadership positions in the WTO.

The Election of Roberto Azevêdo

At the beginning of Lula's presidency, Brazil suffered several setbacks regarding the placement of Brazilian candidates in international organisations (Bourne 2008: 162). Two prominent cases are the leadership election in the WTO in 2004/05 and the IADB leadership election in 2005.

In the WTO leadership race, Brazil initially put forward its own candidate, Luiz Felipe Seixas Corrêa, who was 'knocked out in the first round' (Bourne 2008: 162). This was due to the lack of support from African states for the Brazilian candidate, as several Brazilian diplomats lamented during my interviews. The rationale behind putting up a Brazilian candidate was to represent G-20 in the election, but Brazil had taken the votes of other developing countries for granted (Barreto 2012: 574). In the end, Brazil decided to back the Uruguayan candidate, Carlos Pérez del Castillo, but did not have enough time to rally sufficient support to prevent the European candidate, Pascal Lamy, from winning the vote.

In the IADB leadership race, the Brazilian candidate João Sayad got the vote of only one other MercoSul member, Argentina. The winner, Luis Alberto Moreno from Colombia, was quietly supported by the United States (Rohter 2005a) and gained the support of 20 of 28 countries eligible to vote with 56 per cent of the voting share (Rohter 2005b; IADB 2006: 42). The non-public election was decided quickly and 'delivered a sound defeat to Brazilian diplomacy, not least because the winning rival was also South American' (Malamud 2011: 10). These two experiences made Brazil understand that it could not solely rely on its rhetoric about South–South solidarity but that it had to offer more to the developing world to gather their support.

In the 2013 WTO leadership selection, Brazil's candidate Roberto Azevêdo won the race among nine candidates from Kenya, Ghana, Jordan and Costa Rica (eliminated in the first round), Indonesia, South Korea and New Zealand (eliminated in the second round) and finally the Mexican Herminio Blanco due to both disunity within the European Union and support from African and BRICS countries (Bourcier 2013). By positioning a Brazilian candidate at the top of the WTO, Brazil did not necessarily expect to receive favourable treatment, but rather have certainty over the ability of the DG to understand the different positions within the WTO and to create a process that eventually might lead to a successful conclusion of the Doha Round, as the DG is the master of process (Amorim 2011: 137). Since the election of a Brazilian national as DG of the WTO was viewed as prestigious but also useful in terms of agenda setting, Brazil put more effort into Azevêdo's ultimately successful election campaign. For example, Azevêdo toured over fifty mainly developing countries in the months leading up to the vote and the Brazilian government even put together a campaign website to support their candidate (Costas 2013).

As Monheim (2015: 260) describes, the negotiation management needs to be included as an intervening variable in structural IR analysis. In that sense, Brazil achieved a strategic victory by placing their experienced trade diplomat Roberto Azevêdo at the centre of world trade negotiations. If he succeeds, Brazil will surely add to its soft power reservoir. The central expectation of Azevêdo was to restart the Doha Development Agenda with the Bali ministerial coming up less than a year after his election. The following sections will outline the issues the Doha Round had been facing at that point and how Brazil integrated its ethanol strategy into its wider trade policy.

Bali and Environmental Goods

The Doha Round is the fifth round of negotiations to further develop and liberalise the international trading regime with an emphasis on development in the Global South, which is expressed in its title, the Doha Development Round. With regard to Brazil's ethanol diplomacy, it is interesting to look at three aspects: Brazil's push to introduce the category of 'environmental goods' into WTO language, Brazil's coalitions and Brazil's general preference for the WTO system and its efforts to reach a successful conclusion.

Brazil's Options and Possible Strategies

In 2004, Brazil began to focus its trade policy primarily on the WTO with MercoSul in a distant second place, while the Free Trade Agreement of the Americas (FTAA) was already close to being abandoned (Barreto 2012: 534). A consequence of abandoning FTAA was that Brazil's FPC had to be cautious not to provoke negative reactions by the United States and in particular their agricultural and biofuels lobby (Kloss 2012: 166).

In the Doha Round, Brazil saw the possibility to eliminate agricultural subsidies, to guarantee access to developed markets for the poorest countries, all while strengthening the multilateral governance system (Barreto 2012: 590). These three aspects are relevant for Brazil's ethanol strategy. The elimination of agricultural subsidies puts Brazil's highly competitive agro-industry in an even better position in world markets, while supporting access of poor countries to developed markets not only creates a following for Brazil's leadership aspirations but could also lead to increased trade in ethanol, either produced by or channelled through those countries. Finally, a rules-based multilateral system is beneficial to Brazil's global aspirations and not only helps Brazil in protecting its interests as shown in the WTO disputes but also can be influenced by Brazil in support of a global market for ethanol. It is important to remember that Brazil is the third largest agricultural exporter after the United States and the European Union, without subsidies at corresponding levels (Sangmeister 2013: 134).

Within these parameters, Brazil can place its ethanol strategy within two general venues: liberalisation of agricultural markets, which would allow for tariff-free exports to the big consumers, or a special classification of ethanol (and biofuels) in the WTO system that allows for product- or use-based preferential treatment.

The first is obviously Brazil's preferred outcome, because it would have bigger effects as ethanol would not be the only agricultural product for which Brazil can expand production in a liberalised market, and a fully liberalised market would lead to overall growth with effects for the production base of ethanol. Over this question, Brazil 'broke with India [...], pushing for lowered subsidies' (Hanson 2012), a reflection of Brazil's dominant interests.

The second path had been laid out in the Doha declaration, which encouraged the member states to seek preferential treatment for environmental products. While the first communiqués in this respect were submitted in 2005, the process of biofuels classification accelerated between 2006 and 2008 (Motall 2008: 77). A separate paragraph will analyse the process of the environmental goods negotiations.

A third way of advancing biofuels is through bilateral or regional free trade agreements, which Brazil pursued as a separate strategy. Weiß (2011: 172) argues that the WTO allows for national introduction of subcategories for products, according to their respective end use. This way, countries could introduce a differentiation between fuel-ethanol and ethanol for human consumption and unilaterally lower the import tariffs on fuel-ethanol. An open question remains whether such a fuel-ethanol subcategory then could be subject to further differentiation in sustainable and non-sustainable products with different tariff categories, an option that the European Union had already applied to the ACP countries during the review of the Cotonou agreement (2011: 172, 174).

A fourth way would be to switch the forum and create regulations outside the WTO and subsequently introduce these into the negotiations. Brazil also applied this strategy, which will be discussed towards the end of this chapter.

The State of Doha

In November 2001, the fourth WTO ministerial meeting took place in Doha, Qatar. The final communiqué of the conference launched the Doha

Development Agenda (or Round) of trade negotiations. The aim was to conclude negotiations and come to agreements in the areas of agriculture, services, anti-dumping, environment and the 'Singapore-Issues' by the end of 2004 (Monheim 2015: 177). The WTO agricultural negotiations focus on three areas: domestic support, market access and export competitiveness. These three pillars are particularly relevant to the creation of a global market for ethanol as long as it is traded as an agricultural product.

In the first year of the Lula presidency, Brazil was on the defensive in the WTO but quickly tried to develop an offensive, forward-looking strategy (Amorim 2011b). Even before the infamous Cancun ministerial in 2003, fault lines were visible in the negotiations. These fault lines, however, still followed the primacy of developed countries from the Global North as Blustein (2009: 138) exemplifies with the lashing out of USTR Zoellick at the Japanese delegation at the mini-ministerial in Montreal in July 2003. Monheim (2015) offers a thorough process tracing of the Doha Round from 2001 until the 2013 Bali package. He particularly analyses how after the 'dramatic failure' of the Cancun ministerial in 2003, the 2004 'July framework' was passed relatively quickly and smoothly in Geneva by means of effective negotiation management (2015: 204). The following chapter will be closely linked to his work but will put focus on the power relations that Brazil used to implement its agenda.

Brazil had already approached India in early 2003 to work together to counter Northern dominance in the WTO, with the details to be determined (Blustein 2009: 143). Two possible areas for cooperation were the abolishment of export subsidies and deregulating the agreement on intellectual property (TRIPS). The former is of high interest for Brazil as it competes with the United States and European Union in international markets, while it is not an issue for India, which is a net importer of agricultural products. The latter is important for a number of developing countries, particularly in the area of generic drug manufacturing. Blustein (2009: 147) elaborates how the cause of the Cotton-4 countries was included into the overarching topic of export subsidies and thereby channelled into action by the soon-to-be-founded G-20. Brazil's position in the cotton case added legitimacy for the country to claim leadership of the group (Meyer 2010: 16).

According to Blustein (2009: 153), it was USTR Zoellick who prevented the WTO DG from drafting a final document that incorporated most of the demands of the G-20 and ultimately led to the embarrassing outcome of the Cancun ministerial. In the beginning of 2004, however, USTR Zoellick restarted the Doha Round by inviting Brazil to join a new type of Quad, known as FIPS or 'five interested parties', and by initiating a quasi-ministerial in Geneva for July 2004 (2009: 183). At that point, Brazil had comfortably assumed its role as a spokesperson for the G-20 group, reflected in the statement Brazil (2004) gave on behalf of the group, listing demands towards the developed countries.

During the negotiations for the so-called July framework that was passed in Geneva, the issues of 'Special Products' and 'Special Safeguard Mechanism' came on the table (Amorim 2011: 160). These are categories that developing countries could use to protect special or sensitive products (SP) from market pressures, while the special safeguard mechanism (SSM) is the procedure to limit market access in the case of 'serious injuries' to domestic industries (WTO 2017d). The issue with the July framework was that it incentivised countries to pursue their defensive interests rather than encourage them to play offensive (Blustein 2009: 227). While Brazil was at the centre of decision-making during the negotiations, it relied on the proposals of the United States and the European Union and did not use its position to actively set the agenda.

With agriculture at the heart of the Doha Round in 2005 (Barreto 2012: 576), the lack of Brazilian and developing countries' initiative and EU trade commissioner Mandelson's 'hardball' negotiation tactic (Blustein 2009: 283), the negotiations were 'deadlocked' by the summer of 2005 (Goldberg et al. 2006: 260). But in July 2005, after the G8 meeting at Gleneagles, the Chinese government invited the G-20 for a meeting in Dalian. Here, Brazil was successful in convincing the other members of the new trade block to adopt its positions (Amorim 2015: 317). This is reflected by the final declaration of the Dalian meeting, in particular in the area of agriculture (Bridges Weekly 2005). Amorim (2015: 318–19) points out that Brazil took advantage of its technical capabilities at the subsequent meeting of the G-20 in Bhurban, Pakistan, in preparation of the Hong Kong ministerial. With regard to domestic preparation, Itamaraty used October and November 2005 to further elaborate Brazil's position for the Hong Kong ministerial in collaboration with Brazilian industry representatives (2015: 327). Prior to the Hong Kong ministerial, Amorim expressed that the Cairns group had effectively lost its relevance (Barreto 2012: 577) and Lula successfully put pressure on the United States and the European Union to include G-20 representatives in the negotiations instead (2012: 579).

By the time of the Hong Kong ministerial in December 2005, trade issues were limited to agricultural market access negotiations (AMA) and NAMA, while the Singapore issues played no further role. Brazil had positioned itself at the centre of the negotiations, where no deal could be struck without its significant participation (Amorim 2015: 347). At the Hong Kong ministerial, this elevated position, however, led to several difficulties. For example, the G33 states began severely resisting the G-20s and thereby Brazil's willingness to compromise on agricultural issues (2015: 347). Brazil was able to achieve a minimum compromise among the G-20 and the G90 to push for a defined end of agricultural export subsidies (2015: 349), a step to show Brazil's alignment with developing countries' interests. In terms of market access, however, the European Union had the stronger cards and was able to disintegrate the developing countries' coalition (2015: 350).

Brazil eventually was able to negotiate a minimal compromise and sway the G-20 to support it, which leads Amorim (2015: 354) to claim that Brazil saved the Hong Kong ministerial. It is not clear that Brazil's contribution was that important, but it is clear, however, that after the Hong Kong ministerial, Brazil was publicly seen as a WTO superpower and consequently was more closely involved in the further development of the negotiations with any other party apart from the United States and the European Union. From the Davos Economic Forum 2006 onwards, the G3+1 (the United States, the European Union, Brazil + WTO DG) was a common format to exchange and prepare positions. The most important outcome of the Hong Kong ministerial was the elimination of export subsidies (2015: 489). The final declaration also set a new deadline for concluding the Doha Round to 30 April 2006.

With France blocking the European Union in agricultural concessions and Germany blocking it in industrial concessions, Brazil had to look for a partner within the trade block. The United Kingdom, with its open attitude towards trade, was the perfect partner. From March 2006 onwards, when Lula and Blair published a joint statement on trade (Blair 2006), the two countries worked closely together on WTO issues (Amorim 2015: 364). Already by summer 2006, Amorim (2015: 372) was able to identify a window of opportunity to close a deal with the European Union on AMA.

The meeting on 30 June 2006 in Geneva was conducted by the newly formed G-6, which included the United States, the European Union, Brazil, India, Australia and Japan (Blustein 2009: 229) and did not lead to the desired success. Instead, WTO DG Lamy suspended the negotiations until a staggered re-launch at the end of 2006. The new USTR Schwab made clear that she would not accept a 'Doha Lite' and started engaging further with Brazil to rally its G-20 partners and jointly put pressure on the European Union regarding agricultural matters (da Motta Veiga 2006: 20).

In September 2006, Brazil invited the negotiation groups from developing countries to informal meetings in Rio de Janeiro. This was a 'first attempt at re-starting the negotiations' after unsuccessful meetings in Geneva in July 2006 (Amorim 2015: 384). In the aftermath of this meeting, the fault lines between developing and middle-income countries became clearer and Brazil faced increasing difficulties in coordinating coherent positions. Mexico, for example, expressed that it did not see its interests represented by Brazil (2015: 386). Such expressions of dissatisfaction with Brazil's leadership required top-level (presidential) exchange. In a curious attempt to raise the standing of his top diplomat, Lula gave Amorim full negotiation authority at a meeting in Davos in early 2007 (2015: 389), which in practise weakened Brazil's tactical position in the negotiations.

At the 2006 G8+5 meeting in St. Petersburg in July 2006, President Lula acknowledged that the Doha Round was in crisis and therefore presented Brazil's ethanol proposals to the G8 summit (Barreto 2012: 522). This was underlined by Amorim in the run-up to the 2008 G8 summit by pointing out that no agreement with regard to climate change or energy will be achieved without participation of the BRICS (2012: 523). At the meeting, President Lula made another push for the conclusion of Doha with an emphasis on ethanol (Amorim 2015: 375).

By the time of the G33 meeting in Jakarta in March 2007, which was also attended by the core group, Brazil was under increased pressure from the United States, who saw the G33 'ganging up' on the United States for no substantial reason (Amorim 2015: 397) and perceived Brazil to be the only country in the position to break this Southern blockade. Despite Brazil's efforts, it could not substantially change the G33's defensive position on agriculture.

During his visit to the United States in 2007, Lula and Bush agreed that it was of joint interest to open up India's market for agricultural products and that the European Union posed at that point a bigger hurdle than the developing country (Amorim 2015: 402) for agricultural products. This turned out to be a miscalculation. At informal meetings in Geneva in June 2007, Brazil received severe pushback from Latin American countries, particularly Cuba and Venezuela, who criticised Brazil's cosying up to the United States and the European Union as well its recently more prominent ethanol initiatives (2015: 410). At the same time, the NAMA-11 group of developing countries, who opposed industrial market opening, began to block the G-20 (2015: 411).

The failure of the 2007 Potsdam G4 meeting led to a decrease in top-level negotiations and a return to the negotiations at the technical level where the respective chairs of the negotiations coordinate written statements of the participants (Amorim 2015: 421). The split was between North and South and beyond this excluded a large group of less developed countries, who issued a statement under the name 'G90 Plus'. In this statement, the group that includes the ACP group, the Africa Group and the LDC group, as well as Bolivia and Venezuela, criticised the process of G4 negotiations as well as the offers made by the group (Khor 2007). However, Brazil successfully concerted talks on a G110 declaration on NAMA in Geneva in July 2007 (Amorim 2015: 428), which led to the public declaration in October 2007 and thereby reinforced Brazil's position as the leader of the developing countries.

Brazil's statement at the informal NAMA meeting in Geneva in February 2008 already foreshadowed the upcoming breakdown of the Doha Round. In the statement, Brazil saw a lack of flexibility on NAMA while it made substantial concessions on AMA. This pressure, however, did not lead to the desired outcome of more NAMA flexibility. The 2008 ministerial in Geneva was perceived as the last chance to bring Doha to a successful conclusion with all of the core participants showing signs of nervousness (Amorim 2015: 443). The WTO DG introduced a new core negotiation group, the G7, consisting of the 'usual suspects from the G4 – America's Susan Schwab, the European Union's Peter Mandelson, Brazil's Celso Amorim, India's Kamal Nath – and two new ministers from the other countries in the G-6, Australia's Simon Crean and Japan's Akira Amari' plus China's commerce minister Chen Deming (Blustein 2009: 262). In July 2008, Brazil changed its position and accepted Lamy's offer in Geneva, which led to a division of the G-20, but neither led to a successful agreement due to the continued resistance of India and Argentina (Rossi 2008) that Brazil and Australia jointly opposed (Barreto 2012: 588).

Hopewell (2015: 331) sees the reasons of the July 2008 breakdown in the conflict between the United States and China, the former demanding increased market access for agriculture and manufactured goods, and the latter not conceding to it. Otherwise, 'the Doha Round may well have been concluded in 2008' (2015: 331). Brazil's view differs slightly. Amorim (2011: 171–72) states that the offers of the United States and the European Union were reasonable in NAMA and Brazil had reached close to their maximum demands in AMA. Yet, India was blocking the AMA negotiations (Amorim 2015: 444). At the same time, China was unwilling to accept the United States' suggestions on SP and SSM. While in the eyes of Amorim (2015: 451) Brazil tried to mediate, one should consider Brazil's difficult stance between its tactical and strategic coalitions. In particular, Brazil's rather protectionist stance in terms of NAMA put it at odds with allies like India, while it was already close to consensus with the United States. In AMA, the division was between the European Union and other developed countries and 'less competitive developing countries' like China, India and Indonesia (2015: 453), the latter partners of Brazil in several other coalitions. For the United States, China, and India, the cost of no deal was less than for the other participants (Blustein 2009: 265). In a 2008 ministerial session in Geneva, there seemed to be hope for success. The opposition of China and India in the end 'forced Brazilian retraction' (Fishlow 2010: 3).

Brazil's break with India in the WTO did not come until the 2008 IBSA summit, which was too late and cost a substantial amount of time. This was one of the reasons that the scheduled 2008 ministerial was cancelled due to a lack of technical submissions (Amorim 2015: 471). The lack of unity among the G-20, Brazil's cautious stance regarding India and China's stalling in NAMA led to the 'grand failure' of the July framework (2015: 298). In order to not poison the possibility of further negotiations, MRE and MME pushed back on subsequent demands by UNICA to initiate a case at the dispute resolution mechanism against both US and EU protectionism in the area of biofuels (Kloss 2012: 170). Amorim (2015: 482) notes that by 2009, Doha had basically disappeared from the Brazilian foreign policy agenda. The Doha Round remained a hot potato as Amorim (2010) 'would not risk [...] credibility with [Secretary of State Hillary Clinton] by insisting on the importance of successfully completing the Doha Round of negotiations'. Even a personal intervention of the WTO DG in Brasília in April 2010 did not bear any fruit in terms of putting Doha back on the Brazilian agenda (Amorim 2015: 485). Brazil instead chose to return to its successful strategy of engaging with the WTO on the basis of its institutional framework rather than the negotiations (2015: 487).

After the sobering outcomes of Brazil's participation in elite meetings, particularly in the G8+ meetings, MRE from 2010 onwards did not pursue this route and tried instead to widen participation in negotiations, something that Amorim (2015: 409) sees as a tactical mistake. At the 2011 meeting of G-20 agricultural ministers in Paris, Brazil and the United States made clear to other participants that biofuels should be kept apart from the food-security discussion at political and trade levels (Murphy 2011: 2). Biofuels were put back on the agenda for the upcoming Bali ministerial, the first under the leadership of the new WTO DG. The pressure was high as the likely consequence of a Doha failure would be a drive towards bilateral trade agreements (Macias 2008), something that would be less desirable from Brazil's political and tactical point of view.

The Bali Ministerial

The Bali ministerial took place in early December 2013, shortly after the new WTO DG had taken office and identified the 'success [of] the Bali Ministerial Conference [as] vital [and as the WTO's] first priority' (Azevêdo 2013). By mid-September 2013, negotiations were intensified upon pressure by the new WTO DG and focused heavily on agricultural topics next to trade facilitation and development (Bridges Weekly 2013a). Negotiations were tough, and in agriculture, three proposals, two from the G-20 and one from the G33, were on the table (Bridges Weekly 2013b). Unlike during the 2005 Hong Kong ministerial, where Brazil jointly with India organised the G110 coalition of developing countries, Brazil struggled to repeat a similar success in Bali (Hopewell 2015: 324). This led to a fragmentation of the developing countries' coalitions.

During the second half of 2012, in preparation for the scheduled 2013 ministerial, the G-20 and the G33 submitted two separated proposals on tariff rate quota (TRQ) administration and food security provisions, respectively (CTA 2013a: 2). While the G-20 proposals remained in the realm of technical specifications, the proposal of the G33 (WTO 2014) demanded a political decision on so-called box-shifting, to shift certain domestic subsidies from the amber to the green box and thereby allow for more market distortions but also potentially prevent food shortages. Brazil's role in these negotiations was minor. While Brazil was still part of the new core negotiation group, it was not able to weigh in significantly. Rather, the negotiations were between the United States and India, which led the G33 and almost broke down the negotiations (Hopewell 2015: 327).

In the end, the Bali ministerial passed the Bali Package, the first WTO agreement in years. The content of this declaration encompasses the area of agriculture provisions on public stockholding for food security, an understanding on TRQ administration provisions of agricultural products as well as provisions on export competition (WTO 2013). After its 'rollercoaster ending' (Bridges Daily 2013), the main success was that the Doha Round had been restarted and confidence had been restored so that the body could successfully progress.

Neither with regard to the position of the United States, who maintained its tariff on ethanol, nor with regard to the European Union's position, which aimed at keeping ethanol in the agricultural product category, was Brazil able to make significant progress (Kloss 2012: 191). What is striking is that Brazil, as the self-proclaimed spokesperson of the developing countries and leader of the G-20, was not able to mobilise a coalition to push beyond the status quo and create new norms. While Brazil is able to organise veto coalitions and is often presented as a 'norm-entrepreneur' (Benner 2013), it still lacks the necessary capabilities to be an effective norm marketer.

The Outcome of Bali: Agriculture and the Volatility of Brazilian Leadership

The Bali ministerial resulted in the first WTO agreement since the start of the Doha Round, the so-called Bali Package (WTO 2013). The agreement covered three areas: trade facilitation, agriculture (with cotton as a separate sub-section) and development issues for the least developed countries. It furthermore included a working plan for the future. Gal-Or (2014: 2) identifies three main successes of the Bali Package: the legalisation of grain stockpiling to prevent food shortages, the introduction of monitoring mechanisms to understand the preferential treatment of LDCs and the introduction of a more transparent customs reporting system. But the scepticism in Brazil remained, since at the conclusion of the Bali conference, the main points of criticism that Brazil had voiced for several years remained (Neto and Albres 2012: 84).

Throughout the Doha Round, one can observe Brazil's rise and levelling in the international arena. At the beginning of the Doha Round, the WTO was dominated by the Global North without contestation. Decisions were made ('prepared') by the Quad – the United States, the European Union, Japan and Canada – and formally approved by the other member states. After Cancun, the old power base had cracked, and the G-20 emerged. Due to its diversity of interests combined with attacks from the United States and the European Union, the G-20 remained the base of power for Brazil in the WTO but was relegated to second place with Brazil's ascendance to the exclusive circle of the new G4 (the United States, the European Union, Brazil and India) and G6 (Japan, Brazil, India, Australia, the United States and the European Union). China did not have a significant role in the negotiations until the 2008 informal meeting in Paris (Amorim 2011: 347).

The outcome of the Bali Package is mixed for Brazil. While some estimate that the Bali Package would increase global GDP by up to 1 trillion USD (Bridges Weekly 2013c), and the inclusion of agriculture provisions would benefit Brazil to a certain extent, one can also observe the erosion of Brazilian leadership. The Bali Package was created without crucial Brazilian contributions, apart from the WTO DG. One desirable outcome of the Bali Package for Brazil, however, was that negotiations toward a WTO Environmental Goods Agreement (EGA) were officially launched in July 2014 after years of talks about modalities.

Brazil's Suggestion: Environmental Goods

The negotiations on Environmental Goods and Services (EGS) are based on Article 31(iii) of the WTO Doha Development Agenda, aiming for 'the reduction or, as appropriate, elimination of tariff and non-tariff barriers to environmental goods and services'. The idea behind this is to liberalise markets for goods (and services) that are beneficial for environmental protection purposes. This section will solely focus on environmental goods as these negotiations are relevant for ethanol. It was Brazil's hope that establishing ethanol as an environmental good would support the creation of a global market irrespective of the outcomes of AMA negotiations (Weiß 2011: 170). It was expected that EGS negotiations would yield relatively quick results based on a consensus that environmental issues were to be collectively addressed (Cottier 2009: 1). This assumption turned out to be a miscalculation, as negotiation modalities, possible lists of goods and services, and new ways of assessing likeness and difference in the WTO context posed bigger challenges than anticipated (Cosbey et al. 2010: 10). Additionally, the negotiations 'to clarify the concept of an environmental good and establish a list' take place in the Committee on Trade and Environment in Special Session (CTESS), including the 'labelling requirements for environmental purposes' (Weiß 2011: 182) and (non-)tariff barriers are part of NAMA (Cottier 2009: 1).

The first problem that the negotiators faced was finding a definition of environmental good. The lack of definition has been one of the basic problems for EGS negotiations. In July 2005, Brazil submitted communiqué (TN/TE/W/5) (WTO 2005a) that suggested that whatever definition modality was going to be decided on, it should include renewable energy sources, such as ethanol and biodiesel (Gehring 2009: 4). This made Brazil's intentions clear with a focus on the outcome, rather than the definition modalities. There are basically three approaches to market liberalisation (Cosbey et al. 2010: 13): the list approach, request and offer (suggested by Brazil in 2007) and project-based liberalisation (counter-proposal by India and Argentina in 2007).

The list approach defines an 'environmental product' through a list of products that is negotiated in the CTESS and was opposed by developing countries as it might include agricultural products such as organically farmed produce and biofuels (Cosbey et al. 2010: 13). The list was initially based on the Organisation for Economic Cooperation and Development's (OECD) and Asia Pacific Economic Cooperation's (APEC) suggestions on environmental goods lists (Sugathan 2004). The OECD list already included ethanol (Steenblik 2005: 18). Cosbey et al. (2010: 12) identify three levels of environmental goods,

> Goods that are environmentally superior in end use (e.g. electric cars); Goods for which environmental improvement is a primary object (e.g. carbon capture and storage technology); Goods that are environmentally superior in production and processing (e.g. organic agriculture).

As Cottier (2009: 4) points out, the list approach for environmental goods and environmentally preferable goods – the former possibly describing hardware like wind turbines, the latter possibly covering 'similar substitute goods' like biofuels – seemed to turn EGS into a subset of NAMA negotiations.

While the list approach is undoubtedly compatible with current WTO rules, the submissions by developing countries to designate authority to national institutions to define the products under a certain set of parameters (project approach) raised concerns about WTO compatibility (Cottier 2009: 11). Members could negotiate and create the necessary legislative framework to integrate a project approach into WTO regulation (2009: 21), which would obviously come at a cost in terms of negotiations and resulting uncertainty.

In 2007, Brazil submitted a new proposal that would not rely on one list of environmental goods, but rather on country-specific lists that each WTO member would elaborate based on sustainable development criteria, which Brazil submitted as an official working document (WTO Job(09)/184) to the WTO on 15 December 2009 (Kloss 2012: 161). Due to the difficulty of creating legislation that would allow for a project approach and due to the lack of support that Brazil faced regarding its 'request and offer' proposal, the only way forward was following the list approach. This approach, however, faced credible criticism mainly by developed countries. Brazil supported the demand to only liberalise trade in 'environmental goods that serve a single environmental end-use' (Sugathan 2013: 8). Vikhlyaev (2011: 7) underscores the problem of dual use for environmental products, by the fact that only 1.5 per cent of the almost five hundred submitted products are single-use environmental products.

In early 2007, therefore, the United States and the European Union submitted a list that covered only 43 environmental goods and did not include biofuels, which made a Brazilian success in EGS regarding biofuels unlikely (Weiß 2011: 172). Brazil wanted to include biofuels and organically grown agricultural products into the category and suggested using the UNCTAD definition of 'environmentally preferable products' (EPPs) as a baseline for the definition of environmental good (Kloss 2012: 161). This, however, faced resistance from the WTO as the UNCTAD list would be inconsistent with WTO's rules on 'like products'; that is, the production and process methods cannot be used to discriminate against products (2012: 160). Based on the submitted list, Kloss (2012: 160) accuses the developed countries of using the category of environmental goods as a shortcut through the stalling NAMA negotiations, exemplified by the absence of agricultural products in the OECD suggestion.

Dual use and the resulting possible discrimination of like products would turn out to be the central criticism of IBSA plus China, Argentina and Egypt that led to the suspension of the negotiations in summer 2007 (Vikhlyaev (2011: 12). The main point of criticism by the G33 was that the proposed lists did not cover any of their respective export-relevant products, while only Brazil proposed ethanol to be added to the list (Sugathan 2013: 9). These issues and the lack of agreement on 'a common approach and methodology to EGS' ultimately led to the pause of EGS until the Bali Package (Cottier 2009: 2). Any successful outcome in terms of market liberalisation for ethanol would depend on sustainability criteria that would have to be negotiated in other fora, such as GBEP or IBF (Kloss 2012: 168).

Forum Shopping and Parallel Initiatives

While the UN Food and Agricultural Organisation (FAO) is not the focus of the following paragraphs, it is noteworthy that the FAO issued warnings against biofuels, and Senegalese FAO director general Jacques Diouf spoke out critically against biofuels in 2008. Nevertheless, Brazil was successful in installing a former Brazilian minister of food security, José Graziano da Silva, in 2011 as the new FAO director general, who subsequently lowered the biofuel critics' voices within the FAO.

While Brazil was successful in lowering the resistance to biofuels in the FAO, the active work had to be done in other fora. If technical and sustainability standards for biofuels were agreed upon outside the WTO, the adoption of these standards would support the promotion of these products within the WTO framework (Weiß 2011: 203)

International Biofuels Forum

In 2006, the Brazilian government issued an internal concept paper about an international mechanism to set standards for biofuels, which would become the International Biofuels Forum (IBF) in February 2007 (Kloss 2012: 125–26). Medeiros and Froio (2012: 44) see the IBF as an 'information exchange channel' that tackled four main issues: biofuel blends, production increase, technical norms and participation of ethanol in international finance. The first preparatory meetings took place in Brazil in September and November 2006 (Kloss 2012: 127).

On 2 March 2007, the IBF was officially launched for an initial period of one year at the Permanent Mission of Brazil to the United Nations with its founding members Brazil, the European Union, the United States, China, India and South Africa (UN 2007). The technical standardisation of ethanol had already been subject to technical review in the International Sugar Organisation (ISO) subcommittee (ISO/TC 28/SC 7), but the IBF aimed at securing political solutions to technical questions (Kloss 2012: 25). Observers saw this as an 'important milestone [to] provide an initial framework' for a global market of ethanol (Matthews 2007: 3568), as it was a mechanism to include new biofuels actors like China and South Africa into the discussion about the commodification of biofuels (Motaal 2008: 65). Due to its inception within the UN framework, the IBF was initially more widely known and accepted among developing countries than GBEP (Kloss 2012: 131–32).

The 2007 shift in US energy trade policy elevated the IBF to a well-regarded policy space, without which Brazil probably could not have attracted the European Union or China to work on standards and global biofuels marketing (Mol 2007: 308). Even with US support, initial enthusiasm remained low, which led to a reshuffle of the original structure and Brazil coordinating the working groups before the second IBF conference (Kloss 2012: 134).

While the main protagonists in the IBF, Brazil and the United States, focused on promotion of technical standards to attract global investment in biofuels (Masiero 2011: 113), the other partners had different interests. Both countries opposed a European suggestion for top-down creation of sustainability criteria and instead hoped for an industry-driven initiative for more sustainability after the second IBF meeting (Kloss 2012: 133). This initiative, however, did not gain traction, resulting in the surrender of the sustainability question to GBEP (2012: 136).

One of the main results of the IBF was the creation of the Tripartite Task Force among the United States, the European Union and Brazil that produced a 'White Paper on Internationally Compatible Biofuels Standards', which was published at the end of 2007. The White Paper (IBF 2007) establishes different standards in ethanol purity and encourages the respective national standardisation organisations to work towards standard convergence. The White Paper furthermore sees the most difficult issue to resolve in the low permitted water content of the EU standard and recommends that 'Europe reviews the water content specification at the earliest opportunity' (2007: 69). The level of permitted water content of ethanol is the biggest obstacle to achieving a technical harmonisation of standards (Kloss 2012: 149).

Brazil's leadership in the IBF aimed at creating a scientific consensus about biofuels standards (Jesus 2013: 505) that would favour Brazil's interests, mainly by not disrupting the sugar–ethanol connection with biofuels, which was of highest priority to MAPA and the Brazilian private sector (Kloss 2012: 140). Three years after its inauguration, the IBF depended mainly on Brazil's initiatives and contributions (2012: 188). It has been dominated by the group of three big ethanol producers, Brazil, the United States and the European Union, who maintained a working relationship. They preferred, however, to delegate the technical work to their national standards organisations and thereby to the ISO. Brazil in this respect lacked leadership to engage developing countries to actively participate in the IBF.

From 2009 onwards, the IBF experienced inactivity that culminated in the cancellation of the scheduled 2010 conference to update the White Paper due to lack of submissions and participants (Kloss 2012: 139). After the cancellation of the IBF conference, Brazil, the European Union and the United States decided to push the technical topic forward at ISO level through their national norm agencies.

Already during the second international Biofuels Conference in Brussels in March 2009, Brazil had noticed that environmental and social concerns were rising topics and that they should put more emphasis on factors such as rural development, health effects and other factors that can be addressed under the sustainability umbrella (Kloss 2012: 152). From that point onwards, Brazil shifted its main focus to GBEP.

Global Bioenergy Partnership

GBEP can be traced back as an initiative of the G8 Gleneagles summit in 2005 and was formally incorporated at the UN Commission on Sustainable Development in 2006. It is based at the FAO secretariat in Rome and financially supported by the Italian government. Brazil did not join until 2007, but already in 2008 became co-chair with Italy (Jesus 2013: 505). GBEP's mission and plan of work was developed and published as a White Paper in October 2005 (GBEP 2005), with the following objectives: to create dialogue on bioenergy, to encourage collaboration, to promote knowledge exchange, to facilitate biofuel energy market integration, to promote the use of biofuels and to foster research on biofuels (GBEP 2006). Due to its inception by the G8, GBEP lacks support and participation by developing countries, a fact that Brazil wanted to but was unable to change. Brazil therefore sees itself as a 'spokesperson of developing countries' that watches their interests, for example, that sustainability criteria do not effectively turn into non-tariff/technical trade barriers (Kloss 2012: 172).

After the G8 renewed the GBEP's mandate in 2006, the organisation was recognised as an institutional UN Conference on Sustainable Development (CSD) partnership organisation in 2007. In 2013, GBEP was recognised and endorsed by the G-20 (FIN) (G-20 2013), which continues to support the work of GBEP. The two main working groups are on sustainability and greenhouse gases methodology. Apart from the technical specifications in all areas of sustainability (environmental, including land use, social and economic sustainability), Brazil suggested to publish step-by-step guides for developing countries on how to implement a sustainable bio-energy economy (Kloss 2012: 177). This methodology was adopted and the working groups submitted progress reports biannually until 2011, when both working groups presented their final reports. Since then, GBEP has been working on capacity building and dissemination of information, while updating the technical specifications.

The GBEP process can be regarded as a success and its results will sooner or later enter global regulations, either through ISO or by means of the WTO EGS. The most likely outcome is through both channels. The negotiations were quiet but not without contention. Kloss (2012: 180), for example, accuses the US delegation of attempting to water down agreed definitions following the 2010 Tunis meeting. Nevertheless, the final reports were unanimously approved and Brazil succeeded in defining sustainability criteria that match its ethanol production model. Brazil furthermore gained a crucial institutional partner in the GBEP. Afionis et al. (2016: 143) point out that after the budget cuts in Brazil, the country increasingly relies on GBEP to organise and finance international biofuels promotion events.

Since Brazil has achieved a certain level of standardisation in the realm of sustainability, as well as an agreed methodology to assess the greenhouse gas (GHG) impact of biofuels, these results can be transferred to the next, higher political level in global governance, the UN Climate Change negotiations.

UN Climate Change Negotiations

From the beginning of the Lula administration, Brazil maintained a formal and explicit commitment to the achievements of global climate diplomacy (Barreto 2012: 500). However, the main decision-makers in the Lula administration did not put strong emphasis on climate change until the legally binding initiation of the Kyoto Protocol mechanism in 2005 (Viola 2011: 7). Climate change was a personal issue to science and technology minister Sergio Rezende, and environment minister Marina Silva (Barreto 2012: 502), who did not share the reservations regarding loss of sovereignty through international agreements.

Brazil advocated biofuels as a means to reduce GHG emissions, citing its own success. Apart from its clean energy mix, Brazil can also bring in deforestation efforts in its GHG emissions reduction (Figure 11). Looking at the numbers, it becomes clear that Brazil's peak emissions reduction in 2009 was due to control of deforestation and the financial crisis (Viola 2011: 5). Brazil plays a multifaceted role in international climate change efforts. As a country

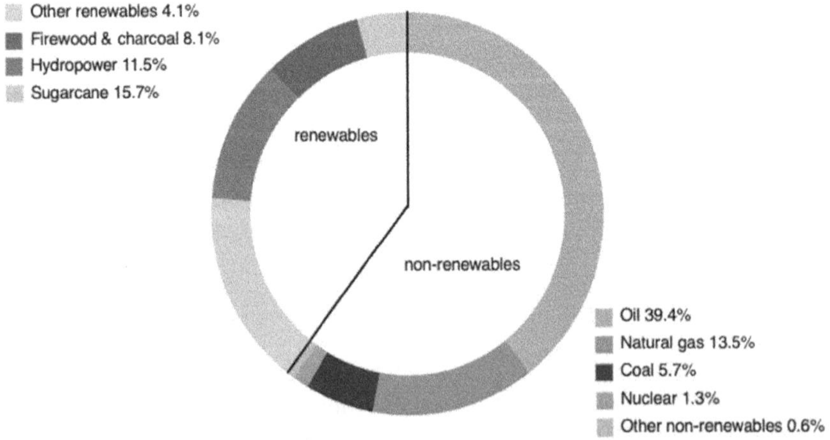

Figure 11 Brazil's energy mix in 2014 (*data source*: MME (2015: 4)).

with a comparatively green energy mix, and a big green reservoir, Brazil faces different challenges in terms of GHG emissions than most countries. The main emissions of GHGs in Brazil are caused by agriculture (kettle) and deforestation (Steinhilber 2009: 3–4). Agriculture is an important economic sector in Brazil. Because of this, Brazil represented the position that developing countries should not be required to reduce their emissions (2009: 5). In particular, the Clean Development Mechanism as developed by the Kyoto Protocol, was a source of constant rhetorical attention from Brazil (Barreto 2012: 501).

The internal lobbying of Marina Silva led to a slow adjustment of Brazil's position by the Nairobi Conference in late 2006, suggesting a global fund against deforestation (Viola 2011: 8). Silva's strong position in the cabinet and the pressure of NGOs put climate change higher on the foreign policy agenda, which led to the creation of an under-secretary of climate change in MRE (2011: 13).

In 2007, President Lula also started to put ethanol into the climate change equation (Barreto 2012: 502). Brazil's hope for a fossil fuel bonanza based on the pre-salt discoveries and the central role that Petrobras plays in the Brazilian political and economic system made the country reluctant to support efforts to transition away from a carbon-based economy. In 2008, Brazil further adapted its position and was willing to accept national commitments to reduce GHG emissions mainly through limits in deforestation. Internally, MMA increased its influence versus MRE, and after the National Plan for Climate Change was launched, MMA representatives took leading positions in Brazil's delegation to the December 2008 Poznan UNFCCC–COP negotiations (Viola 2011: 8).

This re-positioning towards the European Union and Japanese positions regarding climate change cost Brazil leadership acceptance among the G77 and was therefore not exactly welcomed by Itamaraty (Steinhilber 2009: 5). Viola (2011: 13–14) shows how several different industry coalitions attempted to influence Brazil's standing on climate change with open letters and lobbying efforts prior to the Copenhagen Conference. From the documents, one can see a stark division among industries and level of preparedness – a situation that allowed the government to formulate its policies more freely and allowed for more influence of civil society actors, which led to Brazil's voluntary commitment to reduce GHG emissions above the required amount of the Kyoto Protocol. Viola (2010: 101) furthermore shows how the electoral cycle with the candidacy of Marina Silva on the Green Party's platform mainstreamed climate change issues in advance of the Copenhagen Conference and thereby supported MMA's influence in the FPC, in particular vis-à-vis MRE. It is noteworthy that Brazilian ambassador André Amado omits MMA's role in Brazilian foreign policy making while stressing the trade dimension of Brazilian diplomacy that involves MAPA, MCTI and MME alongside Itamaraty (2013: 105).

At the 2009 Climate Conference in Copenhagen, Brazil was one of the main authors and negotiators of the final document among the United States, China, the European Union, India and South Africa (Barreto 2012: 505) but was not able to push its partners towards an agreement that could have been seen as a Brazilian success. Since Brazil might be adversely affected by climate change, as recent droughts have shown, the country is now part of the ambitious group in the negotiations. Brazil joined the coalition of major emitters who were willing to make a substantial contribution to GHG emissions reduction. Deforestation countermeasures and ethanol were two points that the Brazilian delegation stressed at the conference. On the last day in Copenhagen, effectively IBSA plus China and the United States negotiated a non-binding agreement (Viola 2010: 106).

In 2012, the Rio+20 UN Conference on Sustainable Development (UNCSD) took place in Rio de Janeiro. While not technically part of the UNFCCC, hopes were high that the conference would contribute to further climate change mitigation. In the end, Rio+20 produced a final document that introduces a set of 'Sustainable Development Goals' (SDGs) but does not address renewable energy or ethanol (UN 2012).

While Brazil successfully engaged in global climate change negotiations, it was not able to present ethanol as a global solution to the issue. Its own credentials point more towards its success in countering deforestation than in mitigating GHG emissions through biofuels. In the climate change arena, Brazil was never able to develop the same clout as it did in WTO negotiations, an indicator that Brazil's attraction depends more on hard (financial) power than on ideas. Brazil's lack of problem-solving capabilities – or the lack of adequate presentation of ethanol as such – might have played a significant role in Brazil not receiving more attention in climate change negotiations. Additionally, Viola (2011: 8) points out, Brazil applied a traditional approach that overemphasised national sovereignty for too long and therefore was unable to fully realise its potential.

Outcomes of Brazil's Multilateral Ethanol Diplomacy

During the Doha Round, Brazil showed leadership and created veto coalitions. The lack of a substantial agreement, and the lack of ethanol provisions in particular, show that Brazil has not arrived in the league of the major powers yet. While Brazil was able to stall WTO negotiations 'until its concerns on agricultural subsidies were addressed' (Brands 2011: 31), it was not able to prevent India from applying a similar approach.

In the standardisation realm, Brazil made significant progress in enabling the creation of a global market for ethanol in terms of sustainability in GBEP.

The negotiations in the IBF stalled, and while they have expressed concerns and recommendations, these do not have legal authority. The question of technical standardisation, in particular of the water content of ethanol in the European Union, will likely be subject to future WTO contention through a trade dispute regarding non-tariff barriers.

In the climate change negotiations, Brazil initially refused to take an active and ambitious approach due to its traditional understanding of sovereignty. After a reshuffle in the power dynamics of the cabinet, Brazil entered the climate change negotiations with higher ambitions, even if ethanol was only second in the suggested methods.

In either of these arenas, one can see the influence of Brazilian agribusiness dominating the Brazilian FPC (Hopewell 2013: 3) and how policy changed via the changing attitudes of the actors involved.

Summary

When examining Brazil's multilateral approach in its international ethanol strategy, the first conspicuity is the high complexity. It is difficult to argue that ethanol diplomacy was at the centre of the WTO or the climate change negotiations. Ethanol diplomacy certainly was the driving force behind Brazil's ambitions in biofuels standardisation, but the results are mixed as well. Looking at the WTO, it is Brazil's explicit interest to create a situation of multipolarity in the WTO (Amorim 2016: 230), a goal that Brazil has achieved to a certain extent. Brazil's leadership position in the G-20 increased its clout in the WTO (Brands 2011: 35), despite technical positions, especially in AMA, that 'most developing countries are fiercely opposed' (Hopewell 2013: 12). Nevertheless, Brazil was successful at this double-play in the WTO. It continuously pursued trade liberalisation while maintaining the support of developing countries through its rhetoric of South–South solidarity.

An assessment of Brazil's activities within the WTO therefore must be made under the two different perspectives: the organisation perspective and the negotiation perspective. Within the organisation, Brazil is able to use the conflict resolution mechanism to its advantage as shown in the cotton case against the United States and the sugar case against the European Union. It also showed that its nationals are qualified and trusted enough to be accepted as leaders within the organisation. This assessment, however, is different from a negotiation perspective. Ultimately, apart from presenting its ability to form veto coalitions at ministerial meetings, Brazil was not able to push forward its active agenda to facilitate ethanol trade. But the formation of and disruption caused by the creation of the G-20 is seen as more important by Brazil than the actual output of the meeting in Cancun (Amorim 2011: 159).

While the WTO was never truly a unipolar institution, the core group of Northern economies used to dominate its decision-making and development. Brazil recognised that through the WTO's legal framework, it could bind to the power of the dominant countries from the Global North. Already in the days of the Quad, Brazil used the WTO to promote its interests that it otherwise could not push through the resistance of powerful players like the United States. It consequently aimed for shaping the rules that bind stronger powers. Hence, Brazil created a coalition to disrupt the traditional power structure – that never was unipolar – under the banner of multipolarity and multilateralism. Its effective veto coalition in the form of the G-20 helped Brazil enter the inner circle of decision-making. Structurally, this has not changed the WTO; it rather exchanged some pieces of the same clockwork.

One of the most important aspects of creating a global ethanol market is standardisation. GBEP was initiated by the G8 and Brazil only joined later. Its focus was sustainability and GHG emissions methodology. The work of GBEP has been successful and Brazil was able to influence the discussion, as well as gain significant institutional support in the promotion of ethanol through GBEP.

Brazil's initial outsider status at the GBEP led to the creation of the IBF, increased 'activism on the global stage' that is based on the 'belief that it should have a more influential role' (Hanson 2012). This forum explored possibilities of harmonising technical properties of ethanol but, in the end, could change the status quo. The answer why Brazil chose to create its own mechanism rather than integrate its agenda into an existing organisation needs to be explored within the Brazilian FPC. In retrospect, it is not surprising that the plan (Kloss 2012: 59) to separately discuss technical questions regarding ethanol in the IBF, sustainability questions regarding ethanol in GBEP and trade questions regarding ethanol in the WTO did not bear significant fruit.

Brazil entered the active group of climate change negotiations too late. In the early stages, Brazilian FPC was suspicious regarding potential cuts to Brazilian sovereignty. Seeing that Brazil's ethanol diplomacy did not progress quickly, however, changed the approach of the FPC. Paired with societal pressure to engage in climate change talks, this brought climate change onto the Brazilian foreign policy agenda. As a latecomer, Brazil never gained the influence it had in the Doha Round, and its unique properties with a legacy of green energy and the Amazon rainforest as a device for cost-effective GHG emissions reduction impeded Brazil from presenting itself as a credible partner for the developing world. It therefore could not repeat the coalition-building efforts that yielded so much prestige in the WTO.

Despite its mediocre performance, Brazil's leadership was based on its technical capacity, its well-prepared negotiators and a powerful narrative

(Hopewell 2013: 12). While the first two can be classified as somewhere in between hard and soft power, the third factor definitely adds to Brazil's soft power position in terms of convincing developing countries of the sincerity of its leadership of the Global South.

The contribution of the Neoclassical Realist approach for understanding international trade negotiations is best exemplified by Hopewell (2013: 5): 'The relationship between the state and agribusiness is better understood as an alliance or partnership, involving a conscious alignment of the Brazilian state with agribusiness, based on shared interests and ideology.' Or in other words: Brazilian agribusiness was part of and had considerable influence on the Brazilian FPC. Brazilian foreign policy makers represented domestic interests in international fora, which does not necessarily mean that there is a convergence of interests at play; for example, the agricultural lobby that was represented by MAPA in the WTO negotiations met domestic resistance from the Ministry of Rural Development (MDA), which represents smallholder farming.

It is worth taking a closer look at the power asymmetries in the G-20 and whether it actually represents the dominance of the strongest, as Hopewell (2013: 17) suggests. Realists would expect that hard power capabilities determine the success in the international arena, but Brazil and India were able to achieve a higher degree of autonomy without hard power resources and instead through leadership and coalition building (Hopewell 2015: 333). By following Brazil, the developing countries effectively created a counterbalance to the established powers and leveraged their collective bargaining position (Hopewell 2013: 13). Brazil, on the other hand, could position itself in a way that gained acceptance by the established powers and thereby elevated its status in the international system. But counter-intuitively, 'developing country coalitions have [also] constrained Brazil's offensive interests' in the WTO (WWC 2008: 2).

With an ambiguous structural environment in the multilateral setting, Brazil can only present mixed results of its multilateral ethanol diplomacy. With adequate strategies of bandwagoning with the United States and the European Union outside the WTO and balancing inside, Brazil deployed different strategies in different set-ups. While one can certainly attribute part of the lack of success to the international structure, the overconfidence of Brazil's FPC to reach consensus on Brazil's terms certainly did not facilitate successful negotiations.

This chapter has shown that one can agree with Brands's (2011: 32) assessment that 'Brazilian diplomacy featured three characteristics of a middle-power grand strategy': the support for international norms that could bind stronger countries, coalition building to increase its own leverage and applying the rules to seek its own benefits. The way these tactics are applied has its roots in the Brazilian FPC and how they assess the structural environment.

Chapter 7

SUMMARY AND OUTLOOK

This study is the first to examine Brazil's international ethanol strategy from a Neoclassical Realist perspective. Under Presidents Lula da Silva and Dilma Rousseff, Brazil had the explicit foreign policy goal to create a global market for fuel ethanol comparative to the global oil market. Given the benevolent international environment for greater use of biofuels in the early 2000s, with questions of energy security, climate change and South–South cooperation on the top of the international agenda, it is puzzling why Brazil failed to create a global ethanol market despite the beneficial international context. This research question was guided by a set of sub-questions:

- What is Brazil's international ethanol strategy?
- How was Brazil's international ethanol strategy elaborated and by whom?
- Who are the central stakeholders within Brazil and abroad that are involved in the process of implementing Brazil's international ethanol strategy?
- What power relationships are at play within Brazil and towards its partners that influence the implementation of Brazil's international ethanol strategy?
- What are the turning points in Brazil's ethanol diplomacy and how did these happen?
- How can the processes and outcomes be explained within the realm of IR theory?

The study relied on a case study design with three empirical chapters. The first two empirical chapters represented two dimensions of bilateral relations, Brazil–US and Brazil–Mozambique, where Brazil is in a relatively weak position in the former and in a strong position in the latter. The third empirical chapter analysed Brazil's multilateral ethanol diplomacy, in particular Brazil's actions in the WTO.

Process tracing was applied to test Neoclassical Realist hypotheses at the necessary points of analysis. The data for this work was gathered by document and literature research as well as during field work that led to almost 80 expert interviews.

The three empirical chapters showed mixed results of Brazilian foreign policy making. As Ricupero (2010: 29) states, 'Progress varies just as the distance between Brazil's pretensions and reality', and in none of the cases were objectives fully achieved. Three main threads continue through all of the chapters:

- Ethanol was not of the highest priority and was subordinate to other strategic goals.
- The heterogeneity and lack of coordination within Brazil's foreign policy complex (FPC) made its foreign policy less effective.
- The Brazilian FPC overestimated Brazil's ability to solve problems and produce results (soft power) in all three cases, which was particularly detrimental in the relation with the United States and within the multilateral arena.

Brazil and the United States

The Brazil–US ethanol relationship is defined by one major event, the 2007 MoU on biofuels. It is the result of the strategic energy dialogue of the two countries that began in Lula's first term as a sign of rapprochement after the failure of the FTAA and Venezuela's rising influence in South America. Despite coinciding interests in the expansion of fuel ethanol and in the creation of a global ethanol market, the cooperation yielded few results and virtually stopped after the NSA scandal.

Organisationally, Brazil could not follow suit with the strongly structured US State Department, which might be one reason why the Brazilian industry that lobbied both governments, in particular UNICA, abandoned the project and focused on domestic support instead. Conceptually, Brazil's ethanol diplomacy towards the United States represents bandwagoning in a general relationship that was characterised by balancing since the Lula government came to power.

Brazil and Mozambique

With clear leverage over Mozambique, the Brazilian FPC expected its ethanol diplomacy to be fruitful with one of its closest African partners. An example of South–South cooperation in practice, Brazil can account for some successes in Mozambique.

In the case of Mozambique, two main points guided the analysis: the 2007 MoU on biofuels and the trilateral cooperation project ProSavana. Brazil was able to gain some successes with respect to both projects. The 2007 MoU represented a catalogue of Brazilian demands towards Mozambique and Brazil was successful in inserting its specialists in the Mozambican public sector. Furthermore, an ethanol blend-in mandate was introduced in Mozambique after Brazil put pressure on the government. Apart from this, the results in terms of increasing the producer base for ethanol remained lower than expected. ProSavana has thus far not been a success. The project failed in terms of production and reputation. The goals in rural development were not achieved, and through the threat of and actual land grabbing, Brazil lost a significant amount of credibility and therefore soft power in the region. Furthermore, the image of South–South cooperation was damaged as 'Brazil's economic, institutional, scientific or diplomatic stature' outpaces Mozambique's in every aspect and therefore undermines the balanced nature of South–South cooperation (Cabral and Shankland 2013: 21). Brazil took advantage of the 'moment of economic growth and political stability' (Hardt et al. 2017: 58) when it could not only project hard economic power but also attract smaller countries with its reservoir of soft power.

A particularly interesting aspect in the Brazil–Mozambique ethanol relationship is the role of Brazilian mining giant Vale. The company instigated much of Brazil's ethanol approach towards Mozambique without a clear motive, apart from getting the Brazilian government involved in Mozambique. This reflects how the political parts of the FPC were driven by particular interests, rather than strategic calculus. The interaction between Vale and the Brazilian government in Mozambique is one more indicator that ethanol was a means to an end, rather than an end in itself.

Brazil's Multilateral Ethanol Diplomacy

Brazil's multilateral ethanol diplomacy is highly complex. The main venue for it is the WTO, but this is complemented by other fora, such as IBF, GBEP and the UN climate change negotiations (Kloss 2012: 59).

In the WTO, Brazil emerged as a leader of the G-20 group of developing countries with a difficult stance. Unlike most of its partners, Brazil advocated the opening of agricultural markets, which would have positive effects for Brazilian exports in general and for ethanol in particular. On the other hand, Brazil advocated mechanisms that would allow developing countries to shield their industrial and service markets from competition from developed countries and China. As Ferrando (2015: 356) points out, the 'economic nationalism [...] and the internationalisation process are the two faces of the same government'. This difficult position combined with a structural environment that makes deals difficult resulted in mediocre outputs at best.

Several successes can nevertheless be recognised. Brazil's ability to litigate the WTO as seen in the cotton and sugar cases increased Brazil's soft power by displaying concrete problem-solving capabilities. These victories and Brazil's drive to form coalitions like IBSA (India, Brazil, South Africa), which balanced US and EU power (initially outside, later within the WTO), set the foundation for Brazil's rise as a leader of the developing world in the WTO.

By the time of Dilma Rousseff's presidency, however, lack of negotiation success and Brazil's apparent conflicts of interest led to a decline in Brazilian influence. Furthermore, Brazil did not make significant progress in classifying ethanol as an environmental product, which would potentially break down all market barriers. In the IBF, Brazil achieved a strong victory in the final white paper but still struggles to implement the suggestions of the white paper globally.

In the GBEP, on the other hand, Brazil's influence was less apparent, and the process is still ongoing and shaping biofuels policy world-wide. Brazil has found its most important institutional partner in the G8-sponsored GBEP, which after budget cuts in Brazil took over the role as a principal promoter of biofuels globally. In the UN climate change negotiations, Brazil arrived late and never attracted a comparable clout to its position in the WTO.

In its multilateral ethanol strategy, Brazil worked towards creating international norms that constrain its stronger partners, formed coalitions and used international rules to its advantage – a typical 'middle-power grand strategy' (Brands 2011: 32). Here its lack of success can equally be attributed to a difficult structural environment and a lack of problem-solving capability. The former is determined by Brazil's interests that would not allow for clear alignment with the United States, the European Union or its developing partners. Particularly, the latter aspect is determined by an idea of strength derived from the litigation successes that could not be replicated in negotiations. In the climate change arena, Brazil's FPC was too late to the party due to reservations against cuts to sovereignty and fossil fuel production.

Answering the Research Question

Given this empirical background, we can answer the research questions the following way.

What Was the Ethanol Strategy?

Brazil pursued a multi-level strategy to promote a global market for ethanol. The core of the strategy was to increase the user and producer bases of ethanol as a renewable fuel. This strategy was adapted according to the respective partners.

In the case of Brazil–US ethanol relations, Brazil aimed at opening the US market for ethanol and for joining forces with the United States to promote ethanol internationally. One can understand this as a reluctant bandwagoning strategy.

In the case of Brazil–Mozambique ethanol relations, Brazil aimed for the development of significant ethanol production in Mozambique and Africa more generally. This production was incentivised by the introduction of a mandatory ethanol blend that Brazilian representatives pushed through legislation. Based on a developmentalist narrative of South–South cooperation, Brazil was using its soft power as well as its financial dominance to achieve results in Mozambique. One can understand this as soft economic imperialism.

In the case of Brazil's multilateral ethanol diplomacy, the country had a number of goals, ranked according to its preferences. The ideal outcome for Brazil would be the full liberalisation of agricultural markets. Second to this was the classification of ethanol as an environmental product which would liberalise the international ethanol market. Parallel initiatives hoped for technical and sustainability standardisation of ethanol as well as incentivising ethanol within the global climate debate. In the WTO, the most important forum in this respect, Brazil initially applied politics of prestige in the WTO disputes to attract followers for its G-20 coalition. The G-20 reversed the status quo of the WTO from an oligopoly of power to a multipolar set-up, a fuzzy set with an intertwined network of interests and changing alliances. Being left out of GBEP initially, Brazil applied soft balancing by initiating the IBF to compensate for its failure to substantially alter GBEP's agenda.

This patchwork of strategies represents Brazil's multi-level ethanol strategy. It is questionable whether this strategy was ever applied coherently by the government, not to mention the non-governmental actors that form part of the FPC. This outline, however, shows the paths that Brazil followed and aimed at uniting to achieve its goal of a global market for ethanol.

Why Did Brazil Fail to Achieve the Global Market for Ethanol?

Brazil failed to achieve the global market for ethanol for a number of reasons. As previously outlined, a lack of strategy was not the primary reason.

Overall, there seems to be a *lack of focus*. One has to agree with Birle (2013: 150) that Brazil's foreign policy is marked by universalism, the expectation to have substantial relations with all parts of the world and autonomy, the lack of willingness to bear the cost – financial or otherwise – for this international insertion. Expanding on this assessment, this lack of investment in commitment and ethanol diplomacy contributed to the outcome that did not fulfil expectations. As Trinkunas (2015) points out, one of Brazil's main issues is its reluctance to bear costs. This includes financial cost but also limitations on its own sovereignty as well as the willingness to bend rules that it created for a perceived benefit, such as the accession of Venezuela to MercoSul.

Additionally, *ethanol did not rank high enough* in the priorities for the Brazilian government to be pursued with enough pressure to be successful. P. Almeida (2009: 172) sees two strategic goals in Lula's foreign policy, the UNSC seat and dominance in South America. Apparently, it was Foreign Minister Amorim who convinced Lula to put the strategic goal of a permanent seat in the UNSC visibly and publicly high on Brazil's foreign policy agenda (Bourne 2008: 161), which shows that the two main protagonists of Brazilian foreign policy were subsuming all other goals to the UNSC seat.

Ricupero (2010: 29) identifies four strategic goals of Brazilian foreign policy in the Lula era: increase international recognition and ultimately a permanent seat in the UNSC by means of other groups, like BRICS, G-20 and IBAS; create a favourable international economic regime through the WTO and in financial terms through the G-20; become a leader in and of the Global South through South–South initiatives such as BRICS, IBAS and CLPL; and create a political and economic space in South America under Brazilian leadership. *None of Brazil's strategic goals* include renewable energy or ethanol.

Cabral (2014: 18) even goes further and claims that Brazil's international ethanol strategy was nothing more than 'simply a set of uncoordinated actions in response to different Brazilian interests (including business interests)'. This statement does not fully reflect reality, however, as renewable energies and in particular ethanol were prominently elevated to department level at Itamaraty and the MAPA ethanol coordinator internationalised their work. It is more likely that the global ambitions overstretched Brazil's capabilities to be present in a plethora of different international fora with the goal of realising Brazil's interests, as Souza (2009: 16) suggests.

During the second Lula term, the *focus of the FPC further shifted away from ethanol.* After the discovery of pre-salt oil, Brazil's international push for renewable energies softened (Rohter 2010: 189). Like many others in Brazil and beyond, Ricupero (2010: 41) falls into the trap of thinking that Brazil's strategic position was elevated due to the pre-salt discovery. This proved to be a political and diplomatic miscalculation since they led to the dropping of diplomatic initiatives like ethanol diplomacy that were the backbone of Brazil's international insertion.

Former diplomat Paulo Roberto de Almeida (2009: 172) identifies an ideological takeover of Brazilian foreign policy by the Workers' Party (PT) and sees this as the reason for the failure of Brazil's international initiatives. Ricupero

(2010: 36) seconds that to a certain extent but sees the lack of success as rooted in a crisis of the foreign policy consensus. Afionis et al. (2016: 140) see that the 'domestic standstill' negatively affected Brazil's ethanol diplomacy and that it is not clear whether the lower priority was re-assigned or whether 'it had gradually died off'.

Either way, the support of the Brazilian FPC for ethanol diplomacy decreased significantly, and with constrained resources after the financial crisis and the drop in oil prices, the implementation phases of many projects lost their political support.

Contribution to the Literature

Apart from putting together a coherent narrative of Brazil's international ethanol strategy on the bilateral level as well as the multilateral level, this study adds to the existing literature on several points. By understanding Brazil's international ethanol strategy and recognising its shortcomings, one can draw broader conceptual conclusions about the application of the Neoclassical Realist approach, Brazilian foreign policy making and the behaviour of emerging powers in the international arena.

Expanding on Neoclassical Realism

Fuser (2008: 108) offered the critique that Realism cannot grasp the actions of smaller powers and equally lacks explanatory power for changing state preferences in IR. He furthermore points out the blindness of Liberal theories towards interdependence as a source of conflict especially in the area of natural resources (2008: 211). While the basic argument that interdependence is generally seen as a stabilising factor is valid, the question arises to what extent globalisation with its diversification of trade, combined with increased energetic self-sufficiency and 'peak energy demand', outdated his arguments. Opening the black-box state and analysing the decision-making process within the FPC allows for a more nuanced understanding of foreign policy and IR within a Neoclassical Realist framework.

While most Neoclassical Realist studies have focused on major powers in a security context, the work on Brazil's international ethanol strategy shows how Neoclassical Realism can inform our understanding of the foreign policy of a rising (middle) power in the areas of trade and energy. This can also address the issue mentioned by Fuser (2008: 125) of large transnational corporations, particularly in the mining and energy sector, which are relevant to this study, that are not captured by traditional IR theories even though they often have budgets and influence that exceed the power of small to medium-size states.

Neoclassical Realism can include such corporations into the analysis by attributing them a role in the FPC of a country. This study expands on the question that Ripsman et al. (2016: 97) pose regarding national and international NGOs. The example of UNICA shows that not only does the FPC consist of formal policy makers but NGOs also have their role in it, for example, by lobbying a foreign government.

This study lies in between what Ripsman et al. (2016: 12) describe as Type II and Type III Neoclassical Realism, where Type II explains foreign policy outputs and Type III explains the international outcomes that result from the interaction of these outputs. Such Type III analyses typically rely on assessments of power. It seems prudent to add soft power to the understanding of power relations; as Kitchen (2010: 127) points out, 'The impact of ideas [should be placed] alongside the imperatives of material power' which combines the traditional understanding of soft power, as a pull factor with the active engagement of the FPC to produce soft power capabilities. I would suggest adding political problem solving as soft power capability that is dependent on a country's FPC and an effective way of attracting partners, as shown in this study. Political problem solving does not necessarily depend on large material resources and can generate international prestige at a relatively low cost. This, in turn, is a pull factor that attracts followers and thereby enhances a country's coalition-building efforts.

If power relations are the primary determinant to explain international political outcomes, Neoclassical Realism plays a crucial role in understanding soft power that needs to be included into the calculation of these structures.

Insights into Brazilian Foreign Policy Making

Through my analysis of Brazil's FPC in its ethanol diplomacy, we can better understand how Brazilian foreign policy is actually made. While the president and his/her closest advisors are the main agents in foreign policy making and define the general direction, it is worth looking at the FPC and its capabilities closely. Itamaraty increasingly needs to share its prerogative in foreign policy making due to President Lula's personality – to a lesser extent under President Rousseff – and due to the democratisation of Brazilian society with increased government accountability (Cason and Power 2009: 118).

The Brazilian FPC can in certain cases project power in an effective manner, as seen in the WTO disputes and in the case of influencing legislation in Mozambique, but at the same time, a misalignment of preferences within the FPC makes it difficult to reach foreign policy goals.

The FPC around ethanol was created due to President Lula's personal affinity for the product; however, the drought of 2005/06 combined with currency devaluation and rising debt levels led agriculture minister Rodrigues 'to revitalise the agricultural policy network', as expressed by civil servants in MAPA during my interviews. This corporatist turn lead to a conflict between Rodrigues and then finance minister Antonio Palocci. Mueller (2009: 140) assesses that the conflict was resolved at the highest level by President Lula with a decision in favour of a revitalisation of the agro-industrial complex but ultimately increased the speed of the resignation of both Rodrigues and Palocci. The ministers left, but the ethanol FPC was established. From this point onwards, several ministries and organisations in the Brazilian FPC tried to implement their own form of ethanol diplomacy, with Itamaraty insisting on its prerogative in international affairs. This internal competition led to a lack of coordination, which in turn harmed the overall goal. But it is questionable to what extent all actors in the FPC subscribed to a common agenda. As one interviewee from the Brazilian sugarcane sector mentioned, the Brazilian ethanol industry strongly preferred domestic support over spending resources abroad, which might yield better collective outcomes but at the same time could harm individual domestic producers. And as mentioned before, ethanol diplomacy had to serve and follow Itamaraty's higher-ranking goals, like the UNSC seat. This competition of individual and organisational interests in the Brazilian FPC is one defining factor of Brazilian foreign policy making that has thus far been under-researched.

Implications for Emerging Powers Research

Brazil has been included in research regarding emerging markets, rising powers or middle powers. All of these categories express that Brazil aims to improve its position in the international system, while at the same time lacks the capabilities that established major powers have. Brands (2010: 17) argues that 'achieving global influence thus necessitates punching above their own weight' through diplomacy, soft balancing, coalition building and region formation. But it does not suffice to apply these strategies; one must be accepted as the leader of such alliances. Malamud (2011: 3) defines leadership 'as the capacity to win and influence followers'. Thus, how can a country attract a following? One way is through soft power. While some might claim that soft power is inconsistent with the Realist approach, I argue that it is a modern form of politics of prestige.

Brazil's way of actively seeking soft power through cultural capital and problem-solving capital adds to the understanding of the term in the Realist literature. It brings back Morgenthau's definition of 'prestige', with Brazil displaying their power in the WTO and thereby shaping preferences of stronger and weaker partners in the absence of hard military or economic power.

Venues for Further Research

While this study proposes answers to the questions what Brazil's international ethanol strategy was, and why it failed, there remain further venues of possible research.

Expand Neoclassical Realism

As Harig and Kenkel (2017: 641) show, 'States can no longer usefully be conceived of as unitary actors on the international scene [and one needs] to open the black box of the state to examine the complex nature of tensions between foreign policy formulation and its implementation'. This assessment is widely shared by researchers who apply Neoclassical Realism. One way to move this approach forward would be to formalise how to open the black box, that is, define and analyse the FPC. While some authors limit their analyses to the formal foreign policy executive (e.g. Ripsman et al. 2016), I suggested the inclusion of semi- and non-state actors in the analysis. A debate about the formal definitions of the FPC would certainly increase the acceptance of this strain of Realism.

This brings us to the question that has already been raised by Ripsman et al. (2016: 97–98), how to conceptualise the role of NGOs within a Neoclassical Realist theory of foreign policy or even international politics. Looking at the case at hand, the Brazilian sugar lobby group UNICA was present and instrumental at all stages of Brazil's ethanol diplomacy. And UNICA even succeeded in several lobbying efforts in the United States, something that advanced ethanol trade between the two countries more than most government interventions. How can this be conceptualised? Many of these actions were in some form coordinated with (or at least known to) the Brazilian government. Can this be understood as part of Brazil's foreign policy even though it formally is not? And this question can be extended from national NGOs that act internationally to truly international NGOs, for example, Oxfam.

Generalisation for Brazilian Foreign Policy

According to Stolte (2015: 82), Brazil is not pursuing a strategy of soft balancing but rather a new approach to present itself as independent actor and possible partner at the same time. In the case of Brazil's ethanol diplomacy, however, one can see that different strategies are applied at different levels. What does that mean for other areas of foreign policy? Can the same patterns of reluctant bandwagoning towards a stronger power be observed, for example, in the area of intellectual property rights? A general understanding of Brazilian foreign policy based on case studies of different policy fields has the potential to achieve clearer statements than the one by Stolte.

In order to generate such a deeper understanding, one would have to analyse how different FPCs within Brazil interact. How would the interests within the government be mitigated if, to stay with the example, one party represents open intellectual property rights (e.g. Brazilian generic pharmaceutical producers) and another party prefers restrictive intellectual property rights (e.g. Brazilian green biotech companies)?

Generalise the Research for Emerging Powers

Once these questions about Brazilian foreign policy have been clarified to a satisfactory level, one could expand the research to the global level, Type III analysis. Can we observe similar actions in other emerging powers, for example, India? Why did India not receive the same prominence in trade and climate negotiations as Brazil despite its bigger population and interests that are potentially more compatible with the majority of developing countries?

And one step removed, how can we conceptualise the impacts of coalition building? Are there predictable leaders? And how do coalitions affect those leaders, as in this case the G-20 increased Brazil's leverage but also may have limited its potential due to diverging interests?

Final Remarks

Brazil tried to make up for its lack of military-strategic power by exporting its clean energy mix through ethanol diplomacy (P. Almeida 2009: 180). This can be understood as a type of power projection. If the aim of alliances is military security, Brazil offered an alternative via energy security for its partners. Despite a favourable environment, Brazil was not able to convince enough partners of the benefits of its sugarcane-based fuel alternative.

With the advent of electric vehicles in the industrialised world, the window of opportunity to create a global market for ethanol is closing for Brazil. The technology will remain a strong factor in Brazil's domestic energy policy and will continue to offer a development model for developing countries in the tropical belt. This offers the prospect of new attempts at ethanol diplomacy in the South–South context. To succeed, Brazil will need to align its domestic interests and focus on understanding the interests and constraints of its developing partners. This way, ethanol has still a chance to be the fuel of the future.

APPENDIX

List of Interviews[1]

Name	Organisation	Position	Category	Anonymity**
Joaquim Pedro Penna	Brazilian permanent representation to the international organisations in London	Counsellor	Politics	No
Claudia Detsch	Friedrich Ebert Foundation (FES)	Latin America Officer	Think tank	No
Fatima Mello	Federação de Órgãos para Assistência Social e Educacional (FASE)	Diretora	Think tank	No
Emerson Coraiola Yinde Kloss	MRE	Head of division, New and Renewable Energy Office	Politics	No
Paulo Roberto Barbosa Lima	ABC	Africa and Asia manager	Politics	No
Tina Henneken	Friedrich Ebert Foundation (FES)	Former deputy head of São Paulo Office, head of Maputo Office	Think tank	No
[*Name redacted*]	Barral M Jorge Consultores	Trade consultant	Politics/ Ind	Yes
[*Name redacted*]	Diputado Federal	PPS-SP (Frente Parlamentar pela Valorização do Setor Sucroenergético	Politics	No
[*Name redacted*]	German Foreign Office	[redacted]	Politics	Yes

(continued)

1. In chronological order.

Name	Organisation	Position	Category	Anonymity**
[*Name redacted*]	CAMECO	Head of Latin America Desk	Press	No
[*Name redacted*]	Ministério da Ciência, Tecnologia e Inovação	Coordinadora General de Cooperación Internacional	Politics	Semi
[*Name redacted*]	MRE	[redacted]	Politics	Yes
Cid Caldas	MAPA	Coordenador-Geral de Açúcar e Etanol	Politics	No
Luis Job	MAPA	Advisor	Politics	No
[*Name redacted*]	PT	Special advisor [redacted]	Politics	Yes
Marlon Arraes Jardim	MME	General coordinator for ethanol	Politics	No
[*Name redacted*]	MDS	[redacted]	Politics	Yes
[*Name redacted*]	BNDES	Deputy managing director international division	Politics	Semi
[*Name redacted*]	Forum Nacional Sucroenergético	[redacted]	Industry	Yes
[*Name redacted*]	Audi do Brasil	Communication manager	Industry	Semi
[*Name redacted*]	Barral M Jorge Consultores	Trade consultant	Industry	Semi
Elisabeth Farina	UNICA	President and CEO	Industry	No
[*Name redacted*]	ANFAVEA	Analyst – flex-fuel markets	Industry	Yes
[*Name redacted*]	Volkswagen do Brasil	[redacted]	Industry	Yes
[*Name redacted*]	UNICA	Institutional relations coordinator	Industry	Semi
[*Name redacted*]	Odebrecht Agroindustrial	VP	Industry	Semi
[*Name redacted*]	Raizen	VP	Industry	Semi
[*Name redacted*]	Datagro	[redacted] Senior person	Industry	Semi
Antônio José Ferreira Simões	MRE	Ambassador	Politics	No
[*Name redacted*]	HSBC	Trader biofuels	Industry	Yes
Celso Amorim	MRE	Former foreign minister	Politics	No

Name	Organisation	Position	Category	Anonymity**
[*Name redacted*]	GIZ Brazil	Advisor to the director	Politics	Semi
[*Name redacted*]	Brazilian Embassy London	[redacted]	Politics	Yes
[*Name redacted*]	International Sugar Journal	[redacted]	Press	Yes
[*Name redacted*]	EC	Advisor agricultural development	Politics	Yes
Jose Orive	ISO	President	Politics	No
Leonardo Rocha	ISO	Chief economist	Politics	No
[*Name redacted*]	Politica Externa	Editor	Press	Semi
[*Name redacted*]	LatAm Investor	Editorial managing director	Press	No
[*Name redacted*]	The Public Ledger	Deputy head of bulk commodities	Press	No
[*Name redacted*]	F.O. Licht	Sugar analyst	Industry	No
Geraldine Kutas	UNICA	Head of international affairs & senior international adviser to the president of UNICA	Industry	No
Peter Baron	International Sugar Organisation	Former president	Politics	No
Alexandre Strapasson	MAPA	Former Coordenador-Geral de Açúcar e Etanol	Politics	No
[*Name redacted*]	High Commission of the Republic of Mozambique	Diplomat	Politics	Yes
[*Name redacted*]	High Commission of the Republic of Mozambique	Diplomat	Politics	Yes
Arnaldo Vieira	IADB	Ethanol expert	Politics	No
Maria Cameron	US Department of Commerce	Desk officer	Politics	No
Braeden Young	US Department of Commerce	Desk officer	Politics	No
Cora Dickinson	US Department of Commerce	Advisor	Politics	No
Antonio Josino Meirelles	Brazil Industries Coalition, Washington, D.C.	Executive director	Industry	No

(continued)

Name	Organisation	Position	Category	Anonymity**
[Roberto Rodrigues]	FGV	Coordenador do Centro de Agronegocio da FGV; Presidente de LIDE Agronegocios; Former Ministro da Agricultura, Former Presidente da UNICA (until 20 May 2014)	Cross	Interview scheduled
Carlos Guimarães	ED&F Man Brasil S.A	President	Industry	No
Eduardo Puertas	ED&F Man Brasil S.A.	Head of ethanol	Industry	No
Tarcilo Rodrigues	bioagencia	President	Industry	No
Paulo Trucco	bioagencia	Sugar expert	Industry	No
Giorgio Romano Schutte	UniFABC		Academia	No
[*Name redacted*]	IPEA	Planning and research specialist	Academia	Semi
José Goldemberg	USP		Academia	No
[*Name redacted*]	US Embassy BSB	Representative of USDA	Politics	Yes
[*Name redacted*]	Tate & Lyle plc	Public affairs manager	Industry	Yes
Claudia Santos	MRE	Head of division, New and Renewable Energy Office	Politics	No

** Anonymity was optional in the study. On the information and consent sheet, interviewees could choose between three levels of anonymity:
Fully identified: 'no'/Partially identified: 'semi' and [name redacted]/Full anonymity: 'yes' and [name redacted]

Key Events in Brazil's WTO Insertion (2003–14)

Date	Event	Description
6 December 2013	Bali ministerial	9th ministerial meeting, WTO Bali Declaration
17 December 2011	Geneva ministerial	8th ministerial meeting

Date	Event	Description
2 December 2009	Geneva ministerial	7th ministerial meeting
9 December 2008	Doha Round stalls	WTO DG Lamy postpones scheduled ministerial
2 March 2007	United Nations International Biofuels Forum	Brazil, South Africa, China, the United States, India and the European Commission Objective: to promote the sustainable production and use of biofuels around the world
13 September 2006	IBSA Brasília	1st IBSA Summit – Brasília Declaration
13 December 2005	Hong Kong ministerial	6th ministerial meeting
12 July 2005	G-20 Dalian meeting	Brazil reinforces leadership role
8 July 2005	G8 Gleneagles summit	Inception of GBEP
7 July 2005		World Trade Organization (WTO) (2005). 'Environmental Goods for Development, Submission by Brazil', TN/TE/W/59, Word Trade Organization, Geneva, Switzerland.
28 April 2005	WTO Appellate Body Report DS266	Appellate Body largely confirms initial ruling
15 October 2004	WTO Panel Report DS266	Brazil wins in first instance, EC appeals
31 July 2004	Mini-ministerial Geneva	'July Framework' agreement
10 September 2003	Cancún ministerial	5th ministerial meeting; G-20 formation
6 June 2003	IBSA inception	Creation of IBSA Dialogue Forum in Brasília
27 September 2002	Brazil instigates sugar and cotton cases	Sugar dispute DS266 Cotton dispute DS267
9 November 2001	Doha ministerial	4th ministerial meeting; Inception of the Doha Development Round

Key People in Brazil's Ethanol Diplomacy (2003–14)

Brazil–US

List of Brazilian Foreign Ministers
Celso Amorim 1 January 2003–31 December 2010
Antonio Patriota 1 January 2011–26 August 2013
Luiz Alberto Figueiredo 28 August 2013–1 January 2015

List of Ambassadors of Brazil to the United States (2002–14)
Rubens Antonio Barbosa 8 June 1999–31 March 2004
Roberto Abdenur 3 April 2004–21 November 2006
Antonio de Aguiar Patriota 7 January 2007–4. October 2009
Mauro Vieira 6 January 2010–31 December 2014

List of Permanent Representative of Brazil to the United Nations
Ronaldo Mota Sardenberg 2003–7
Maria Luiza Ribeiro Viotti 25 July 2007–16 January 2013
Luiz Alberto Figueiredo 28 January 2013–28 August 2013
Antonio Patriota 28 August 2013–1 January 2015

List of Ambassadors of the United States to Brazil
Donna J. Hrinak 23 April 2002–26 June 2004
John J. Danilovich 02 September 2004–07 November 2005
Philip T. Chicola November 2005–November 2006 (Chargé d'Affaires ad interim)
Clifford M. Sobel 7 November 2006–August 2009
Thomas A. Shannon 24 December 2009–September 2013
Liliana Ayalde 12 September 2013–ongoing

Key People in Brazil-US Relations
Assistant Secretary of State for Western Hemisphere Affairs Roberta S. Jacobson
Ambassador to Brazil (2009–13) and Assistant Secretary, Bureau of Western Hemisphere Affairs (2005–9) Thomas Shannon
Special Representative for Global Intergovernmental Affairs Reta Jo Lewis
Special Representative for Global Partnerships Kris Balderston
Assistant Secretary Ann Stock
Deputy Secretary William J. Burns
State Department Bureau of Energy Resources, headed by Ambassador Carlos Pascual (founded by Hillary)
Tom Donohue US Chamber of Commerce
Arturo Valenzuela, assistant secretary for the Western Hemisphere (2009–11)
Assistant Secretary for Economic, Energy and Business Affairs Jose W. Fernandez
Nicholas Burns, 'number three in the US State Department'
'US State Department spokesperson' Sean McCormack
Carlos Pascual, special envoy and coordinator for international energy affairs (2011–14)
David Goldwyn, (first) special envoy and coordinator for international energy affairs (2009–11)

Brazil in the WTO

WTO Director General
Roberto Azevêdo Since 1 September 2013
Pascal Lamy 1 September 2005–1 September 2013
Supachai Panitchpakdi 1 September 2002–1 September 2005

Brazilian Representative to the WTO
Evandro Didonet Since 2016
Roberto Azevêdo 2008–12
Clodoaldo Hugueney 2005–8
Luiz Felipe de Seixas Corrêa 2002–5

US Trade Representative (2001–17)
Robert Zoellick 20 January 2001–22 February 2005
Rob Portman 17 May 2005–29 May 2006
Susan Schwab 8 June 2006–20 January 2009
Ron Kirk 18 March 2009–15 March 2013
Demetrios Marantis (acting) 15 March 2013–23 May 2013
Miriam Sapiro (acting) 23 May 2013–21 June 2013
Michael Froman 21 June 2013–20 January 2017

EU Trade Commissioner
Karel de Gucht 9 February 2010–1 November 2014
Benita Ferrero-Waldner 1 December 2009–9 February 2010
Catherine Ashton 3 October 2008–1 December 2009
Peter Mandelson 22 November 2004–3 October 2008
Pascal Lamy 13 September 1999–22 November 2004

Stakeholder Mapping

This list gives an overview of the main actors and entities relevant for Brazil's ethanol diplomacy. The list is not exhaustive. WTO neogotiation groups are mapped in the following section.

Brazilian Ethanol Complex
President Lula da Silva (2003–10), Dilma Rousseff (2010–14)
Ministro Chefe da Casa Civil) J. Dirceu (2003–5), D. Rousseff (2005–10)
Ministério das Relações Exteriores (MRE – Itamaraty)
Ministério da Agricultura, Pecuária e Abastecimento (MAPA)
Ministério de Minas e Energia (MME)
Agência Nacional do Petróleo, Gás Natural e Biocombustíveis (ANP)
Ministério do Meio Ambiente (MMA)
Ministério do Desenvolvimento, da Indústria e Comércio Exterior (MDIC)
Frente Parlamentar Sucroalcooleira
União da Indústria de Cana-de-Açúcar (UNICA)
Conselho dos Produtores de Cana-de-Açúcar, Açúcar e Álcool (Consecana)
Fundação Getúlio Vargas (FGV)
Empresa de Pesquisa Energética (EPE)
Informal Council of 4 (MRE, MAPA, MME, MinFacenda)
Associação Brasileira de Normas Técnicas (ABNT)
Datagro Consulancy

(continued)

Agência Brasileira de Cooperação (ABC)
Ministério do Meio Ambiente (MMA)
Ministério do Desenvolvimento, da Indústria e Comércio Exterior (MDIC)

International Entities
Global Bioenergy Partnership (GBEP)
IEA Bioenergy Implementing Agreement: Task 40 on Sustainable International Bioenergy Trade
Renewable Energy Policy Network for the 21st Century (REN21)
International Panel on Climate Change (IPCC)
Kyoto Protocol to the United Nations Framework Convention on Climate Change (UNFCCC)
International Sugar Organisation (ISO)
Tripartite Task Force (ABNT, CEN, ASTM)
Food and Agricultiural Organisation (FAO)
World Trade Organisation (WTO)
F.O. Licht Consultancy
ISO (International Organisation for Standardisation) Project Committee 248 – Sustainability criteria for Bioenergy

US Stakeholders
The President of the United States
US Department of State
US Department of Energy (DOE)
US Department of Agriculture (USDA)
American Society for Testing and Materials (ASTM)
Renewable Fuel Association (RFA)
Environmental Protection Agency (EPA)
American Coalition for Ethanol

Mozambique Stakeholders
Presidency of the Republic
Foreign Ministry
Centro de Promoção da Agricultura (CEPAGRI)
Centro de Promoção de Investimento (CPI)
Direção Nacional de Terras e Florestas (DNTF)
Mozambique Principle Energy Ltd (MPEL)
Ministry of Agriculture of Mozambique (MINAG)
Econenergy Corporation
ProSavana

Relevant groups in the WTO Doha Round Negotiations

Groups*	Description/Issues	Countries
ACP*	African, Caribbean and Pacific countries with preferences in the European Union **Issues:** Agricultural preferences **Nature:** Geographical **Website:** http://www.acpsec.org	**WTO members (61):** Angola, Antigua and Barbuda, Barbados, Belize, Benin, Botswana, Burkina Faso, Burundi, Côte d'Ivoire, Cabo Verde, Cameroon, Central African Republic, Chad, Congo, Cuba, Democratic Republic of the Congo, Djibouti, Dominica, Dominican Republic, Fiji, Gabon, Gambia, Ghana, Grenada, Guinea, Guinea-Bissau, Guyana, Haiti, Jamaica, Kenya, Lesotho, Madagascar, Malawi, Mali, Mauritania, Mauritius, *Mozambique*, Namibia, Niger, Nigeria, Papua New Guinea, Rwanda, Saint Kitts and Nevis, Saint Lucia, Saint Vincent and the Grenadines, Samoa, Senegal, Seychelles, Sierra Leone, Solomon Islands, South Africa, Suriname, Swaziland, Tanzania, Togo, Tonga, Trinidad and Tobago, Uganda, Vanuatu, Zambia, Zimbabwe **WTO observers (7):** Bahamas, Comoros, Equatorial Guinea, Ethiopia, Liberia, Sao Tomé and Principe, Sudan **Not WTO members or observers (11):** Cook Islands, Eritrea, Kiribati, Marshall Islands, Micronesia, Federated States of, Nauru, Niue, Palau, Somalia, Timor-Leste, Tuvalu
African group*	African members of the WTO **Issues:** General **Nature:** Regional	**WTO members (43):** Angola, Benin, Botswana, Burkina Faso, Burundi, Côte d'Ivoire, Cabo Verde, Cameroon, Central African Republic, Chad, Congo, Democratic Republic of the Congo, Djibouti, Egypt, Gabon, Gambia, Ghana, Guinea, Guinea-Bissau, Kenya, Lesotho, Madagascar, Malawi, Mali, Mauritania, Mauritius, Morocco, *Mozambique*, Namibia, Niger, Nigeria, Rwanda, Senegal, Seychelles, Sierra Leone, South Africa, Swaziland, Tanzania, Togo, Tunisia, Uganda, Zambia, Zimbabwe

(continued)

Groups*	Description/Issues	Countries
ASEAN	Association of Southeast Asian Nations **Issues:** General **Nature:** Regional **Website:** http://www.asean.org	**WTO members (10):** Brunei Darussalam, Cambodia, Indonesia, Lao People's Democratic Republic, Malaysia, Myanmar, Philippines, Singapore, Thailand, Viet Nam
EU*	European Union **Issues:** General **Nature:** Customs union **Website:** http://ec.europa.eu	**WTO members (29):** Austria, Belgium, Bulgaria, Croatia, Cyprus, Czech Republic, Denmark, Estonia, *European Union* (formerly EC), Finland, France, Germany, Greece, Hungary, Ireland, Italy, Latvia, Lithuania, Luxembourg, Malta, Netherlands, Poland, Portugal, Romania, Slovak Republic, Slovenia, Spain, Sweden, United Kingdom
MercoSul*	Common Market of the Southern Cone, a customs union (MercoSul in Portuguese) **Issues:** General **Nature:** Customs union **Website:** http://www.MercoSul.int	**WTO members (4):** Argentina, *Brazil*, Paraguay, Uruguay
G-90*	African Group + ACP + least-developed countries **Issues:** General	**WTO members (70):** Angola, Antigua and Barbuda, Bangladesh, Barbados, Belize, Benin, Botswana, Burkina Faso, Burundi, Côte d'Ivoire, Cabo Verde, Cambodia, Cameroon, Central African Republic, Chad, Congo, Cuba, Democratic Republic of the Congo, Djibouti, Dominica, Dominican Republic, Egypt, Fiji, Gabon, Gambia, Ghana, Grenada, Guinea, Guinea-Bissau, Guyana, Haiti, Jamaica, Kenya, Lao People's Democratic Republic, Lesotho, Madagascar, Malawi, Maldives, Mali, Mauritania, Mauritius, Morocco, *Mozambique*, Myanmar, Namibia, Nepal, Niger, Nigeria, Papua New Guinea, Rwanda, Saint Kitts and Nevis, Saint Lucia, Saint Vincent and the Grenadines, Samoa, Senegal, Seychelles, Sierra Leone, Solomon Islands, South Africa, Suriname, Swaziland, Tanzania, Togo, Trinidad and Tobago, Tunisia, Uganda, Vanuatu, Yemen, Zambia, Zimbabwe

		WTO observers (9): Afghanistan, Bahamas, Bhutan, Comoros, Equatorial Guinea, Ethiopia, Liberia, Sao Tomé and Principe, Sudan **Not WTO members or observers (12):** Cook Islands, Eritrea, Kiribati, Marshall Islands, Micronesia, Federated States of, Nauru, Niue, Palau, Somalia, South Sudan, Timor-Leste, Tuvalu
Least-developed countries (LDCs)*	Least developed countries: the world's poorest countries. The WTO uses the UN list (pdf) available here: www.un.org/en/development/desa/policy/cdp/ldc_info.shtml **Issues:** General **Website:** http://www.un.org/en/development/desa/policy/cdp/ldc/ldc_list.pdf	**WTO members (34):** Angola, Bangladesh, Benin, Burkina Faso, Burundi, Cambodia, Central African Republic, Chad, Democratic Republic of the Congo, Djibouti, Gambia, Guinea, Guinea-Bissau, Haiti, Lao People's Democratic Republic, Lesotho, Madagascar, Malawi, Mali, Mauritania, *Mozambique*, Myanmar, Nepal, Niger, Rwanda, Senegal, Sierra Leone, Solomon Islands, Tanzania, Togo, Uganda, Vanuatu, Yemen, Zambia **WTO observers (8):** Afghanistan, Bhutan, Comoros, Equatorial Guinea, Ethiopia, Liberia, Sao Tomé and Principe, Sudan **Not WTO members or observers (6):** Eritrea, Kiribati, Somalia, South Sudan, Timor-Leste, Tuvalu
Cairns group*	Coalition of agricultural exporting nations lobbying for agricultural trade liberalisation. **Issues:** Agriculture **Website:** http://www.cairnsgroup.org	**WTO members (20):** Argentina, Australia, Bolivia, Plurinational State of, *Brazil*, Canada, Chile, Colombia, Costa Rica, Guatemala, Indonesia, Malaysia, New Zealand, Pakistan, Paraguay, Peru, Philippines, South Africa, Thailand, Uruguay, Viet Nam
G-10	Coalition of countries lobbying for agriculture to be treated as diverse and special because of non-trade concerns (not to be confused with the Group of Ten Central Bankers) **Issues:** Agriculture	**WTO members (9):** Chinese Taipei, Iceland, Israel, Japan, Korea, Republic of, Liechtenstein, Mauritius, Norway, Switzerland

(continued)

Groups*	Description/Issues	Countries
G-20*	Coalition of developing countries pressing for ambitious reforms of agriculture in developed countries with some flexibility for developing countries (not to be confused with the G-20 group of finance ministers and central bank governors, and its recent summit meetings) **Issues:** Agriculture **Website:** http://www.g-20.mre.gov.br	**WTO members (23):** Argentina, Bolivia, Plurinational State of, *Brazil*, Chile, China, Cuba, Ecuador, Egypt, Guatemala, India, Indonesia, Mexico, Nigeria, Pakistan, Paraguay, Peru, Philippines, South Africa, Tanzania, Thailand, Uruguay, Venezuela, Bolivarian Republic of, Zimbabwe
G-33*	Also called 'Friends of Special Products' in agriculture. Coalition of developing countries pressing for flexibility for developing countries to undertake limited market opening in agriculture **Issues:** Agriculture	**WTO members (47):** Antigua and Barbuda, Barbados, Belize, Benin, Bolivia, Plurinational State of, Botswana, Côte d'Ivoire, China, Congo, Cuba, Dominica, Dominican Republic, Ecuador, El Salvador, Grenada, Guatemala, Guyana, Haiti, Honduras, India, Indonesia, Jamaica, Kenya, Korea, Republic of, Madagascar, Mauritius, Mongolia, *Mozambique*, Nicaragua, Nigeria, Pakistan, Panama, Peru, Philippines, Saint Kitts and Nevis, Saint Lucia, Saint Vincent and the Grenadines, Senegal, Sri Lanka, Suriname, Tanzania, Trinidad and Tobago, Turkey, Uganda, Venezuela, Bolivarian Republic of, Zambia, Zimbabwe
NAMA-11*	Coalition of developing countries seeking flexibilities to limit market opening in industrial goods trade **Issues:** NAMA	**WTO members (10):** Argentina, *Brazil*, Egypt, India, Indonesia, Namibia, Philippines, South Africa, Tunisia, Venezuela, Bolivarian Republic of

Note: Groups that are directly or indirectly involved in Brazil's ethanol diplomacy are marked with an *.
Relevant countries have been set in italics.
Source: World Trade Organization (2015): Groups in the Negotiations. https://www.wto.org/english/tratop_e/dda_e/negotiating_groups_e.htm. Accessed 15 May 2015.

Ethanol/Biofuels MoUs Signed by Brazil (2003–14)

Date	Title	Partner	Signature
8 April 2002	Memorando de Entendimento entre o Governo da República Federativa do Brasil e o Governo da República da Índia referente a cooperação tecnolólica na area de mistura de etanol em combustíveis para transportes	India	Sergio Silva do Amaral, Ministro do Desenvolvimento, Industria e Comercio Exterior
1 September 2002	Memorando de Entendimento entre o Ministério do Meio Ambiente da República Federativa do Brasil e a Conferencia das Nações Unidas para o Comércio e o Desenvolvimento (UNCTAD) da Organização das Nações Unidas para o estabelecimento de um programa de cooperação técnica em comércio e investimento em produtos e serviços da biodiversidade	UNCTAD	José Carlos Carvalho, Ministro de Estado do Meio Ambiente
25 August 2004	Memorando de Entendimento entre o Governo da República Federativa do Brasil e da República do Equador sobre cooperação no setor de energia	Ecuador	Dilma Rousseff, Ministra de Minas e Energia
12 November 2004	Memorando de Entendimento entre o Ministério do Desenvolvimento, Indústria e Comércio Exterior da República Federativa do Brasil e a Comissão Nacional de Desenvolvimento e Reforma da República Popular da China em cooperação industrial	China	Luiz Fernando Furlan, Ministro do Desenvolvimento, Indústria e Comércio Exterior
22 November 2004	Declaração Conjunta sobre os resultados das conversações oficiais entre o Presidente da República Federativa do Brasil, Luiz Inácio Lula da Silva, e o Presidente da Federação da Rússia, Vladimir V. Putin	Russia	Pres. Lula
14 February 2005	Memorando de Entendimento para cooperação na área da indústria do etanol combustível entre o Ministério de Minas e Energia da República Federativa do Brasil e o Ministério de Energia e Petróleo da República Bolivariana da Venezuela	Venezuela	Dilma Rousseff, Ministra de Minas e Energia do Brasil + José Eduardo Dutra, Presidente da Petrobrás

(continued)

Date	Title	Partner	Signature
16 May 2005	Memorando de Entendimento entre o Governo da República Federativa do Brasil e o governo da Jamaica na área de açúcar e de etanol	Jamaica	Celso Amorim, Ministro das Relações Exteriores
5 July 2005	Declaração Conjunta por ocasiaão da visita do Ministro Dos Negócios Estrangeiros da Itália, Gianfranco Fini	Italy	Celso Amorim, Ministro das Relações Exteriores
15 July 2005	Protocolo de Intenções entre o Governo da República Federativa do Brasil e o governo da República Francesa referenta à cooperação na área das tecnologias avançadas e de suas aplicações	France	Celso Amorim, Ministro das Relações Exteriores
8 September 2005	Visita de Estado do Presidente da República Federal da Nigéria, Olusegun-Obasanjo	Nigeria	Pres. Lula
12 September 2005	Protocolo de Intenções entre o Governo da República Federativa do Brasil e o governo da República da Guiana para cooperação técnica na área de técnicas de produção e uso de etanol combustível	Guyana	Samuel Pinheiro Guimarães, Secretário-Geral das Relações Exteriores
12 September 2005	Visita ofocial do Excelentíssimo Senhor Luiz Inácio Lula da Silva, Presidente da República Federativa do Brasil, à Guatemala, Cidade de Guatemala, 12 September 2005	Guatemala	Pres. Lula
12 September 2005	Protocolo de Intenções entre o Governo da República Federativa do Brasil e o governo da República da Guatemala sobre cooperação técnica na área de técnicas de produção e uso de etanol combustível	Guatemala	Celso Amorim, Ministro das Relações Exteriores
13 September 2005	Protocolo de Intenções entre o Governo da República Federativa do Brasil e o governo de Belize sobre cooperação técnica na área de técnicas de produção e uso de etanol combustível	Belize	Celso Amorim, Ministro das Relações Exteriores
13 September 2005	Protocolo de Intenções entre o Governo da República Federativa do Brasil e o governo da República de Costa Rica sobre cooperação técnica na área de técnicas de produção e uso de etanol combustível	Costa Rica	Celso Amorim, Ministro das Relações Exteriores

13 September 2005	Protocolo de Intenções entre o Governo da República Federativa do Brasil e o governo da República de EL Salvador sobre cooperação técnica na área de técnicas de produção e uso de etanol combustível	El Salvador	Celso Amorim, Ministro das Relações Exteriores
13 September 2005	Protocolo de Intenções entre o Governo da República Federativa do Brasil e o governo da República de Honduras sobre cooperação técnica na área de técnicas de produção e uso de etanol combustível	Honduras	Celso Amorim, Ministro das Relações Exteriores
13 September 2005	Protocolo de Intenções entre o Governo da República Federativa do Brasil e o governo da República da Nicarágua sobre cooperação técnica na área de técnicas de produção e uso de etanol combustível	Nicaragua	Celso Amorim, Ministro das Relações Exteriores
13 September 2005	Protocolo de Intenções entre o Governo da República Federativa do Brasil e o governo da República do Panamá sobre cooperação técnica na área de técnicas de produção e uso de etanol combustível	Panama	Celso Amorim, Ministro das Relações Exteriores
13 September 2005	Protocolo de Intenções entre o Governo da República Federativa do Brasil e o governo da República Dominicana sobre cooperação técnica na área de técnicas de produção e uso de etanol combustível	Dominican Republic	Celso Amorim, Ministro das Relações Exteriores
30 September 2005	Memorando de Entendimento entre o Ministério do Desenvolvimento, Indústria e Comércio Exterior da República Federativa do Brasil e a Comissão Nacional de Desenvolvimento e Reforma da República Popular da China em cooperação industrial	China	Representatnte do Ministério do Desenvolvimento, da Indústria e Comércio Exterior, República Federativa do Brasil
13 October 2005	Declaração Conjunta do Primeiro Ministro da República Portuguesa e do Presidente da República Federativa do Brasil por ocasião da VIII Cimeira Luso-Brasileira	Portugal	Pres. Lula

(continued)

Date	Title	Partner	Signature
18 October 2005	Declaração Conjunta sobre os resultados das conversações oficiais entre o Presidente da República Federativa do Brasil, Luiz Inácio Lula da Silva, e o Presidente da Federação da Rússia, Vladimir V. Putin	Russia	Pres. Lula
26 October 2005	Ajuste complementar entre o Governo da República Federativa do Brasil e o Instituto Interamericano de Cooperação para a Agricultura, fundada na carta da Organização dos Estados Americanos, na convenção sobre o Instituto Interamericano de Cooperação para a Agricultura e no acordo básico entre o governo da República Federativa do Brasil e o Instituto Interamericano de Cooperação para a Agricultura, para a gestão e modernização da tecnologia de informação e implementação do modelo de gestão de segurança da informação do Ministerio da Agricultura, Pecuária e Abastecimento	Instituto Interamericano de Cooperação para a Agricultura	Emb. Lauro Barbosa da Silva Moreira, Diretor-Geral da Agência Brasileira de Cooperação – ABC/ MRE
7 March 2006	Declaração Conjunta do Governo da República Federativa do Brasil e do Governo do Reino Unido da Gra-Bretanha e Irlando Norte sobre o diálogo de alto nível Brasil – Reino Unido sobre desenvolvimento sustentável	United Kingdom	Celso Amorim, Ministro das Relações Exteriores
23 May 2006	Protocolo de Intenções entre o Governo da República Federativa do Brasil e o governo da República do Haiti sobre cooperação técnica na área de técnicas de produção e uso de etanol combustível	Haiti	Celso Amorim, Ministro das Relações Exteriores
25 May 2006	Declaração sobre biocombustíveis	France	Celso Amorim, Ministro das Relações Exteriores
31 May 2006	Ajuste complementar ao acordo básico de cooperação científica e técnica entre o Governo da República Federativa do Brasil e o governo da República do Peru para implementação do projeto 'Desenvolvimento de cultivos alternativos para produção de biocombustíveis'	Peru	Emb. Luiz Augusto de Araujo Castro

5 June 2006	Memorando de Entendimento sobre o estabelecimento da subcomissão de energia e recursos minerais da comissão Sino-Brasileira de alto nível de concertação e cooperação entre o Ministério de Minas e Energia da República Federativa do Brasil e a Comissão Nacional de Desenvolvimento e Reforma da República Popular da China em cooperação industrial	China	Silas Rondeau Cavalcante Silva, Ministro das Minas e Energia
13 September 2006	Memorando de Entendimento entre os membros do forum de diálogo Índia-Brasil-África do Sul, o Governo da República Federativa do Brasil, o Governo da República da África do Sul e o Governo da República da Índia, para estabelecer força-tarefatrilateral sob biocombustíveis	IBSA	Silas Rondeau Cavalcante Silva, Ministro das Minas e Energia
9 November 2006	Memorando de Entendimento para o estabelecimento de uma comissão mista permanente em matéria energética, geológica e de mineração entre o Ministério de Minas e Energia da República Federativa do Brasil e o Ministério de Energia e Minas da República do Peru	Peru	Silas Rondeau Cavalcante Silva, Ministro das Minas e Energia
23 November 2006	Ajuste complementar ao acordo de cooperação técnica entre o Governo da República Federativa do Brasil e o governo da República do Paraguai para implementação do projeto 'Desenvolvimento de técnicas para a produção de materias-primas de biocombustíveis no Paraguai'	Paraguay	Celso Amorim, Ministro das Relações Exteriores
23 November 2006	Comunicado Conjunto dos Ministros das Relações Exteriores da República Federativa do Brasil e da República do Paraguai	Paraguay	Celso Amorim, Ministro das Relações Exteriores
15 December 2006	Memorando de Entendimento entre o Governo da República Argentina, o Governo da República Federativa do Brasil, o Governo da República do Paraguai, o Governo da República Oriental do Uruguai, e o Governo da República Bolivariana da Venezuela, para Estabelecer um Grupo de Trabalho Especial Sobre Biocombustíveis	MercoSul	Celso Amorim, Ministro das Relações Exteriores

(continued)

Date	Title	Partner	Signature
15 February 2007	Ajuste complementar ao acordo de cooperação técnica entre o Governo da República Federativa do Brasil e o governo da Jamaica para para implementação do projeto 'Formação de recursos humanos e tranferencia de técnicas para apoio ao programa Jamaicano de modernização do setor sucroalcoleiro	Jamaica	Celso Amorim, Ministro das Relações Exteriores
26 February 2007	Protocolo de Intenções entre o Governo da República Federativa do Brasil e o governo da República Oriental do Uruguai sobre programa de cooperação na área de biocombustíveis	Uruguay	Celso Amorim, Ministro das Relações Exteriores
9 March 2007	Memorando de Entendimento entre o Governo da República Federativa do Brasil e o Governo dos Estados Unidos da America para avançar a cooperação em biocumbustíveis	USA	Celso Amorim, Ministro das Relações Exteriores
4 April 2007	Memorando de Entendimento entre o Governo da República Federativa do Brasil e o Governo da República do Equador sobre cooperação no setor de energia	Ecuador	Silas Rondeau Cavalcante Silva, Ministro das Minas e Energia
4 April 2007	Protocolo de Intenções entre o Governo da República Federativa do Brasil e o governo da República do Equador sobre cooperação técnica nas áreas de energia e de minas	Ecuador	Celso Amorim, Ministro das Relações Exteriores
4 April 2007	Ajuste complementar ao acordo básico de cooperação técnica entre o Governo da República Federativa do Brasil e o governo da República do Equador para implementação do projeto 'Desenvolvimento de processos agroprodutivos para biocombustíveis'	Ecuador	Celso Amorim, Ministro das Relações Exteriores
26 April 2007	Declaração Conjunta do Presidente da República Federativa do Brasil, Luiz Inácio Lula da Silva, e da Presidente da República do Chile, Michelle Bachelet Jeria	Chile	Pres. Lula
26 April 2007	Memorando de Entendimento entre o Governo da República Federativa do Brasil e o Governo daRepública do Chile na área de biocombustíveis	Chile	Celso Amorim, Ministro das Relações Exteriores + Silas Rondeau Cavalcante Silva, Ministro das Minas e Energia

16 May 2007	Ajuste complementar ao acordo básico de cooperação científica e técnica entre o Governo da República Federativa do Brasil e o governo da República do Senegal para implementação do projeto 'Apoio ao combate ao gafanhoto no Senegal'	Senegal	Ruy Nunes Pinto Nogueira, Ministro de Estado, Interino, das Relações Exteriores
16 May 2007	Ajuste complementar ao acordo básico de cooperação científica e técnica entre o Governo da República Federativa do Brasil e o governo da República do Senegal para implementação do projeto 'Apoio ao programa nacional de biocombustíveis no Senegal '	Senegal	Ruy Nunes Pinto Nogueira, Ministro de Estado, Interino, das Relações Exteriores
21 May 2007	Memorando de Entendimento entre o Governo da República Federativa do Brasil e o governo da República do Paraguai para o estabelecimento de plano de ação para o desenvolvimento dos biocombustíveis no Paraguai	Paraguay	Celso Amorim, Ministro das Relações Exteriores + Silas Rondeau Cavalcante Silva, Ministro das Minas e Energia (stepped down 22 May 2007)
21 May 2007	Declaração Conjunta	Paraguay	Pres. Lula
5 July 2007	Diálogo regular de política energética Brasil – Comunidade Européia – Termos de referencia	EU	Celso Amorim, Ministro das Relações Exteriores
6 August 2007	Memorando de Entendimento em material de cooperação energética entre o Governo da República Federativa do Brasil e o governo dos Estados Unidos Mexicanos	Mexico	Celso Amorim, Ministro das Relações Exteriores
7 August 2007	Declaração do Governo da República Federativa do Brasil e o governo da República de Honduras sobre cooperação técnica na área de técnicas de produção e uso de etanol combustível	Honduras	Celso Amorim, Ministro das Relações Exteriores
8 August 2007	Memorando de Entendimento entre o Governo da Federativa do Brasil e o governo da República da Nicarágua sobre cooperação nas áreas de energia e mineração	Nicaragua	Celso Amorim, Ministro das Relações Exteriores
10 August 2007	Memorando de Entendimento entre o Governo da República Federativa do Brasil e o governo da República do Panamá para estabelecer força-tarefa na área de biocombustíveis	Panama	Celso Amorim, Ministro das Relações Exteriores

(continued)

Date	Title	Partner	Signature
15 August 2007	Protocolo de Intenções entre o Governo da República Federativa do Brasil e o governo da República do Benin sobre cooperação técnica na área biocombustíveis	Benin	Celso Amorim, Ministro das Relações Exteriores
6 September 2007	Memorando de Entendimento entre o Governo da República Federativa do Brasil e o governo da República de Moçambique na área de biocombustíveis	Mozambique	Celso Amorim, Ministro das Relações Exteriores + Nelson Hubner, Ministro interino, de Minas e Energia
11 September 2007	Memorando de Entendimento entre o Governo da República Federativa do Brasil e o Governo do Reino da Suécia sobre cooperação na área de bioenergia, incluindo biocombustíveis	Sweden	Celso Amorim, Ministro das Relações Exteriores
13 September 2007	Memorando de Entendimento entre o Governo da República Federativa do Brasil e o Governo do Reino da Dinamarca sobre cooperação nas áreas de energias renovaveis e eficiencia energetica	Denmark	Celso Amorim, Ministro das Relações Exteriores
15 October 2007	Memorando de Entendimento entre o Governo da República Federativa do Brasil e a União Economica e Monetária do Oeste Africano na Área de biocombustíveis	ECOWAS – UEMOA	Celso Amorim, Ministro das Relações Exteriores
15 October 2007	Protocolo de Intenções entre o Governo da República Federativa do Brasil e o governo do Burquina Faso sobre cooperação técnica na área de técnica de produção de cana-de-açucár	Burkina Faso	Celso Amorim, Ministro das Relações Exteriores
17 October 2007	Memorando de Entendimento entre o Governo da República Federativa do Brasil, o Governo da República da Índia e o Governo da República da África do Sul sobre Cooperação em Recursos Eólicos	IBSA	Celso Amorim, Ministro das Relações Exteriores
5 December 2007	Ajuste complementar ao acordo de cooperação técnica, científica e tecnológica entre o Governo da República Federativa do Brasil e o governo da República de El Salvador para implementação do projeto 'Adoção de tecnologias modernas para a produção de etanol em El Salvador'	El Salvador	Samuel Pinheiro Guimarães, Ministro Interino, das Relações Exteriores

7 February 2008	Plano de Ação em ciencia e tecnologia entre o Governo da República Federativa do Brasil e o governo do Reino da Espanha	Spain	Celso Amorim, Ministro das Relações Exteriores
27 February 2008	Protocolo de Intenções entre o Governo da República Federativa do Brasil e o governo da República Socialista do Vietnã sobre cooperação técnica na área de técnicas de produção e uso de etanol combustível	Vietnam	Celso Amorim, Ministro das Relações Exteriores
11 April 2008	Memorando de Entendimento entre o Governo da República Federativa do Brasil e o Governo dos Países Baixos sobre cooperação na área de bioenergia, incluindo biocombustíveis	Netherlands	Celso Amorim, Ministro das Relações Exteriores
19 April 2008	Ajuste complementar ao acordo básico de cooperação científica e técnica entre o Governo da República Federativa do Brasil e o governo da República de Gana para implementação do projeto 'Desenvolvimento das bases para o estabelecimento da agricultura de energia em Gana'	Ghana	Celso Amorim, Ministro das Relações Exteriores
14 May 2008	Acordo entre o Governo da República Federativa do Brasil e o governo da República Federal da Alemanha sobre cooperação no setor de energia com foco em energias renováveis e eficiencia energética	Germany	Samuel Pinheiro Guimarães, Ministro de Estado interino, das Relações Exteriores
17 May 2008	Ajuste complementar ao acordo básico de cooperação científica e técnica entre o Governo da República Federativa do Brasil e o governo da República do Peru para implementação do projeto 'Promoção de cultivos alternativos para a produção de biocombustíveis – Fase II'	Peru	Samuel Pinheiro Guimarães, Secretário Geral das Relações Exteriores
17 May 2008	Comunicado Conjunto dos Presidentes da República Federativa do Brasil, Luiz Inácio Lula da Silva, e da República do Peru, Alan García Pérez	Peru	Pres. Lula

(continued)

Date	Title	Partner	Signature
12 July 2008	Protocolo de Intenções entre o Governo da República Federativa do Brasil e o governo da República da Indonésia sobre cooperação técnica na área de técnicas de produção e uso de etanol combustível	Indonesia	Celso Amorim, Ministro das Relações Exteriores
23 July 2008	Memorando de Entendimento para cooperação no campo da energia entre o Governo da República Federativa do Brasil e o governo da República de Trinidad e Tobago	Trinidad and Tobago	
30 July 2008	Ajuste complementar ao acordo de cooperação técnica entre o Governo da República Federativa do Brasil e o governo da República da Costa Rica para implementação do projeto 'Alternativas de produção de biocombustíveis em Costa Rica'	Costa Rica	Samuel Pinheiro Guimarães, Ministro, interino, das Relações Exteriores
8 September 2008	Declaração Conjunta Visita de Estado ao Brasil da Presidenta da República Argentina, Cristina Fernandez de Kirchner	Argentina	Pres. Lula
18 November 2008	Memorando de Entendimento entre o Governo da República Federativa do Brasil e o Governo da República da Indonésia sobre cooperação no campo da agricultura	Indonesia	Celso Amorim, Ministro das Relações Exteriores
26 November 2008	Declaração Conjunta Visita Oficial à República Federativa do Brasil do Presidente da Federação da Rússia, Dmitry Medvedev Rio de Janeiro, 24 a 26 de novembro de 2008	Russia	Pres. Lula
23 December 2008	Parceria Estratégica entre a República Federativa do Brasil e a República Francesa Plano de Ação	France	Pres. Lula
19 February 2009	Protocolo entre o Governo da República Federativa do Brasil e o governo da República Popular da China sobre cooperação em energia e mineração	China	Márcio Pereira Zimmermann, Secretário-Executivo do Ministério das Minas e Energia
10 March 2009	Declaração Conjunta	Uruguay	Pres. Lula
13 March 2009	Ata DAI Comissão Mista de Cooperação Brasil – Benim	Benin	Roberto Jaguaribe, Subsecretário Geral de Assuntos Políticos do Ministério das Relações Exteriores

23 April 2009	Declaração Conjunta Visita de Trabalho à República Argentina do Presidente da República Federativa do Brasil, Luiz Inácio Lula da Silva	Argentina	Pres. Lula
19 May 2009	Comunicado Conjunto entre a República Federativa do Brasil e a República Popular da China sobre o contínuo fortalecimento da parceria estrateegica	China	Pres. Lula
28 May 2009	Acordo de cooperação em agricultura entre o Governo da República Federativa do Brasil e o governo da República do Uzbequistão	Uzbekistan	Reinhold Stephanes, Ministro da Agricultura, Pecuária e Abastecimento
1 June 2009	Visita de estado a la República de Guatemala del Excelentísimo Senõr Presidente de la República Federativa de Brasil, Luiz Inacio Lula da Silva	Guatemala	Pres. Lula
24 June 2009	Memorando de Entendimento entre o Governo da República Federativa do Brasil e o Governo da República das Filipinas sobre cooperação no campo da agricultura	Philippines	Reinhold Stephanes, Ministro da Agricultura, Pecuária e Abastecimento
24 June 2009	Memorando de Entendimento sobre cooperação na área de bioenergia, incluindo biocombustíveis, entre o Ministério de Minas e Energia da República Federativa do Brasil e o Departamento de Energia da República das Filipinas	Philippines	Edison Lobão, Ministro das Minas e Energia
29 July 2009	Memorando de Entendimento em material de cooperação na área de energia entre a República Federativa do Brasil e a República Federal da Nigéria	Nigeria	Edison Lobão, Ministro das Minas e Energia
29 July 2009	Ajuste complementar ao acordo de cooperação economica, técnica e científica entre o Governo da República Federativa do Brasil e o governo da República Federal da Nigéria na área de biotecnologia	Nigeria	Celso Amorim, Ministro das Relações Exteriores
	Programa executivo de cooperação educacional entre o Governo da República Federativa do Brasil e o Governo da República do Peru para o period de 2009 a 2012, Annexo II	Peru	

(continued)

Date	Title	Partner	Signature
10 September 2009	Ajuste Complementar ao Acordo Básico de Cooperação Científica e Técnica entre o Governo da República Federativa do Brasil e o Governo da República do Suriname para a implementação do projeto 'Apoio ao desenvolvimento da produção de biocombustíveis no Suriname'	Surinam	Celso Amorim, Ministro das Relações Exteriores
10 November 2009	Ajuste Complementar ao Acordo Básico de Cooperação Técnica entre o Governo da República Federativa do Brasil e o Governo da Colômbia para Implementação do Projeto 'Cooperação Técnica para o Incremento do Conhecimento sobre a Palma Azeiteira e a Mamona como Fontes de Biomassa para a Produção de Biodiesel	Colombia	Marco Farani, Diretor da ABC
18 November 2009	Declaração Conjunta – Visita de Trabalho à República Federativa do Brasil da Presidenta da República Argentina, Cristina Fernández de Kirchner	Argentina	Pres. Lula
2 December 2009	Declaração Conjunta do Presidente da República Federativa do Brasil, Luiz Inácio Lula da Silva, e do Presidente da Ucrânia, Victor Yushchenko	Ukraine	Pres. Lula
3 December 2009	Memorando de Entendimento sobre Cooperação no Combate à Mudança do Clima entre O Governo da República Federativa do Brasil e o Governo da República Federal da Alemanha	Germany	Antonio Patriota, Secretario Geral das Relações Internacionais
3 March 2010	Memorando de Entendimento entre o Governo da República Federativa do Brasil e o Governo dos Estados Unidos da América sobre a Implementação de Atividades de Cooperação Técnica em Terceiros Países	USA	Celso Amorim, Ministro das Relações Exteriores
3 March 2010	Memorando de Entendimento entre o Governo da República Federativa do Brasil e o Governo dos Estados Unidos da América sobre Cooperação em Mudança do Clima	USA	Celso Amorim, Ministro das Relações Exteriores

7 April 2010	Memorando de Entendimento entre o Governo da República Federativa do Brasil e o Governo da República da Libéria sobre Cooperação em Minas e Energia	Liberia	Márcio Zimmermann, Ministro de Minas e Energia
12 April 2010	Parceria Estratégica entre a República Federativa do Brasil e a República Italiana	Italy	Pres. Lula
15 April 2010	Plano de Ação Conjunta entre o Governo da República Federativa do Brasil e o Governo da República Popular da China, 2010-2014	China	Pres. Lula
17 May 2010	Memorando de Entendimento entre o Governo da República Federativa do Brasil e o Governo da República Islâmica do Irã sobre Cooperação Agrícola	Iran	Celso Amorim, Ministro das Relações Exteriores
27 May 2010	Action Plan for Strategic Partnership between the Federative Republic of Brazil and the Republic of Turkey	Turkey	Pres. Lula
6 July 2010	Acordo entre o Governo da República Federativa do Brasil e o Governo da República do Quênia sobre Cooperação no Setor de Energia	Kenia	Celso Amorim, Ministro das Relações Exteriores
8 July 2010	Ajuste Complementar ao Acordo de Cooperação Técnica entre o Governo da República Federativa do Brasil e o Governo da República da Zâmbia para Implementação do Projeto 'Produção de Biocombustíveis'	Zambia	Celso Amorim, Ministro das Relações Exteriores
4 August 2010	Memorando de Entendimento entre o Governo da República Federativa do Brasil e o Governo da República do Cameroun sobre Cooperação no Campo da Agricultura e Pecuária	Cameroon	Wagner Gonçalves Rossi, Ministro da Agricultura
25 August 2010	Memorando de Entendimento entre o Governo da República Federativa do Brasil e o Governo da República da Guiné-Bissau sobre Cooperação no Campo da Agricultura	Guinea-Bissau	Celso Amorim, Ministro das Relações Exteriores

(continued)

Date	Title	Partner	Signature
1 September 2010	Memorando de Entendimento entre o Governo da República do Brasil e a República da Colômbia sobre Cooperação na Área de Bioenergia, Incluindo Biocombustíveis	Colombia	
22 September 2010	Memorando de Entendimento entre o Governo da República Federativa do Brasil e o Governo da Austrália para o Estabelecimento de Parceria Reforçada	Australia	Celso Amorim, Ministro das Relações Exteriores
16 December 2010	Memorando de Entendimento entre o Governo da República Federativa do Brasil e o Governo da República do Suriname sobre Cooperação na Área de Bioenergia, Incluindo Biocombustíveis	Surinam	
31 January 2011	Memorando de Entendimento entre o Governo da República Federativa do Brasil e o Governo da República Argentina sobre Cooperação na Área de Bioenergia, Incluindo Biocombustíveis	Argentina	
31 January 2011	Declaração Conjunta – Visita oficial da Presidenta da República Federativa do Brasil, Dilma Rousseff, à Presidenta da República Argentina, Cristina Fernández de Kirchner	Argentina	Pres. Dilma
19 March 2011	Parceria para o Desenvolvimento de Biocombustíveis de Aviação	USA	Antonio Patriota, Ministro das Relações Exteriores + Edison Lobão, Ministro das Minas e Energia
31 March 2011	Declaração Conjunta sobre o Intercâmbio na Área de Combustíveis Alternativos e Tecnologias de Propulsão Inovadoras entre o Ministério das Relações Exteriores da República Federativa do Brasil e o Ministério Federal de Transportes, Construção Civil e Desenvolvimento Urbano da República Federal da Alemanha	Germany	Antonio Patriota, Ministro das Relações Exteriores
12 April 2011	Comunicado Conjunto entre a República Federativa do Brasil e a República Popular da China	China	Pres. Dilma
30 March 2012	Memorando de Entendimento entre o Governo da República Federativa do Brasil e o Governo da República da Índia em Cooperação na Área de Biotecnologia	India	Marco Antonio Raupp, Ministro da Ciência Tecnologia e Inovação

9 April 2012	Memorando de Entendimento sobre a Parceria em Aviação entre o Governo da República Federativa do Brasil e o Governo dos Estados Unidos da América	USA	Antonio Patriota, Ministro das Relações Exteriores
21 June 2012	Memorando de Entendimento entre o Governo da República Federativa do Brasil e o Governo da República Italiana sobre Cooperação na Área de Bioenergia	Italy	Edison Lobão, Ministro das Minas e Energia
17 August 2012	Memorando de Entendimento entre o Governo da República Federativa do Brasil e o Governo do Reino da Tailândia sobre o Programa de Cooperação Técnica Trilateral	Thailand	Antonio Patriota, Ministro das Relações Exteriores
23 February 2013	Memorando de Entendimento entre o Governo da República Federativa do Brasil e o Governo da República da Nigéria para o estabelecimento de mecanismo de diálogo estratégico	Nigeria	Antonio Patriota, Ministro das Relações Exteriores
2 October 2013	Memorando de Entendimento sobre o estabelecimento de diálogo político, economico, comercial e de investimentos bilaterais entre o Ministério das Relções Exteriores da República Federativa do Brasil e o Ministério dos Negócios Estrangeiros da República do Cazaquistão	Kasachstan	Luiz Alberto Figueiredo Machado, Ministro das Relações Exteriores
26 November 2013	Declaração Conjunta da I sessão do Mecanismo de Diálogo Estratégico Brasil – Nigéria	Nigeria	VP Michel Temer
16 May 2014	Acordo de complementação economica N° 2 celebrado entre a República Federativa do Brasil e a República Oriental do Uruguai Septuagésimo Quarto Protocolo Adicional	Uruguay	Luiz Alberto Figueiredo Machado, Ministro das Relações Exteriores
16 July 2014	Memorando de Entendimento entre o Governo da República Federativa do Brasil e o Governo da República da Índia sobre cooperação na área de meio ambiente	India	Luiz Alberto Figueiredo Machado, Ministro das Relações Exteriores
30 March 2015	Memorando de Entendimento entre a República Federativa do Brasil e a República de Moçambique sobre a cooperação na área de energias renováveis	Mozambique	Mauro Vieira, Ministro das Relações Exteriores
19 May 2015 (July respectively)	Plano de Ação Conjunta entre o Governo da República Federativa do Brasil e o Governo da República Popular da China 2015-2021	China	Pres. Dilma

(continued)

REFERENCES

All web links last accessed on 23 July 2017.

Abdenur, Roberto. 2006. 'Brazil and the USA: A Strategic Relationship, a Strategic Dialogue'. In *The Ambassadors Review*. Washington, DC: Council of American Ambassadors.

Adriázola, Paola, Alexander Carius, Lena Ruthner, Dennis Tänzler, Joe Thwaites and Stephan Wolters. 2013. *Climate Diplomacy: New Approaches for Foreign Policy*. Berlin: Adelphi Research.

Afionis, Stavros, Lindsay C. Stringer, Nicola Favretto Julia Tomei and Marcos S. Buckeridge. 2016. 'Unpacking Brazil's Leadership in the Global Biofuels Arena: Brazilian Ethanol Diplomacy in Africa'. *Global Environmental Politics* 16, no. 3: 127–50.

Agência Brasil. 2003. 'Celso Amorim Will Visit Six African Countries'. http://memoria.ebc.com.br/agenciabrasil/noticia/2003-04-30/celso-amorim-will-visit-six-african-countries, http://memoria.ebc.com.br/agenciabrasil/noticia/2003-04-30/celso-amorim-inicia-viagem-de-10-dias-africa.

Agrix. 2014. 'Investment Opportunities for Dutch Agrifood Companies in Mozambique: A Challenge for Patient Money'. Report commissioned by the Agricultural Council of the Embassy of the Kingdom of the Netherlands, Pretoria. https://agriprofocus.com/upload/AgrifoodinvestmentopportunitiesMozambique1417448619.pdf.

Agroanalysis. 2012. 'A revista de agronegócio da FGV'. August 2012. São Paulo: FGV. http://www.agroanalysis.com.br/8/2010.

Alden, Chris, and Marco Antonio Vieira. 2005. 'The New Diplomacy of the South: South Africa, Brazil, India and Trilateralism'. *Third World Quarterly* 26, no. 7: 1077–95.

Almeida, Paulo Roberto de. 2009. 'Lula's Foreign Policy: Regional and Global Strategies'. In *Brazil under Lula*, edited by Joseph Love and Werner Baer, 167–86. New York: Palgrave Macmillan.

———. 2010. 'Never before Seen in Brazil: Luis Inácio Lula da Silva's Grand Diplomacy'. *Revista Brasileira de Política Internacional* 53, no. 2: 160–77.

Almeida, Wilson. 2009. 'Ethanol Diplomacy: Brazil and U.S. in Search of Renewable Energy'. *GCG* 3, no. 3: 114–24. doi:10.3232/GCG.2009.V3.N3.06.

Amado, André. 2013. *Por dentro do Itamaraty – impressões de um diplomata*. Brasília: FUNAG.

Amanora, Kojo S., and Sérgio Chichava. 2016. 'South–South Cooperation, Agribusiness, and African Agricultural Development: Brazil and China in Ghana and Mozambique'. *World Development* 81 (May): 13–23.

Amorim, Celso. 2010. 'Remarks at a Press Conference with Secretary of State Hillary Clinton, Brasília', 3 March 2010. https://2009-2017.state.gov/secretary/20092013clinton/rm/2010/03/137774.htm.

———. 2011a. *Conversas Com Jovens Diplomatas*. São Paulo: Benvirá.

———. 2011b. 'Reflections on Brazil's Global Rise'. *Americas Quarterly: The New Brazil and the Changing Hemisphere* 1 (Spring). www.americasquarterly.org/node/2420.

———. 2015a. *Teerã, Ramalá e Doha. Memórias da Política Externa Ativa e Altiva.* São Paulo: Benvirá.

———. 2015b. Interview with the former foreign minister of Brazil, London, 22 November 2015.

———. 2016. *A Grande Estratégia Do Brasil: Discursos, Artigos e Entrevistas da Gestão no Ministério da Defesa (2011–2014).* Brasília: FUNAG.

Argüelles, Lucía, Leah Temper and Beatriz Rodríguez-Labajos. 2014. 'Comercio de biomasa y acaparamiento de tierra: nuevas dimensiones de las relaciones Sur-Sur'. *Ecología Política*, no. 48, (December): 93–96.

Arkhangelskaya, Alexandra A. 2010. 'India, Brazil and South Africa Dialogue Forum: A Bridge between Three Continents. Challenges, Achievements and Policy Options'. The Nordic Africa Institute Policy Notes, August 2010. https://www.files.ethz.ch/isn/124580/2010_8.pdf.

Ashoff, Guido. 2010. 'Triangular Cooperation: Opportunities, Risks, and Conditions for Effectiveness'. *Development Outreach* 12, no. 2: 22–24.

Atanassov, Boris. 2013. *The Status of Biofuels Projects in Mozambique.* London: ODI.

Atkinson, Ben. 2004. 'The CDM, Kyoto Protocol and the Sugar, Ethanol and Bio-Fuels Industry'. *International Sugar Journal* 106, no. 1263: 175–77.

Azevêdo, Roberto. 2013. 'Inaugural Speech as WTO DG. 09.09.2013'. https://www.wto.org/english/news_e/news13_e/gc_09sep13_e.htm, https://www.youtube.com/watch?v=7Uy6HKtfYyg.

Bambo, Tomé Fernando. 2014. 'Cooperação Sul-Sul: o acordo Brasil-Moçambique na área de biocombustíveis'. Dissertation (Mestrado em Relações Internacionais), Universidade de São Paulo.

Barbosa, Rubens. 2011. 'Política externa de dois governos'. Fórum de Economia da Fundação Getúlio Vargas 8.

———. 2015. *The Washington Dissensus: A Privileged Observer's Perspective on US-Brazil Relations.* Nashville: Vanderbilt University Press.

Barreto, Fernando de Mello. 2012. 'A política externa após a redemocratização'. *Tomo II – 2003-2010.* Brasília: FUNAG.

BBC. 2013. 'Brazil "to Write Off" Almost $900m of African Debt'. 25 May. http://www.bbc.co.uk/news/world-latin-america-22669331.

Bellmann, Christophe, Jonathan Hepburn, Ekaterina Krivonos and Jamie Morrison. 2013. 'G-33 Proposal: Early Agreement on Elements of the Draft Doha Accord to Address Food Security'. *ICTSD Programme on Agricultural Trade and Sustainable Development; Information Note.* Geneva: International Centre for Trade and Sustainable Development. http://www.fao.org/fileadmin/templates/est/PUBLICATIONS/g33-proposal-early-agreement-on-elements-of-the-draft-doha-accord-to-address-food-security_1_.pdf.

Belting, Julia. 2008. 'Empirical Methods: Expert Interviews'. Presentation given at ETH Zurich, Switzerland, 5 November.

Beltrame, Cristian. 2008 .'O Etanol na Diplomacia Presidencial do Governo Lula'. siaibib01.univali.br/pdf/Cristian%20Beltrame.pdf.

Benevides, Neil Giovanni. 2011. *Relações Brasil-Estados Unidos no Setor de Energia: do mecanismo de consultas sobre a cooperação energética do memorando de entendimento sobre biocombustíveis (2003–2007).* Brasília: Fundação Alexandre Gusmão.

Benner, Thorsten. 2013. 'Brazil as a Norm Entrepreneur: The "Responsibility While Protecting" Initiative'. GPPI Working Paper, March. http://www.gppi.net/fileadmin/user_upload/media/pub/2013/Benner_2013_Working-Paper_Brazil-RWP.pdf.

Bennett, Andrew, and Alexander L. George. 1997. 'Process Tracing in Case Study Research'. *MacArthur Foundation Workshop on Case Study Methods*, 17–19 October. http://users.polisci.wisc.edu/kritzer/teaching/ps816/ProcessTracing.htm.

Bennett, Andrew, and Colin Elman. 2006. 'Qualitative Research: Recent Developments in Case Study Methods'. *Annual Review of Political Science* 9 (2006): 455-76.

Benson, Todd. 2009. 'US Sees Progress with Brazil on Climate Talks'. Reuters News, 6 August. http://www.wilsoncenter.org/article/us-sees-progress-brazil-climate-talks#.

Berenskoetter, Felix, and Adam Quinn. 2012. 'Hegemony by Invitation: Neoclassical Realism, Soft Power and US–European Relations'. In *Neoclassical Realism in Europe*, edited by Asle Toje and Barbara Kunz, 214–33. Manchester: Manchester University Press.

Biden, Joe. 2013. 'Remarks by the Vice President on US-Brazil Relations'. 29 May. https://www.whitehouse.gov/the-press-office/2013/05/29/remarks-vice-president-us-brazil-relations-rio-de-janeiro-brazil.

Birle, Peter, ed. 2013. 'Brasilien als internationaler Akteur'. *Brasilien. Eine* Einführung, 149–68. Frankfurt: Vervuert Verlag.

Blair, Tony. 2006. 'Joint Statement on Trade by President Lula and Mr Blair'. 9 March. http://webarchive.nationalarchives.gov.uk/20080909021718/http://www.number10.gov.uk/Page9169.

Blustein, Paul. 2009. *Misadventures of the Most Favoured Nations*. New York: PublicAffairs.

Boschi, Renato R. 2016. 'Lobby Groups, the State and the Relationship between the Branches of Government in Brazil'. In *The Political System of Brazil*, edited by Dana de la Fontaine and Thomas Stehnken, 163–82. Berlin: Springer.

Bourcier, Nicolas. 2013. 'Roberto Azevêdo's WTO Appointment Gives Brazil a Seat at the Top Table'. *The Guardian*, 5 May. https://www.theguardian.com/world/2013/may/21/Azevêdo-head-world-trade-organisation.

Bourne, Richard. 2008. *Lula of Brazil – The Story So Far*. London: Zed Books.

Brands, Hal. 2010. *Dilemmas of Brazilian Grand Strategy*. Carlisle: Strategic Studies Institute.

———. 2011 'Evaluating Brazilian Grand Strategy under Lula'. *Comparative Strategy* 30, no. 1: 28–49.

Brawley, Mark. 2009a. 'Political Economy and Grand Strategy: A Neoclassical Realist View'. London: Routledge.

———. 2009b. 'Neoclassical Realism and Strategic Calculations: Explaining Divergent British, French, and Soviet Strategies toward Germany between the World Wars (1919–1939)'. In *Neoclassical Realism, the State, and Foreign Policy*, edited by Norrin M. Ripsman, Jeffrey W. Taliaferro and Steven E. Lobell, 75–98. Cambridge: Cambridge University Press.

Brazil. 2004. 'Agricultural Negotiations, Statement by Brazil on Behalf of G-20', 21 July. https://www.iatp.org/sites/default/files/451_2_36569.pdf.

Bridges Daily. 2013. 'Update #5 – Historic Bali Deal to Spring WTO, Global Economy Ahead'. 7 December. https://www.ictsd.org/bridges-news/bridges-africa/news/bridges-daily-update-5-historic-bali-deal-to-spring-wto-global.

———. 2013a. 'Azevêdo Jump-Starts WTO Talks as Bali Ministerial Approaches'. *Bridges Weekly Brief* 17, no. 30. 19 September. https://www.ictsd.org/bridges-news/bridges/news/azev%C3%AAdo-jump-starts-wto-talks-as-bali-ministerial-approaches.

———. 2013b. 'Azevêdo Extends WTO Negotiating Deadline in Bid to Secure Bali Deal', *Bridges Weekly Brief* 17, no. 38, 14 November. https://www.ictsd.org/bridges-news/bridges/news/azev%C3%AAdo-extends-wto-negotiating-deadline-in-bid-to-secure-bali-deal.

———. 2013c. 'Success in Bali Sparks Questions over Doha, WTO Future', *Bridges Weekly Brief* 17, no. 41, 12 December. https://www.ictsd.org/bridges-news/bridges/news/success-in-bali-sparks-questions-over-doha-wto-future.

Brookings Institution. 2007. 'Energy Security, Energy Urgency: Key Issues Facing the Next President'. Transcript of the event in Washington, DC. 18 December. http://www.brookings.edu/events/2007/12/18-lugar.

Bull, Benedicte. 2013. 'Social Movements and the "Pink Tide" Governments in Latin America: Transformation, Inclusion and Rejection'. In *Democratization in the Global South. International Political Economy*, edited by Stokke K. and Törnquist O. London: Palgrave Macmillan.

Burges, Sean. 2007. 'Building a Global Southern Coalition: The Competing Approaches of Brazil's Lula and Venezuela's Chávez'. *Third World Quarterly* 28, no. 7: 1343–58

———. 2010. 'The Possibilities and Perils of Presidential Diplomacy: Lessons from the Lula years in Brazil'. In *Relations Internationales du Brésil: Les Chemins de la Puissance*, edited by Denis Rolland and Antonio Carlos Lessa. Paris: L'Harmattan.

———. 2012. 'Developing from the South: South-South Cooperation in the Global Development Game'. *Austral: Revista Brasileira de Estratégia e Relações Internacionais – Brazilian Journal of Strategy & International Relations* 1, no. 2: 225–49.

———. 2017. *Brazil in the World: The International Relations of a South American Giant.* Manchester: Manchester University Press.

Burns, E. Bradford. 1966. *The Unwritten Alliance: Rio-Branco and Brazilian-American Relations.* New York: Columbia University Press.

———. 1993. *A History of Brazil.* New York: Columbia University Press.

Burns, William. 2012. 'Building a Deeper Partnership with Brazil'. 1 March. http://www.state.gov/s/d/former/burns/remarks/2012/185063.htm.

Cabral, Lídia. 2014. 'The EU-Brazil Partnership on Development: A Lukewarm Affair'. In *New Donors, New Partners? EU Strategic Partnerships and Development*, edited by Clare Castillejo. ESP – European Strategic Partnership Observatory Report 3, December, pp. 15–24. Fride: Madrid.

Cabral, Lídia, and Alex Shankland. 2013. 'Narratives of Brazil-Africa Cooperation for Agricultural Development: New Paradigms?' CBAA Working Paper 051. Brighton: Future Agricultures Consortium.

Cabral, Lídia, Alex Shankland, Arilson Favareto and Alcides Costa Vaz. 2013. 'Brazil-Africa Agricultural Cooperation Encounters: Drivers, Narratives and Imaginaries of Africa and Development'. *IDS Bulletin* 44, no. 4. https://opendocs.ids.ac.uk/opendocs/handle/123456789/2606.

Cabral, Lídia, Arilson Favareto, Langton Mukwereza and Kojo Amanor. 2016. 'Brazil's Agricultural Politics in Africa: More Food International and the Disputed Meanings of "Family Farming"'. *World Development* 81 (May): 47–60.

Caporaso, James A. 2007. 'Qualitative Methods and EU Studies'. *EUSA Review Spring*,. 5–7. www.eustudies.org/files/eusa_review/websprinG-2007.pdf.

Cárdenas, Mauricio. 2011. 'US–Brazil Relations: A Fresh New Start?' Up Front, Brookings Institution, 8 February. http://www.brookings.edu/blogs/up-front/posts/2011/02/08-brazil-cardenas.

Carmona, Francisco. 2007. 'Através da Intelec Holding Guebuza entra na Vodacom'. www.open.ac.uk/technology/mozambique/sites/www.open.ac.uk.technology.mozambique/files/pics/d75974.doc.

Carr, Edward H. 2011. *The Twenty Years Crisis*, edited by Michael Cox. London: Palgrave Macmillan.

Cason, Jeffrey W., and Timothy J. Power. 2009. 'Presidentialization, Pluralization, and the Rollback of Itamaraty: Explaining Change in Brazilian Foreign Policy Making in the Cardoso-Lula Era'. *International Political Science Review* 30, no. 2: 117–40.

Castro, Neves, and Luiz Augusto de. 2012. 'Relações Brasil-Estados Unidos'. *CEBRI Textos*, 12 December. http://www.cebri.org/midia/documentos/textos12.pdf.

Caverley, Jonathan D., 2013. 'Neoconservatism, Neoclassical Realism, and the Narcissism of Small Differences'. In *After Liberalism: The Future of Liberalism in International Relations*, edited by Rebekka Friedman, Kevork Oskanian and Ramon Pardo, pp. 145–66. London: Palgrave.

CEBEU – Conselho Empresarial Brasil – Estados Unidos. 2006. 'Brasil-EUA: Uma Agenda Estratégica para as Relações Bilaterais'. September.

Cesarino, Letícia. 2016. 'Brazil as an Emerging Donor in Africa's Agricultural Sector: Comparing Two Projects'. *Agrarian South: Journal of Political Economy* 4, no. 3: 371–93.

CFR (Council on Foreign Relations). 2011. 'Task Force Report: Global Brazil and US-Brazil Relations'. Appendix of 2011 and 2010 US–Brazil Bilateral Agreements. http://www.cfr.org/brazil/global-brazil-us-brazil-relations/p25407.

CFR Brazil Task Force. 2011. 'Global Brazil and U.S.-Brazil Relations'. Independent Task Force Report No. 66. Washington, DC: Council on Foreign Relations. https://www.cfr.org/content/publications/attachments/Brazil_TFR_66.pdf.

Cha, Victor. 1997. 'Realism, Liberalism, and the Durability of the U.S.-South Korean Alliance'. *Asian Survey* 37, no. 7: 609–22.

———. 2000. 'Abandonment, Entrapment, and Neoclassical Realism in Asia – The United States, Japan, and Korea'. *International Studies Quarterly* 44, 261–91.

———. 2009. 'Powerplay – Origins of the U.S. Alliance System in Asia'. *International Security* 34, no. 3: 158–96.

Chichava, Sérgio. 2017. 'A "Operação Lava Jato" vista de Moçambique'. *IDeIAS Boletim* 96, no. 11. http://www.iese.ac.mz/wp-content/uploads/2017/07/ideias_96.pdf.

Chichava, Sérgio, Jimena Duran, Lídia Cabral, Alex Shankland, Lila Buckley, Tang Lixia and Zhang Yue. 2013. 'Chinese and Brazilian Cooperation with African Agriculture: The Case of Mozambique'. Future Agricultures CBAA Working Paper 049. March.

Chomthongdi, Jacques Chai. 2005. 'The "G-Guide": Groupings in the WTO Agriculture Negotiations'. https://focusweb.org/node/649.

Clements, Elizabeth Alice, and Bernardo Mançano Fernandes. 2013. 'Land Grabbing, Agribusiness and the Peasantry in Brazil and Mozambique.' *Agrarian South: Journal of Political Economy* 2, no. 1: 41–69.

Clinton, Hillary R. 2010. 'Remarks with Brazilian Foreign Minister Celso Luiz Nunes Amorim'. 3 March. http://www.state.gov/secretary/20092013clinton/rm/2010/03/137774.htm.

———. 2011a. 'Remarks with Brazilian Foreign Minister Antonio Patriota after Their Meeting'. 23 February. http://www.state.gov/secretary/20092013clinton/rm/2011/02/157029.htm.

———. 2011b. 'Remarks at the 41st Washington Conference on the Americas'. 11 May. http://www.state.gov/secretary/20092013clinton/rm/2011/05/163025.htm.

———. 2012. 'Remarks at the Business Leaders' Lunch'. National Confederation of Industries, 16 April. http://www.state.gov/secretary/20092013clinton/rm/2012/04/187956.htm.

Collier, David. 2011. 'Understanding Process Tracing'. *PS: Political Science and Politics* 44, no. 4: 823–30.

Collier, Ruth Berins, and David, Collier. 1991. Shaping the Political Arena: Critical Junctures, the Labor Movement, and Regime Dynamics in Latin America. Princeton: Princeton University Press.

Collier, David, James Mahoney, and Jason Seawright. 2004. 'Claiming Too Much: Warnings about Selection Bias'. In *Rethinking Social Inquiry: Diverse Tools, Shared Standards*, edited by Henry E. Brady and David Collier, pp. 85–102. Lanham: Rowman & Littlefield.

Cosbey, Aaron, Soledad Aguilar, Melanie Ashton and Stefano Ponte. 2010. 'Environmental Goods and Services Negotiations at the WTO: Lessons from Multilateral Environmental Agreements and Ecolabels for Breaking the Impasse'. 31 March. https://ssrn.com/abstract=1730402 or http://dx.doi.org/10.2139/ssrn.1730402.

Cosh, Colby. 2007. 'Ethanol Diplomacy: A Rare Display of Commie Common Sense?' *Western Standard Online*. 4 June. http://www.westernstandard.ca/website/article.php?id=2575.

Costa, Thomaz Guedes da. 2010. 'Grand Strategy for Assertiveness: International Security and U.S.-Brazil Relations'. Expanded paper of the presentation delivered at the first session of the Challenges to Security in the Hemisphere Task Force on 24 March.

Costas, Ruth. 2013. 'Brasileiro perto de posto-chave no comércio global'. BBC Brazil London, 23 April. http://www.bbc.co.uk/portuguese/noticias/2013/04/130415_omc_eleicao_ru.shtml.

Cottier, Thomas. 2009. 'WTO Negotiations on Environmental Goods and Services: A Potential Contribution to the Millennium Development Goals'. *UNCTAD Report UNCTAD/DITC/TED/2008/4*. New York: United Nations. http://unctad.org/en/Docs/ditcted20084_en.pdf.

Crandall, Britta. 2011. 'Hemispheric Giants: The Misunderstood History of U.S.-Brazilian Relations'. Plymouth: Rowman & Littlefield.

DAI. 2017. 'The Shop That Changed Lives'. https://daiglobal.exposure.co/the-seeds-of-transformation.

Dalgaard, Klaus. 2012. 'The Energy Statecraft of Brazil: Promotin Biofuels as an Instrument of Brazilian Foreign Policy, 2003–2010'. Dissertation, London School of Economics and Political Science, University of London.

Dávila, Sérgio. 2006. 'Mudança no governo Lula começa por Embaixada de Washington'. *Folha de São Paulo*, 1 November. http://www1.folha.uol.com.br/folha/brasil/ult96u86272.shtml.

Defraigne, Jean-Christophe. 2012. 'The Evolution of Brazil's Trade Policy'. Presentation given at the Conference Strategic Challenges in the EU-Brazil Relationship, Brussels. 7–8 May. http://ghum.kuleuven.be/ggs/projects/eu_brazil/documents/slides-defraigne.pdf.

Deutsche Welle. 2020. 'Fim do ProSavana: Uma oportunidade para o desenvolvimento agrícola em Moçambique? By Romeu da Silva'. 27 July. https://www.dw.com/pt-002/fim-do-prosavana-uma-oportunidade-para-o-desenvolvimento-agr%C3%ADcola-em-mo%C3%A7ambique/a-54339235.

Dyson, Tom. 2016. Neoclassical Realism and Defence Reform in Post-Cold War Europe. London: Palgrave Macmillan.

Dueck, Colin. 2004. 'Ideas and Alternatives in American Grand Strategy 2000–2004'. *Review of International Studies* 30: 511–35.

. 2005. 'Realism Culture and Grand Strategy Explaining America's Peculiar Path to World Power'. *Security Studies* 14, no. 2: 195–231.

———. 2009. 'Presidents, Domestic Politics, and Major Military Interventions'. In *Neoclassical Realism and the State*, edited by Steven Lobell, Norrin Ripsman and Jeffrey Taliaferro, pp. 139–69. Cambridge: Cambridge University Press.

Economist. 2007. 'Ethanol – Fuel for Friendship: America and Its Neighbours Discover a Common Interest'. 1 March. http://www.economist.com/node/8780213.

Einaudi, Luigi R. 2011. 'Brazil and the United States: The Need for Strategic Engagement'. National Defense University Strategic Forum (SF) No. 266. March.

Embrapa. 2011. *Seminário dá bases para investimento em agronegócio moçambicano.*https://www.embrapa.br/busca-de-noticias/-/noticia/18144462/seminario-da-bases-para-investimento-em-agronegocio-mocambicano.

Enríquez, Laura. 2013. 'The Paradoxes of Latin America's "Pink Tide": Venezuela and the Project of Agrarian Reform'. *Journal of Peasant Studies* 40, no. 4: 611–38. doi:10.1080/03066150.2012.746959.

Environmental Justice Atlas. 2013. 'Principle Capital Holdings Biofuel Project in Dombe, Mozambique'. https://ejatlas.org/conflict/principle-capital-holdings-biofuel-project-in-dombe-mozambique.

Ewing, Reese. 2015. 'US Ethanol Exports to Brazil to Suffer from Big Tariff Hike'. Reuters Online. 22 June. http://af.reuters.com/article/energyOilNews/idAFL1N0Z81CG-20150622.

Fagundes, Paloma de Mattos. 2013. 'As relações internacionais de interdependência no setor de etanol e suas implicações na cadeia de produção brasileira'. Doctoral Thesis. Universidade Federal do Rio Grande do Sul, Centro de Estudos e Pesquisas em Agronegócio, Porto Alegre.

Falleti, Tulia G. 2006. 'Theory Guided Process-Tracing: Something Old, Something New'. *APSA-CP, Newsletter of the Organized Section in Comparative Politics of the APSA* 17, no. 1: 9–14

FAO (Food and Agriculture Organization of the United Nations). 2017. 'Mozambique at a Glance'. http://www.fao.org/mozambique/fao-in-mozambique/mozambique-at-a-glance/en/.

Farina, Elizabeth. 2015. Interview with Elizabeth Farina, CEO of UNICA. São Paulo.

FASE (Federação de Órgãos para Assistência Social e Educacional). 2015. 'Fundo Nacala – Estrutura Original e Desdobramentos'. Rio de Janeiro: Fase & Oxfam. https://fase.org.br/wp-content/uploads/2015/04/Fundo_Nacala_Final.pdf.

Fátima Mello, Ana Toni. 2013. *Sustentabilidade do Desenvolvimento no Brasil pós-Rio+20. FES Análise Novembro de 2013. Friedrich-Ebert-Stiftung (FES).* Brasil: São Paulo.

Ferrando, Tomaso. 2015. 'Dr. Brasilia and Mr. Nacala: The Apparent Duality behind the Brazilian State-Capital Nexus'. *Revista de Economia Política* 35, no. 2: 343–59.

Ferreira Capellaro, Angélica, Anamaria Guimarães Gandra, Lara Bartocci Liboni and Simone Vasconcelos Ribeiro Galina. 2012. 'Internationalisation of Brazilian Ethanol: An Analysis of the Current Scenario'. *African Journal of Business Management* 6, no. 42: 10677–86. http://www.academicjournals.org/AJBM.

FGV Projetos. 2012. 'Nacala Corridor Fund'. https://www.oecd.org/forum/issues/NACALA%20CORRIDOR%20FUND-FGV%20Projetos.pdf.

Finger, J. Michael. 2009. 'Trade and Development: Systemic Lessons from WTO Experience with Implementation, Trade Facilitation, and Aid for Trade'. In *Developing Countries in the WTO Legal System*, edited by Thomas Chantal and Joel P. Trachtman, 75–104. Oxford: Oxford University Press.

Fingermann, Natalia. 2013. 'Os mitos por trás do ProSavana'. *IDeIAS*, no. 49, 29 May. Maputo: Instituto de Estudos Sociais e Económicos (IESE). http://www.iese.ac.mz/lib/publication/outras/ideias/ideias_49.pdf.

Fishlow, Albert. 2010. 'The United States and Brazil: In Search of a Stable Relationship'. Documento para el Centro para la Política Hemisférica, Universidad de Miami 18.

Flemes, Daniel. 2007. 'Emerging Middle Powers' Soft Balancing Strategy: State and Perspectives of the IBSA Dialogue Forum'. GIGA Working Paper 57/2007. Hamburg: German Institute of Global and Area Studies (GIGA).

Flick, Uwe. 2002. 'Qualitative Research – State of the Art'. *Social Science Information* 41: 5–24.

Fogarty, Ed. 2013. *Projecting Polities: States, Nonstate Actors, and Global Governance.* London: Routledge.

Fontaine, Dana de la. 2016. 'Brazil's Foreign Policy: Between Self-Determination and Dependency'. In *The Political System of Brazil*, edited by Dana de la Fontaine and Thomas Stehnken, 393–414. Berlin: Springer.

Foodtank. 2016. 'Land Grab Update: Mozambique, Africa Still in the Crosshairs'. https://foodtank.com/news/2016/10/land-grab-update-mozambique-africa-still-in-the-crosshairs/.

Franco, Jennifer, Les Levidow, David Fig, Lucia Goldfarb, Mireille Hönicke and Maria Luisa Mendonça. 2010. 'Assumptions in the European Union Biofuels Policy: Frictions with Experiences in Germany, Brazil and Mozambique'. *Journal of Peasant Studies* 37, no. 4: 661–98. doi:10.1080/03066150.2010.512454.

Frey, Adrian. 2016. 'Brazil's Investment Reaches US$10 Billion – Mining, Construction and Agriculture'. http://clubofmozambique.com/news/mining-construction-and-agriculture-brazils-investment-reaches-eur-10-billion/.

Funada-Classen, Sayaka. 2013a. 'Analysis of the Discourse and Background of the Prosavana Programme in Mozambique – Focusing on Japan's Role'. Paper presented at the 2013 Legal and Development Implications of International Land Acquisitions conference, Kyoto. http://afrikagrupperna.se/sodraafrikaidag-uploads/2013/06/ProSavana-Analysis-Japanese-University.pdf, http://farmlandgrab.org/uploads/attachment/ProSavana%20Analysis% 20based%20on%20Japanese%20source%20(FUNADA2013).pdf.

———. 2013b. 'Post-Fukushima Anatomy of Studies on ProSavana: Focusing on Natalia Fingermann's "Myths behind ProSavana"' (English version). *Observador Rural No. 13*, December. https://www.farmlandgrab.org/uploads/attachment/Observador_Rural_N%C2%BA_13,_vers%C3%A3o_inglesa.pdf.

Funada-Classen, Sayaka. 2019. 'The Rise and Fall of Prosavana: From Triangular Cooperation to Bilateral Cooperation in Counter-resistance'. *Observador Rural* 82 (December). Maputo: Observatório do Meio Rural. https://omrmz.org/omrweb/wp-content/uploads/OR82-ProSAVANA-English.pdf.

Furtado, André. 2009. 'Biocombustibles y comercio internacional: una perspectiva latinoamericana'. CEPAL – Colección Documentos de proyectos LC/W.247. Santiago de Chile.

Fuser, Igor. 2008. 'Os recursos energéticos e as teorias das relações internacionais'. In *A Energia, a Política Internacional e o Brasil*, edited by José Alexandre Hage, vol. 1, 105–27. São Paulo: Instituto Memória.

G-20. 2013. 'G-20 Leaders' Declaration'. http://en.G-20russia.ru/load/782795034.

Gal-Or, Noemi. 2014. 'The WTO Bali Package'. *Does It Mark the Resurgence of Trade Multilateralims? Global Governance Spotlight 1-2014*. Bonn: Stiftung Entwicklung und Frieden.

Gallagher, Paul W. 2007. 'A Look at US–Brazil Ethanol Trade and Policy'. *Biofuels, Bioproducts Biorefining* 1: 9–13. doi:10.1002/bbb.9.

GBEP (Global Bioenergy Partnership). 2005. 'White Paper'. http://www.globalbioenergy.org/fileadmin/user_upload/docs/WhitePaper-GBEP.pdf.

GBEP. 2006. 'Terms of Reference'. http://www.globalbioenergy.org/fileadmin/user_upload/gbep/docs/TOR_text_only_updated_November_2012.pdf.

Geertz, Clifford. 2008. Thick Description: Toward an Interpretive Theory of Culture. Milton Park: Routledge.

George, Alexander L., and Andrew Bennett. 2005. Case Studies and Theory Development in the Social Sciences. Cambridge, MA: MIT Press.

Gehring, Markus. 2009. 'Biofuels in the WTO – Challenges and Opportunities for Sustainable Development?' Presentation given at IUCN Academy for Environmental Law, 15 December. http://www.iucnael.org/en/documents/doc_download/318-gehring-markus-biofuels-in-the-wto.html.

———. 2004. 'What Is a Case Study and What Is It Good for?' *American Political Science Review* 98, no. 2: 341–54.

———. 2007. 'Is There a (Viable) Crucial-Case Method?' *Comparative Political Studies* 40, no. 3: 231–53.

———. 2011. 'How Good Is Good Enough? A Multidimensional, Best-Possible Standard for Research Design'. *Political Research Quarterly* 64, no. 3: 625–36.

Gladys, Lechini. 2012. 'BRICS e Africa: A grande terra incognita'. *Boletim de economia e política internacional* 9 (January/March): 139–50.

Gläser, Jochen, and Grit Laudel. 2009. *Experteninterviews und qualitative Inhaltsanalyse: als Instrumente rekonstruierender Untersuchungen*. Wiesbaden: Springer-Verlag.

Globo. 2007. Lula recebe secretário do tesouro dos EUA com um relatório de queixas. 11 July.

Goldberg, Ray, Robert Lawrence and Katie Milligan. 2006. 'Brazil's WTO Cotton Case: Negotiation hrough Litigation'. *HBS Case Collection*, September (revised January 2005). http://www.hbs.edu/faculty/Pages/item.aspx?num=31569 and edited and revised version of the Harvard Business School case with the same name: https://piie.com/publications/chapters_preview/3632/05iie3632.pdf.

Gorter, Harry de, David R. Just and Qinwen Tan. 2009. 'The Socially Optimal Import Tariff and Tax Credit for Ethanol with Farm Subsidies'. *Agricultural and Resource Economics Review* 38, no. 1: 65–77. http://purl.umn.edu/49865.

GRAIN. 2013. 'Leaked ProSavana Master Plan Confirms Worst Fears'. 30 April. https://www.grain.org/article/entries/4703-leaked-ProSavana-master-plan-confirms-worst-fears.

Gratius, Susanne. 2003. 'Is the FTAA at an Impasse? The Key Players US and Brazil'. *SWP-Comments*, 13 October.

Guest, Greg, Arwen Bunce, and Laura Johnson. 2006. 'How Many Interviews Are Enough? An Experiment with Data Saturation and Variability'. *Field Methods* 18, no. 1: 59–82.

Gunter, Janet. 2010. 'Mozambique/Brazil: "Ethanol diplomacy" meets criticism'. Global Voices. https://globalvoices.org/2010/07/22/mozambiquebrazil-ethanol-diplomacy-meets-criticism/.

Haddad, Lawrence. 2011. 'The FAO Candidates Speak. Are We Moved?' Commentary on the Guardian Development Blog, 26 April. https://www.theguardian.com/global-development/poverty-matters/2011/apr/26/fao-candidates-director-general-statements, https://www.scribd.com/document/53951193/Fao-Candidates-Haddad-Table-April-26.

Hall, Ian. 2006. *The International Thought of Martin Wight*. London: Palgrave MacMillan.

Hanlon, Joseph. 2015. *A Decade of Mozambique: Politics, Economy and Society 2004-2013*. Leiden: Brill.

———. 2016. 'Mozambique: Brazil Cuts Dam Funding over Corruption'. http://allafrica.com/stories/201610180155.html.

Hanson, Stephanie. 2012. 'Brazil on the International Stage'. CFR Backgrounder, 2 July. http://www.cfr.org/brazil/brazil-international-stage/p19883.

Hardt, Matheus Soldi, Fernando Mouron and Laerte Apolinário Júnior. 2017. 'Rising Donors in a Transitional World: Challenges and Opportunities for Brazilian Technical Cooperation'. *Rising Powers Quarterly* 2, no. 2: 55–82. http://risingpowersproject.com/wp-content/uploads/2017/07/Rising-Powers-Quarterly-Volume-2-Issue-2.pdf.

Harmer, Toni. 2009. 'Biofuels Subsidies and the Law of the WTO'. ICTSD Programme on Agricultural Trade and Sustainable Development, issue paper no. 20, International Centre for Trade and Sustainable Development, Geneva, Switzerland.

Henry, Joseph Jr. 2013. Flex Fuel Vehicles in Brazil. Presentation given at the Global Bioenergy Partnership Study Tour for Capacity Building 'Bioenergy Week', Brasília, 22 March.

Hira, Anil. 2011. 'Sugar Rush: Prospects for a Global Ethanol Market'. *Energy Policy* 39, no. 11: 6925–35.

Hira, Anil, and Luiz Guilherme de Oliveira. 2009. 'No Substitute for Oil? How Brazil Developed Its Ethanol Industry'. *Energy Policy* 37, no. 6: 2450–56. doi:10.1016/j.enpol.2009.02.037.

Hirst, Monica. 2005. 'The United States and Brazil'. *A Long Road of Unmet Expectations*. New York: Routledge.

———. 2013. *Understanding Brazil-United States Relations: Contemporary History, Current Complexities and Prospects for the 21st Century*. Brasília: Funag.

Hollander, Gail. 2010. 'Power Is Sweet: Sugarcane in the Global Ethanol Assemblage'. *Journal of Peasant Studies* 37, no. 4: 699–721.

Hopewell, Kristen. 2013. 'New Protagonists in Global Economic Governance: Brazilian Agribusiness at the WTO'. *New Political Economy*. doi:10.1080/13563467.2013.736957.

———. 2015. 'Different Paths to Power: The rise of Brazil, India and China at the World Trade Organization'. *Review of International Political Economy* 22, no. 2: 311–38. doi:10.1080/09692290.2014.927387.

Howse, Robert, Petrus van Bork and Charlotte Hebebrand. 2006. 'WTO Disciplines and Biofuels: Opportunities and Constraints in the Creation of a Global Marketplace', IPC Discussion Paper, International Food & Agricultural Trade Policy Council, Washington, DC, October.

Hugueney, Clodoaldo. 2004. 'The G-20: Passing Phenomenon or Here to Stay?' FES Briefing Paper. March. http://library.fes.de/pdf-files/iez/global/02021.pdf.

Husar, Jörn, and Stormy-Annika Mildner. 2007. Indien, Brasilien und Süd-Afrika in der Doha-Runde. Handelspolitische Interessen und Entscheidungsstrukturen, SWP Diskussionspapier FG 4/3.

IADB (Inter-American Development Bank). 2006. 'Informe Annual 2005'. Washington, DC: IADB. http://idbdocs.iadb.org/wsdocs/getdocument.aspx?DOCNUM=37177813.

IBF (International Biofuels Forum). 2007. 'White Paper on Internationally Compatible Biofuel Standards – Tripartite Task Force Brazil, European Union & United States of America', 31 December. https://www.nist.gov/sites/default/files/documents/2017/05/09/biofuels_report.pdf.

IBSA (Dialogue Forum India, Brazil, South Africa). 2003. 'Brasília Declaration'. http://ibsa.nic.in/brasil_declaration.htm.

———. 2006a. 'Joint Declaration of the 1st Summit Meeting'. http://www.ibsa-trilateral.org/images/stories/documents/declarations/1st_summit_declaration.pdf.

———. 2006b. 'Memorandum of Understanding on Establishing a Trilateral Task Team on Biofuels'. http://www.ibsa-trilateral.org/images/stories/documents/agreements/20060913IBSABiofuels.pdf.

———. 2007. 'India-Brazil-South Africa Dialogue Forum'. Second Summit of Heads of State/Government. Tshwane Declaration, 17 October. http://www.ibsa-trilateral.org/images/stories/documents/declarations/2nd_IBSA_Summit_Declaration_-_Tshwane_2007.pdf.

———. 2008. 'India-Brazil-South Africa Dialogue Forum'. Third Summit of Heads of State/Government. New Delhi Declaration, 15 October. http://www.ibsa-trilateral.org/images/stories/documents/declarations/3rd_IBSA_Summit_Declaration_-_New_Delhi_2008.pdf.

———. 2010. 'India-Brazil-South Africa Dialogue Forum'. Fourth Summit of Heads of State/Government. Brasília Declaration, 15 April. http://www.ibsa-trilateral.org/images/stories/documents/declarations/Final%20Summit%20Declaration%20-%204th%20IBSA%20Summit%202010.pdf.

ICTSD (International Centre for Trade and Sustainable Development) . 2003. 'Developments since the Fourth WTO Ministerial Conference'. *Doha Round Briefing Series* 1, no. 6. https://www.ictsd.org/sites/default/files/downloads/2008/06/doha6-singaporeissues.pdf.

Jacobson, Roberta. 2012. 'Remarks on US-Brazil Relations on the Eve of President Dilma Rousseff's First Visit to Washington, DC'. 12 March. http://www.state.gov/p/wha/rls/rm/2012/185622.htm.

James Tiburcio, Fernanda Lira Gomes. 2010. Os BRIC e a África. Desafios de Desenvovimento. Ano 8. Edição 60 - 28/05/2010. IPEA online. http://ipea.gov.br/desafios/index.php?option=com_content&view=article&id=1086:catid=28&Itemid=23.

Jeffrey, W. Legro, and Andrew Moravcsik. 1999. 'Is Anybody Still a Realist?' *International Security* 24, no. 2: 5–55. doi: https://doi.org/10.1162/016228899560130.

Jesus, Diego Santos de Vieira. 2013. 'Lighting the Fire: Brazil's Energy Diplomacy, 2003-2010'. *Diplomacy and Statecraft* 24: 499–515.

Joerißen, Britta, and Jochen Steinhilber. 2009. 'Rendezvous von Nord und Süd'. *Ein Blick auf die US-amerikanisch- brasilianischen Beziehungen*. FES BrasilInfo August. library.fes.de/pdf-files/bueros/brasilien/06660.pdf.

Joint Action Plan. 2010. 'Between the Department of Energy of the United States of America and the Ministry of Mines and Energy of the Federative Republic of Brazil'. 20 July. http://energy.gov/eere/downloads/us-brazil-binational-energy-working-group-joint-action-plan.

Joint Remarks. 2008. 'US Secretary of State Condoleezza Rice, Brazilian Foreign Minister Amorim'. http://iipdigital.usembassy.gov/st/english/texttrans/2008/03/20080314144343xjsnommis0.238949.html#ixzz4IgRUN3kP.

———. 2012. 'From the Fourth US-Brazil Global Partnership Dialogue, October 2012'. 24 October. http://www.cfr.org/brazil/joint-statement-fourth-us-brazil-global-partnership-dialogue-october-2012/p29340.

JornalDomingo. 2012. 'Agromoz arranca com o plantio de culturas'. http://www.jornaldomingo.co.mz/index.php/nacional/177-agromoz-arranca-com-o-plantio-de-culturas.

José, Goldemberg. 2013. 'Sugarcane Ethanol: Strategies to a Successful Program in Brazil'. In *Advanced Biofuels and Bioproducts*, edited by J. Lee. New York: Springer. https://doi.org/10.1007/978-1-4614-3348-4_2.

Josling, Tim. 2009. 'Agricultural Trade Disputes in the WTO'. In *Trade Disputes and the Dispute Settlement Understanding of the WTO: An Interdisciplinary Assessment*, edited by Hartigan James, 245–82. Bingly: Emerald. http://www.emeraldinsight.com/doi/pdfplus/10.1108/S1574-8715%282009%290000006013.

———. 2015. 'Agricultural Trade Disputes in the WTO'. *Farm Policies and World Markets: Monitoring and Disciplining the International Trade Impacts of Agricultural Policies.* 206–43.

Junginger, Martin, Jinke van Dam, Simonetta Zarrilli, Fatin Ali Mohamed, Didier Marchal and Andre Faaij. 2011. 'Opportunities and Barriers for International Bioenergy Trade'. *Energy Policy* 39, no. 4: 2028–42.

Kapoor, Radhika, and Ritika Tewari. 2010. 'FDI in the BRICs: Changing the Investment Landscape'. *The Perspective of the World Review* 2, no. 2: 147–70.

Kaufman, Robert. 2005. 'Morgenthau's Unrealistic Realism'. *Yale Journal of International Affairs* 1: 24.

Kaup, Felix. 2015. 'The Sugarcane Complex in Brazil'. *The Role of Innovation in a Dynamic Sector on Its Path towards Sustainability*. Heidelberg: Springer.

Keaney, Brian A. 2006. 'The Realism of Hans Morgenthau', dissertation, Tampa: University of South Florida.

Khor, Martin. 2007. '"G90 Plus" Developing Countries Issue Declaration on Doha Talks'. TWN Info Service on WTO and Trade Issues, 7 June http://www.africafocus.org/docs07/tr0706.php.

Kitchen, Nicholas. 2010. 'Systemic Pressures and Domestic Ideas: A Neoclassical Realist Model of Grand Strategy Formation'. *Review of International Studies* 36, no. 1: 117–43. doi:10.1017/S0260210509990532.

Kloss, Emerson Coraiola. 2012. *Transformação do etanol em commodity. Perspectivas para uma ação diplomática brasileira.* Brasília: Fundação Alexandre de Gusmão.

———. 2015. Interview with Emerson Cariola Kloss, head of Renewable Energy Department, Itamaraty. Brasilia.

Langevin, Mark S. 2013. 'O Setor energético e as Relações Brasil- Estados Unidos'. *Universitas Relações Internacionais* 11, no. 1: 13–27.

Lobell, Steven E. 2009. 'Threat Assessment, the State, and Foreign Policy: A Neoclassical Realist Mode'. In *Neoclassical Realism, the State, and Foreign Policy*, edited by Norrin M,

Ripsman, Jeffrey W. Taliaferro and Steven E. Lobell, 42–74. Cambridge: Cambridge University Press.

Locke, Anna. 2009. 'Managing the Biofuels Boom (and Bust?) – Mozambique's Experience'. Presentation given at Sustainable Biofuels and Human Security: A Comparison of Brazil and Southern Africa – A Hewlett Conference at the University of Illinois at Urbana-Champaign', 16–17 April. https://www.open.ac.uk/technology/mozambique/sites/www.open.ac.uk.technology.mozambique/files/pics/d128239.pdf.

Lowenthal, Abraham F. 2010a. 'América Latina en la política exterior de los EE.UU.: Políticas, prioridades e intereses cambiantes'. In *América Latina: Transformaciones geopolíticas y democracia*, edited by Bernardo Sorj and Sergio Fausto, 181–205. Buenos Aires: Siglo XXI Editora Iberoamericana S.A.

———. 2010b. 'United States-Brazil Relations are Critical'. *San Diego Union – Tribune Opinion*, 5 March. http://www.brookings.edu/research/opinions/2010/03/05-united-states-brazil-lowenthal.

MacauHub. 2011. 'Brazil's Petrobras to Build Ethanol Factory in Mozambique'. https://macauhub.com.mo/2011/08/12/brazil%E2%80%99s-petrobras-biocombustivel-to-build-ethanol-factory-in-mozambique/.

Macias, Carlos. 2008. 'Dealing without Doha'. Americas Society/Council of the Americas blog, 1 August. http://www.as-coa.org/articles/dealing-without-doha.

Macias, Carlos, and Carin Zissis. 2008. 'Predicting US-Brazil Ethanol Policy'. Americas Society/Council of the Americas weblog, 10 November. http://www.as-coa.org/articles/predicting-us-brazil-ethanol-policy.

Malamud, Andrés. 2011. 'A Leader without Followers? The Growing Divergence between the Regional and Global Performance of Brazilian Foreign Policy'. *Latin American Politics and Society* 53, no. 3: 1–24.

MAPA (Ministério da Agricultura, Pecuária e Abastecimento do Brasil). 2000. 'Declaração conjunta que fazem o Departamento de Agricultura dos Estados Unidos e o Ministério da Agricultura e do Abastecimento da República Federativa do Brasil relativa à criação de um Comitê Consultivo Agrícola (cca)', Washington, DC, 17 October.

Marx, Johannes. 2010. 'Is There a Hard Core of IR? Eine wissenschaftstheoretische Betrachtung der Theorien der Internationalen Beziehungen'. Zeitschrift für internationale Beziehungen: 41–74.

Masiero, Gilmar. 2011. 'Developments of Biofuels in Brazil and East Asia: Experiences and Challenges'. *Revista Brasileira de Polítca Internacional* 54, no. 2: 97–117.

Mathews, John A. 2007. 'Viewpoint: Biofuels: What a Biopact between North and South Could Achieve'. *Energy Policy* 35: 3550–70.

Medeiros, Marcelo de Almeida, and Liliana Froio. 2012. 'Actors, Interests and Strategies of Brazilian Foreign Policy on Biofuels'. *Brazilian Political Science Review* 6, no. 1: 37–52.

Meirelles. 2016. Interview with Antonio Josino Meirelles, executive director of the Brazilian Industries Coalition, Washington, DC.

Meyer, Peter J. 2010. 'Brazil-US Relations'. Congressional Research Service Report 7-5700, RL33456, 5 March.

MINAG (Ministério da Agricultura do Moçambique). 2013a. 'Estratégias do Governo e Oportunidades de Investiments no Agronegócio em Moçambique'. Presentation given at the Lançamento da Nova Aliança para a Segurança Alimentar e Nutricional, Maputo, 11 April. http://fsg.afre.msu.edu/mozambique/caadp/Apresentacao_Nova_Alianca_Intro_CEPAGRI.pdf.

———. 2013b. 'Oportunidades do Agronegocio em Moçambique'. Presentation given at the Lançamento da Nova Aliança para a Segurança Alimentar e Nutricional, Maputo, 11 April. http://www.portugalglobal.pt/PT/Acoes/abcMercado/Documents/ApresentacaoAbcMocambiqueAgronegocio_CEPAGRI.pdf.

Mol, Arthur P. J. 2007. 'Boundless Biofuels? Between Environmental Sustainability and Vulnerability'. *Sociologia Ruralis* 47, no. 4: 297–315.

Monheim, Kai. 2015. *How Effective Negotiation Management Promotes Multilateral Cooperation. The Power of Process in Climate, Trade, and Biosafety Negotiations.* Abingdon: Routledge.

Moniz-Bandeira, Luiz Alberto. 2006. 'Brazil as a Regional Power and Its Relations with the United States'. *Latin American Perspectives* 33, no. 3: 12–27.

———. 2009. *Geopolítica e política exterior: Estados Unidos, Brasil e América do Sul.* Brasília: Fundação Alexandre de Gusmão.

Monteiro, Nathalia, Ira Altman and Sajal Lahiri. 2012. 'The Impact of Ethanol Production on Food Prices: The Role of Interplay between the US and Brazil'. *Energy Policy* 41: 193–99.

Mononen, Juha. 2009. 'War or Peace for Finland? Neoclassical Realist Case Study of Finnish Foreign Policy in the Context of the Anti-Bolshevik Intervention in Russia 1918–1920'. MS thesis.

Moravcsik, Andrew. 1992. 'Liberalism and International Relations Theory'. Paper No. 92-6. www.princeton.edu/~amoravcs/library/Liberalism_working.pdf.

Morgenthau, Hans J. 1978. *Politics among Nations: The Struggle for Power and Peace.* brief edition, revised by Kenneth W. Thompson. New York: McGraw-Hill 1993.

Motaal, Doaa Abdal. 2008. 'The Biofuels Landscape: Is There a Role for the WTO?'. *Journal of World Trade* 42, no. 1: 61–86.

Mozambique. 2009. 'Resolução 22/2009'. *Boletím da República*, 4. June, I Série – Número 22. http://extwprlegs1.fao.org/docs/pdf/moz119871.pdf.

MRE (Ministério das Relações Exteriores do Brasil). 2013. *Guia de Negócios – Moçambique.* Brasília: MRE. https://investexportbrasil.dpr.gov.br/arquivos/Publicacoes/ComoExportar/GNMocambique.pdf.

Mueller, Charles C. 2009. 'Agricultural, Agrarian, and Environmental Policy Formation under Lula: The Role of Policy Networks'. In *Brazil under Lula*, edited by Joseph Love and Werner Baer, 135–50. New York: Palgrave Macmillan.

Mukwereza, Langton. 2015. 'Zimbabwe-Brazil Cooperation through the More Food Africa Programme'. Future Agricultures China and Brazil in African Agriculture Working Paper Series, Working Paper 116. http://www.future-agricultures.org/publications/research-and-analysis/working-papers/1946-zimbabwe-brazil-cooperation-through-the-more-food-africa-programme/file.

Murphy, Sofia. 2011. *G-20 Agriculture Ministers Meet in Paris with Little Result.* Washington, DC: Institute for Agriculture and Trade Policy. https://www.iatp.org/sites/default/files/2011_07_15_SophiaMurphy_G-20_boell.pdf.

Murtagh & Associates. 2016. 'Beverage, Fuel and Industrial Alcohol Production Consultants: Ethanol Specifications Worldwide'. http://www.distill.com/specs/.

Negroponte, Diana Villiers. 2012. 'US-Brazilian Relations: Understanding President Rousseff's Visit to Washington and Secretary Clinton's Visit to Brasilia'. Brookings Institution Opinion. 20 April. http://www.brookings.edu/research/opinions/2012/04/20-rousseff-clinton-negroponte.

Neto, Walter Antonio Desiderá, and Hevellyn Menezes Albres. 2012. 'Relações Brasil-Estados Unidos no governo Dilma: A agenda das visitas presidenciais oficiais em 2011 e 2012'. *Boletim de economia e política internacional/Instituto de Pesquisa Econômica Aplicada. Diretoria de Estudos e Relações Econômicas e Políticas Internacionais*, no. 11 (Jul/Sep), 77–88. Brasília: Ipea. Dinte.

Nhachote, Luis. 2012. 'Mozambique's "Mr Guebusiness"'. https://mg.co.za/article/2012-01-06-mozambiques-mr-guebusiness.

Nhantumbo, Isilda, and Alda Salomão. 2010. 'Biofuels, Land Access and Rural Livelihoods in Mozambique'. London: IIED. http://pubs.iied.org/pdfs/12563IIED.pdf.

Nogueira, Isabela. 2013. 'Agricultural Systems with Pro-Poor Orientation in Mozambique? ProSavana and the Forgotten Risks of Contract Farming'. Paper presented at the UNU-WIDER Conference on Inclusive Growth in Africa: Measurements, Causes, and Consequences. Helsinki, 20–21 September.

Nogueira, Isabela, and Ossi Ollinaho. 2013. *From Rhetoric to Practice in South-South Development Cooperation: A Case Study of Brazilian Interventions in the Nacala Corridor Development Program.* Geneva: Institute of Socioeconomics University of 2013. http://www.ie.ufrj.br/intranet/ie/userintranet/hpp/arquivos/2732nogueira_ollinaho_workingpaper_nacala_corridor.pdf.

Nogueira, Isabela, Ossi Ollinaho, Eduardo Costa Pinto, Grasiela Baruco, Alexis Saludjian, José Paulo Guedes Pinto, Paulo Balanco and Carlos Schonerwald. 2017. 'Mozambican Economic Porosity and the Role of Brazilian Capital: A Political Economy Analysis'. *Review of African Political Economy* 44, no. 151: 104–21.

Nogueira, Saulo. 2009. 'The International Financial Crisis and Brazil in the Doha Development Round'. Working paper prepared for presentation at the 2009 World Trade Organization Forum, Geneva, 28 September. http://www.nsi-ins.ca/wp-content/uploads/2012/11/2009-Brazil-at-Doha-Paper.pdf.

Nolte, Detlef, and Christina Stolte. 2007. 'Machtressource Bioenergie: Eine neue strategische Partnerschaft zwischen Brasilien und den USA'. GIGA Focus Lateinamerika #3-2007. http://www.giga-hamburg.de/dl/download.php?d=/content/publikationen/pdf/gf_lateinamerika_0703.pdf.

Nye, Joseph S. Jr. 1990. 'Soft Power'. *Foreign Policy*, no. 80: 153–71.

O'Keefe, Thomas Andrew, and Diana Villiers Negroponte. 2012. 'Promoting Energy Security and Tackling Climate Change: Missed Opportunities at the Cartagena Summit'. In *The Road to Hemispheric Cooperation: Beyond the Cartagena Summit of the Americas*, 45–58. Washington, DC: Brookings Institution. http://www.brookings.edu/research/reports/2012/07/07-summit-of-the-americas/climate-change.

Obama and Lula. 2009. 'Remarks by President Obama and President Lula da Silva of Brazil'. The White House, Office of the Press Secretary, 14 March. https://www.whitehouse.gov/the-press-office/remarks-president-obama-and-president-lula-da-silva-brazil.

Ondetti, Gabriel, and Sybil Rhodes. 2010. 'Courting the South: Lula's Trade Diplomacy'. *Documentos de Trabajo Nro* 430, September. Buenos Aires: Universidad del CEMA.

Onea, Tudor. 2012. 'Putting the "Classical" in Neoclassical Realism: Neoclassical Realist Theories and US Expansion in the Post-Cold War'. *International Relations* 26, no. 2: 139–64.

Patriota, Antonio de Aguiar. 2013. 'Remarks with Foreign Minister of Brazil Antonio de Aguiar Patriota before Their Meeting'. Washington, DC, 20 May. http://www.state.gov/secretary/remarks/2013/05/209664.htm.

Phillips, Leticia. 2011. 'Obamas Visit Signals New Chapter for US-Brazil Energy Partnership'. UNICA blog post, 24 March. http://www.unica.com.br/columns/15497664920334804993/obamas-visit-signals-new-chapter-for-us-brazil-energy-partnership/.

Pianto, Donald Matthew, and Lina Chang. 2006. 'O potencial exportador e as políticas de promoção das exportações da APEX-Brasil'. In *As empresas brasileiras e o comércio internacional*, edited by João Alberto de Negri and Bruno César Pino Oliveira de Araújo, vol. 1, 87–108. Brasília: IPEA. http://www.ipea.gov.br/portal/index.php?option=com_content&view=article&id=5568.

Piccone, Ted. 2012. 'US and Brazil: Together and Apart'. The National Interest. 9 April. http://nationalinterest.org/commentary/us-brazil-together-apart-6746.

Porter, Michael. 2008. 'Venezuela, he United States, and Brazil: Countering Socialism through Regional Economic Balancing'. *Virginia Military Institute – Economics and Business Online Journal*. www.vmi.edu/WorkArea/downloadasset.aspx?id=38941.

Procópio, Argemiro. 2007. 'A volta do dualismo estrutural: fome e bioethanol'. *Meridiano* 47, no. 84: 10–12.

ProSavana. 2015. 'Plano Director Para O Desenvolvimento Agrário Do Corredor De Nacala Em Moçambique'. *Esboço Versão 0*. http://www.ProSavana.gov.mz/wp-content/uploads/2015/09/1.Master_Plan_Draft_Zero_Main_Revisao1.pdf.

Puppim de Oliveira, Jose Antonio. 2002. 'The Policymaking Process for Creating Competitive Assets for the Use of Biomass Energy: The Brazilian Alcohol Programme'. *Renewable and Sustainable Energy Reviews* 6: 129–40.

Purdon, Mark. 2017. 'Neoclassical Realism and International Climate Change Politics: Moral Imperative and Political Constraint in International Climate Finance'. *Journal of International Relations and Development* 20, no. 2: 263–300.

Quinn, Adam. 2013. 'Kenneth Waltz, Adam Smith and the Limits of Science: Hard Choices for Neo-Classical Realism'. *International Politics* 50: 159–82.

———. 2014. 'Does the Flaw Lie within Us? Classical Realism and Unrealistic Policy'. *Global Society* 28, no. 2: 241–65.

Raja, Kanaga. 2007. 'India-Brazil-South Africa Call for Balanced Outcome in Doha Talks'. South North Development Monitor (SUNS) #6347, 19 October. http://www.africafocus.org/docs07/ibsa0711.php.

Reuters. 2008. 'Interview – Principle Energy to Press on with Mozambique Ethanol'. https://uk.reuters.com/article/biofuels-mozambique-idUKLP69047220081126.

———. 2010. 'EU, Brazil, Mozambique to Sign Bioenergy Pact'. 12 July. http://af.reuters.com/article/topNews/idAFJOE66B0SL20100712.

Ribeiro, Marcos Paulo de Araújo. 2007. 'Rodada Doha: atores, temas e interesses'. *Meridiano* 47, no. 81: 23–25.

Ricupero, Rubens. 2010. 'Carisma e prestígio: a diplomacia do período Lula de 2003 a 2010'. *Política Externa* 19, no. 1: 27–42.

Rios, Sandra, Renard P. Aron and Roxana Jordan. 2001. 'The Free Trade Area of the Americas & the Brazil-US Trade Agenda in the US Congress'. CEBRI Project Report BRA/00/001, January. www.cebri.org/midia/documentos/96_PDF.pdf.

Ripsman, Norrin M, Jeffrey W. Taliaferro and Steven E. Lobell. 2009. *Neoclassical Realism, the State, and Foreign Policy*. Cambridge: Cambridge University Press.

———. 2016. *Neoclassical Realist Theory of International Politics*. New York: Oxford University Press.

Risse, Thomas, and Harald Müller. 2001. 'Arguing and Persuasion in Multilateral Negotiations'. Grant Proposal to the Volkswagen Foundation. http://www.polsoz.fu-berlin.de/polwiss/forschung/international/atasp/forschung/projekte_abgeschlossen/argumentieren/vwneuantrag.pdf.

Rodrigues. 2016. Interview with Tarcilo Rodrigues, director of Bioagencia, São Paulo.

Rodrigues de Castro, Eduardo, Erly Cardoso Teixeira and Constanza Valdes. 2012. 'Sugar Cane Expansion: Does It Contribute to Amazon Deforestation?' Paper prepared for presentation at the International Association of Agricultural Economists (IAAE) Triennial Conference, Foz do Iguaçu, Brazil, 18–24 August.

Rodrigues Vieira, Vinícius. 2014. 'Is Politics behind Trade? The Impact of International Trends and Diplomatic Action on Brazil's Exports During Globalisation'. *Bulletin of Latin American Research* 33, no. 2: 140–57.

Rohter, Larry. 2005a. 'As Did O.A.S., Bank Resists a Candidate Backed by U.S'. *New York Times*, 27 July. http://www.nytimes.com/2005/07/27/world/americas/as-did-oas-bank-resists-a-candidate-backed-by-us.html.

———. 2005b. 'Americas: U.S.-Backed Candidate to Lead Development Bank'. *New York Times World Briefing*, 28 July. https://query.nytimes.com/gst/fullpage.html?res=9B07E4D9103FF93BA15754C0A9639C8B63.

———. 2005c. 'With New Chief, Uruguay Veers Left, in a Latin Pattern'. *New York Times*, 1 March. https://www.nytimes.com/2005/03/01/world/americas/with-new-chief-uruguay-veers-left-in-a-latin-pattern.html?_r=0.

———. 2010. *Brazil on the Rise: The Story of a Country Transformed.* New York: Palgrave Macmillan.

Romano Schutte, Giorgio. 2012. 'Avaliação Crítica da Diplomacia do Etanol'. Paper presented at the Associação Brasileira de Relações Internacionais – ABRI 1o Seminário Nacional de Pós-Graduação em Relações Internacionais 12 e 13 de julho de, Brasília.

Romero, Simon. 2012. 'Brazil Gains Business and Influence as It Offers Aid and Loans in Africa'. *New York Times*, 7 August. http://www.nytimes.com/2012/08/08/world/americas/brazil-gains-in-reaching-out-to-africa.html.

Roos, Ulrich. 2012. 'Deutsche Außenpolitik nach der Vereinigung. Zwischen ernüchtertem Idealismus und realpolitischem Weltordnungsstreben'. *Zeitschrift für Internationale Beziehungen* 19: 7–14.

Rose, Gideon. 1998. 'Neoclassical Realism and Theories of Foreign Policy'. *World Politics* 51, no. 1: 144–72.

Rosenau, James N., and Ernst-Otto Czempiel (eds). 1992. 'Governance without Government: Order and Change in World Politics'. *Cambridge Studies in International Relations* (Book 20). Cambridge: Cambridge University Press.

Rossi, Amanda. 2015. *Moçambique – O Brasil é aqui.* São Paulo: Record2.

Rossi, Clóvis. 2008. 'Todos perdem com fracasso de Doha – Brasil perde mais'. *Folha de S. Paulo*, 30 July. http://www1.folha.uol.com.br/fsp/dinheiro/fi3007200807.htm.

Salifu, Uyo, and Lesley Masters (eds). 2011. 'The Global South and the International Politics of Climate Change'. Proceedings Report of the International Workshop: Negotiating Africa and the Global South's Interests on Climate Change, Report No. 1. 25 November. Pretoria: Institute for Global Dialogue. www.igd.org.za/publications/igd-reports/finish/8/215 .

Sanchez, Milani and Carlos Roberto. 2011. 'A importância das relações Brasil – Estados Unidos na politica externa Brasileira'. *Boletim de economia e política internacional/Instituto de Pesquisa Econômica Aplicada. Diretoria de Estudos e Relações Econômicas e Políticas Internacionais*, no. 6: 69–86.

Sandalow, David. 2006. 'Ethanol: Lessons from Brazil'. The Brookings Institution, May. http://www.brookings.edu/research/articles/2006/05/energy-sandalow.

Sangmeister, Helmut. 2013. 'Brasiliens Aufstieg zur weltwirtschaftlichen Großmacht'. In *Brasilien. Eine Einführung*, edited by Birle Peter, 127–48. Frankfurt: Vervuert Verlag.

Schlesinger, Sergio. 2012. *Cooperação e Investimentos Internacionais do Brasil. A internacionalização do etanol e do biodiesel.* Rio de Janeiro: FASE.

———. 2013 Cooperação e investimentos do Brasil na África: O caso do ProSavana em Moçambique. Maputo: Federação de Órgãos para Assistência Social e Educacional.

Schut, Marc, Maja Slingerland and Anna Locke. 2010. 'Biofuel Developments in Mozambique. Update and Analysis of Policy, Potential and Reality'. *Energy Policy* 38, no. 9: 5151–65.

Schweller, Randall L. 2003. 'The Progressiveness of Neoclassical Realism'. *Progress in International Relations Theory: Appraising the Field*: 311-47.

———. 2009. 'Neoclassical Realism and State Mobilization: Expansionist Ideology in the Age of Mass Politics'. In *Neoclassical Realism and the State*, edited by Steven Lobell, Norrin Ripsman, and Jeffrey Taliaferro, pp. 227–50. Cambridge: Cambridge University Press.

Scoones, Ian, Kojo Amanor, Arilson Favareto and Gubo Qi. 2016. 'A New Politics of Development Cooperation? Chinese and Brazilian Engagements in African Agriculture'. *World Development* 81: 1–12.

Seelke, Clare Ribando, and Brent D. Yacobucci. 2007. 'Ethanol and Other Biofuels: Potential for US-Brazil Energy Cooperation'. CRS Report RL34191. Washington, DC: Congressional Research Service.

Shankland, Alex, and Euclides Gonçalves. 2016. 'Imagining Agricultural Development in South–South Cooperation: The Contestation and Transformation of ProSavana'. *World Development* 81: 35–46.

Silva, Antouan Matheus Monteiro Pereira da. 2013. *O BRIC na Política Externa do Governo Lula (2003-2010): Do conceito a coalizão.* Brasilia: UnB. http://repositorio.unb.br/bitstream/10482/13650/1/2013_AntouanMatheusMonteiroPereiradaSilva.pdf.

Simões, Antônio José Ferreira. 2007. 'Biocombustíveis: a experiência brasileira e o desafio da consolidação do mercado internacional'. In *Biocombustíveis no Brasil: Realidades e Perspectivas*, edited by Ministério das Relações Exteriores, 11–33.

Skloven, Danielle. 2008. 'U.S.-Brazil Agricultural Trade Negotiations: One Messy Food Fight'. Paper published on slideshare, 6 February 2013. http://www.slideshare.net/DanielleSkloven/usbrazil-agricultural-trade-negotiations.

Slaughter, Anne-Marie. 1995. 'Liberal International Relations Theory and International Economic Law'. *American University International Law Review* 10, no. 2: 717–43.

Smith, Joseph. 1991. *Unequal Giants: Diplomatic Relations between the United States and Brazil 1889-1930.* Pittsburgh, PA: University of Pittsburgh Press.

———. 2010. *Brazil and the United States: Convergence and Divergence.* Athens: University of Georgia Press.

Soares, Adriano Campolina de Oliveira. 2005. 'G-20, G90 and G33'. Terraviva Blog. 23 January. https://www.globalpolicy.org/component/content/article/209/43775.html.

Sotero, Paulo. 2007. 'Building a Biofuels Alliance'. *Washington Post*, 8 March. http://www.cfr.org/renewable-energy/building-biofuels-alliance/p12803.

———. 2009. 'Emerging Powers: India, Brazil and South Africa (IBSA) and the Future of South-South Cooperation'. Special Report for the Woodrow Wilson International Center for Scholars, August.

Souza, Amaury de. 2009. *A agenda internacional do Brasil: a política externa brasileira de FHC a Lula.* Rio de Janeiro: Elsevier/CEBRI

Stanley Foundation/CEBRI. 2010. 'The Roles of Brazil and the United States for the 21st Century International Agenda'. Discussion summary of the Dialogue on Global Leadership, 12–22 November, Rio de Janeiro.

Steenblik, Ronald. 2005. 'Environmental Goods: A Comparison of the APEC and OECD Lists'. OECD Trade and Environment Working Paper No. 2005-04. https://www.oecd.org/trade/envtrade/35837840.pdf.

Steinhilber, Jochen. 2009. 'Der Wald, das Rind, das Zuckerrohr. Brasilien in der Klimapolitik'. FES BrasilInfo, December. library.fes.de/pdf-files/bueros/brasilien/06872.pdf.

Sterling-Folker, Jennifer. 1997. 'Realist Environment, Liberal Process, and Domestic-Level Variables'. *International Studies Quarterly* 41, no. 1: 1–25.

———. 2009. 'Neoclassical Realism and Identity: Peril Despite Profit Across the Taiwan Strait'. In *Neoclassical Realism, the State, and Foreign Policy*, edited by Norrin M. Ripsman, Jeffrey W. Taliaferro and Steven E. Lobell, 99–138. Cambridge: Cambridge University Press.

Stolte, Christina. 2013. 'Brazil in Africa'. *Harvard International Review Online*, 30 March. http://hir.harvard.edu/the-future-of-democracy/brazil-in-africa.

———. 2015. *Brazil's Africa Strategy: Role Conception and the Drive for International Status*. New York: Palgrave Macmillan.

Stolte, Christina, and Dana de la Fontaine. 2012. 'Neue externe Akteure in Afrika'. *GIGA Focus Afrika*, July.

Strauss, Anselm L., and Barney Glaser. 2017. *Discovery of Grounded Theory: Strategies for Qualitative Research*. London: Taylor & Francis.

Sugathan, Mahesh. 2004. 'Environmental Goods and Services Negotiations: Challenges and Opportunities'. Presentation given at the WTO Workshop on Environmental Goods: Para 31 (iii) of the DDA, Geneva, 11 October. http://www.wto.org/english/tratop_e/envir_e/wksp_goods_oct04_e/sugathan_ictsd_e.ppt.

———. 2013. *Lists of Environmental Goods: An Overview*. Environmental Goods and Services Series. Geneva: International Centre for Trade and Sustainable Development. https://www.ictsd.org/downloads/2013/12/info_note_list-of-environmental-goods_sugathan.pdf.

Taliaferro, Jeffrey W. 2009. 'Neoclassical Realism and Resource Extraction: State Building for Future War'. In *Neoclassical Realism and the State*, edited by Steven Lobell, Norrin Ripsman, and Jeffrey Taliaferro, pp. 194–226. Cambridge: Cambridge University Press.

Tang, Shiping. 2006. 'Reputation Cult of Reputation and International Conflict'. *Security Studies* 14, no. 1: 34–36.

———. 2008a. 'Fear in International Politics – Two Positions'. *International Studies Review* 10: 451–71.

———. 2008b. 'Offence-Defence Theory: Towards a Definitive Understanding'. *Chinese Journal of International Politics* 3: 213–60.

———. 2009a. 'Taking Stock of Neoclassical Realism'. *International Studies Review* 11: 799–803.

———. 2009b. 'The Security Dilemma: A Conceptual Analysis'. *Security Studies* 18, no. 3: 587–623.

———. 2010. *A Theory of Security Strategy for Our Time: Defensive Realism*. New York: Palgrave Macmillan.

Teixeira, Carlos Gustavo Poggio. 2011. 'Brazil and United States: Fading Interdependence'. *Orbis* 55, no. 1: 147–62.

Thomaz, Laís. 2016. 'As coalizões de defesa e as mudanças na política externa comercial e energética dos Estados Unidos para o etanol em 2011'. São Paulo. http://repositorio.unesp.br/bitstream/handle/11449/137930/thomaz_lf_dr_mar.pdf.

Thomaz, Lais, and Carlos Eduardo Carvalho. 2011. 'The Tortilla Crisis in Mexico (2007): The Upward Trend in Commodity Prices, Financial Instability and Food Security'. *Perspective of the World Review* 3, no. 2.

Thorstensen, Vera. 2012. 'The Multisystem of Global Trade Regulation: Proposal for a New Theoretical Reference and a New Analysis Methodology'. *Perspective of the World Review* 3, no. 1: 83–110.

Thorstensen, Vera, Daniel Ricardo Castelan, Daniel Ramos and Carolina Müller. 2012. 'Partiçipação dos BRICS na Rodada Doha'. In *Os BRICS na OMC: políticas comerciais comparadas de Brasil, Rússia, Índia e África do Sul*, edited by Vera Thorstensen and Ivan Tiago Machado Oliveira, 399–448. Brasília: Ipea.

Timossi, Adriano José, and Lucas Assunção. 2012. 'State of South-South and Triangular Cooperation in the Production, Use and Trade of Sustainable Biofuels'. UNCTAD BioFuels Initiative Report UNCTAD/DITC/TED/2011/10. New York: United Nations.

Toke, David, and Sevasti-Eleni Vezirgiannidou. 2013. 'The Relationship between Climate Change and Energy Security: Key Issues and Conclusions'. *Environmental Politics* 22, no. 4: 537–52.

Tomei, Julia, Nicola Favretto, Stavros Afionis and Lindsay Stringer. 2016. 'Brazilian Ethanol Diplomacy in Sub-Saharan Africa: The Case of Mozambique'. Presentation given at the Sugarcane Landscapes Workshop at University College London, 15 July. https://www.ucl.ac.uk/steapp/docs/sugarcane_landscapes_workshop_july_2016/presentation_8.

Torres, Ernani, and Rodrigo Zeidan. 2016. 'The Life-Cycle of National Development Banks: The Experience of Brazil's BNDES'. *Quarterly Review of Economics and Finance* 62, 97–104.

Trinkunas, Harold. 2015. 'Brazil's Global Ambitions'. *Americas Quarterly Winter* and Brookings Institution Online. http://www.americasquarterly.org/content/brazils-global-ambitions, http://www.brookings.edu/research/articles/2015/02/04-brazil-global-ambitions-trinkunas.

Trucco, Paulo. 2016. Interview with Paulo Trucco, Ethanol Trader at Bioagencia, São Paulo.

Tyner, Wallace E. 2008. 'The US Ethanol and Biofuels Boom: Its Origins, Current Status, and Future Prospects'. *BioScience* 58, no. 7: 646–53.

———. 2015. 'US Ethanol Policy – Possibilities for the Future'. Historical Documents of the Purdue Cooperative Extension Service. Paper 1039. http://docs.lib.purdue.edu/agext/1039.

Ubiraci-Sennes, Ricardo, and Thais Narciso . 2008. 'Brazil as an International Energy Player'. In *Brazil as an Economic Superpower? Understanding Brazil's Changing Role in the Global Economy*, edited by Lael Brainard and Leonardo Martinez-Diaz. Washington, DC: Brookings Institution Press.

Ulbert, Cornelia, Thomas Risse and Harald Müller. 2004. 'Arguing and Bargaining in Multilateral Negotiations'. Paper presented to the Conference on Empirical Approaches to Deliberative Politics, European University Institute, Swiss Chair Firenze, 21–22 May. http://www.polsoz.fu-berlin.de/en/polwiss/forschung/international/atasp/publikationen/4_artikel_papiere/26/index.html.

UN (United Nations). 2007. Press Conference Launching International Biofuels Forum, 2 March. http://www.un.org/press/en/2007/070302_Biofuels.doc.htm.

———. 2012. 'The Future We Want'. Report of the Rio+20 Group. Resolution adopted by the General Assembly on 27 July, 66/288. http://www.un.org/ga/search/view_doc.asp?symbol=A/RES/66/288&Lang=E.

UN Comtrade. 2017. 'United Nations Comtrade World Trade Database'. https://comtrade.un.org/data.

UNAC (União Nacional de Camponeses). 2017. 'Quem somos?'. http://www.unac.org.mz/index.php/unac/nossos-membros.

UNAC and GRAIN. 2015a. 'Report: The Land Grabbers of the Nacala Corridor. A New Era of Struggle against Colonial Plantations in Northern Mozambique'. February. https://www.grain.org/article/entries/5137-land-grabbers-of-the-nacala-corridor.pdf.

———. 2015b. 'Colonial Plantations Are Making a Comeback in Mozambique'. Press release, 19 February. https://farmlandgrab.org/24542.

UNAC et al. 2013. 'Open Letter from Mozambican Civil Society Organisations and Movements to the Presidents of Mozambique and Brazil and the Prime Minister of Japan'. Maputo, 28 May. https://www.grain.org/bulletin_board/entries/4738-open-letter-from-mozambican-civil-society-organisations-and-movements-to-the-presidents-of-mozambique-and-brazil-and-the-prime-minister-of-japan.

UNCTAD (United Nations Conference on Trade and Development). 2013. 'FDI in Brief: Brazil – Brazil Largest Recipient of FDI in Latin America'. unctad.org/sections/dite_fdistat/docs/wid_ib_br_en.pdf.

UNICA (União da Indústria de Cana-de-Açúcar). 2010. 'EPA Reaffirms Sugarcane Biofuel Is Advanced Renewable Fuel with 61% Less Emissions Than Gasoline'. Press release, 3 February. http://www.unica.com.br/media-center/103869129203425665 67/epa-reaffirms-sugarcane-biofuel-is-advanced-renewable-fuel-with-61-por-cento-less-emissions-than-gasoline/.

———. 2013. 'The Sugarcane Industry in Brazil'. São Paulo: UNICA.

———. 2014. 'África pode incrementar produção de etanol no mundo'. Press release, 21 May. http://www.unica.com.br/noticia/6551584920342566567/unica-por-cento3A-por-centoC3-por-cento81frica-pode-incrementar-producao-de-etanol-no-mundo/.

———. 2015. 'Histórico de exportação mensal de etanol pelo Brasil'. http://www.unicadata.com.br/listagem.php?idMn=65.

UNICA data. 2016. 'Production Data Sugarcane and Ethanol'. http://www.unicadata.com.br/historico-de-producao-e-moagem.php?idMn=31&tipoHistorico=2.

U.S.-Brazil Innovation Summit. 2007. R. Nicholas Burns, Undersecretary for Political Affairs. Brasilia, Brazil. 12 July. https://2001-2009.state.gov/p/us/rm/2007/88685.htm.

US Energy Independence and Security Act. 2007. Public Law 110-140.

US Energy Policy Act. 2005. Public Law 109–58.

US International Trade Administration. 2006. U.S.–Brazil Commercial Dialogue Launched. International Trade Update, June.

US International Trade Commission. 2002. 'The Year in Trade 2001'. Operations of the Trade Agreements Program, 53rd Report. Washington, DC: USITC.

USDA–FAS (US Department of Agriculture–Foreign Agriculture Service). 2012. 'Biofuels – Ethanol Import Tariff'. Global Agriculture Information Network (GAIN) Report BR12001. 9 January.

USTR (The Office of the United States Trade Representative). 2016. Mission Statement. https://ustr.gov/about-us/about-ustr.

Vieira, Maíra Baé Baladão. 2011. 'The Semi-Periphery in Africa: The Case of Brazil'. Paper presented at the ECAS 2011 – 4th European Conference on African Studies, Uppsala, 15–18 June. http://www.nai.uu.se/ecas-4/panels/1-20/panel-8/Maira_-_First_draft-(3).pdf.

Vieira, Marco. 2012. 'Brazilian Environmental Politics and Global Climate Governance'. Report prepared for the international workshop The Global South and the International Politics of Climate Change, Report no. 1, Institute for Global Dialogue, Durban, South Africa, 25 November. http://www.igd.org.za/archives/latest-news-archive/207-the-global-south-and-the-international-politics-of-climate-change.

———. 2013. 'Brazilian Foreign Policy in the Context of Global Climate Norms'. *Foreign Policy Analysis* 9, no. 4: 369–86.

Vieira, Marco Antonio, and Klaus Guimarães Dalgaard. 2013. 'The Energy-Security–Climate-Change Nexus in Brazil'. *Environmental Politics* 22, no. 4: 610–26.

Vigevani, Tullo. 2011. 'Relações Brasil-Estados Unidos'. *Textos para Discussão CEPAL-IPEA* 30. Brasília, DF: CEPAL. Escritório no Brasil/IPEA.

Vigevani, Tullo, and Gabriel Cepaluni. 2007. 'Lula's Foreign Policy and the Quest for Autonomy through Diversification'. *Third World Quarterly* 28, no. 7: 1309–26.

Vikhlyaev, Alexey. 2011. 'WTO Negotiations on Environmental Goods: Selected Technical Issues'. UNCTAD/DITC/TED/2011/1. United Nations: Geneva. http://unctad.org/en/Docs/ditcted2011d1_en.pdf.

Viola, Eduardo. 2010. 'Global Climate Policy and Brazil: 2005-2010'. *The Perspective of the World Review* 2, no. 2: 79–114.

———. 2011. 'The Shift in Brazilian Climate Policy, Commitment with Global Governance and Perspectives for Transition to a Low Carbon Economy'. Prepared for presentation at the annual conference of the International Studies Association, Montreal, Canada, 16–19 March.

Visentini, Paulo Fagundes. 2010. 'South-South Cooperation, Prestige, Diplomacy or "Soft Imperialism"?' *SÉCULO XXI, Porto Alegre* 1, no. 1: 65–84.

———. 1987. *The Origins of Alliances*. Ithaca: Cornell University Press.

Waltz, Kenneth. 1959. *Man, the State, and War: A Theoretical Analysis*. New York: Columbia University Press.

Weiß, Wolfgang. 2011. 'Biofuels and WTO Law'. In *European Yearbook of International Economic Law*, edited by Christoph Herrmann and Jörg Philipp Terhechte, 169–204. Heidelberg: Springer.

Wheatley, Jonathan. 2008. 'Brazil to Dispute US Subsidies'. *Financial Times Online*, 3 August. http://www.ft.com/intl/cms/s/0/7928a77a-6183-11dd-af94-000077b07658.html#axzz2lbIz6XNr.

———. 2009. 'Brazil Ready to Escalate US Trade Dispute'. *Financial Times Online*, 31 August. http://www.ft.com/cms/s/0/c74abee0-95c4-11de-90e0-00144feabdc0.html#axzz2lbIz6XNr.

———. 2013. 'Emerging Powers in Africa: Is Brazil Any Different?'. *South African Journal of International Affairs* 20, no. 1: 117–36.

Whitehead, Laurence, and Detlef Nolte. 2012. 'The Obama Administration and Latin America: A Disappointing First Term'. GIGA Focus International Edition 6-2012. http://www.giga-hamburg.de/dl/download.php?d=/content/publikationen/pdf/gf_international_1206.pdf.

Winter, Brian. 2012. 'Insight: US and Brazil – At Last, Friends on Ethanol'. *Chicago Tribune Online*, 14 September. http://articles.chicagotribune.com/2012-09-14/news/sns-rt-us-ethanolbre88d195-20120914_1_ethanol-biofuel-tariff.

Wise, Timothy. 2014. 'What Happened to the Biggest Land Grab in Africa? Searching for ProSavana in Mozambique'. Globalization Commentaries blog, 20 December. https://foodtank.com/news/2014/12/what-happened-to-the-biggest-land-grab-in-africa-searching-for-ProSavana-in/.

Wittger, Bea. 2010. 'Der Clean Development Mechanism in Brasilien'. *Nachhaltigkeitsstandard in Theorie und Praxis*. Wuppertal Spezial No 43. Wuppertal Institut für Klima, Umwelt, Energie GmbH.

Woodrow Wilson International Center for Scholars. 2008. 'Brazil and the United States: Trade Agendas and Challenges of the Bilateral Relationship'. Brazil Institute Special Report, April. http://www.wilsoncenter.org/publication/brazil-and-the-united-states-trade-agendas-and-challenges-the-bilateral-relationship.

World Bank. 2015. 'Development Indicators'. http://data.worldbank.org/country.

———. 2017. 'World Trade Data'. http://data.worldbank.org/topic/trade?end=2014&start=2001.

Wright, Alan M. 2008. 'Brazil–U.S. Biofuels Cooperation: One Year Later'. Brazil Institute Special Report, June. Washington, DC: Woodrow Wilson International Center for Scholars.

WTO (World Trade Organization). 2003. Ministerial Conference Fifth Session Cancún, 10–14 September 2003, Agriculture – Framework Proposal. WTO Document symbol: WT/MIN(03)/W/6.

———. 2005a. 'Environmental Goods for Development, Submission by Brazil'. Document TN/TE/W/59, Word Trade Organization, Geneva, Switzerland. http://www.jmcti.org/2000round/com/doha/tn/te/tn_te_w_059.pdf.

———. 2005b. 'NGOs Eligible to Attend the Sixth WTO Ministerial Conference, to be held in Hong Kong, China, from 13 to 18 December. https://www.wto.org/english/thewto_e/minist_e/min05_e/list_ngo_e.pdf.

———. 2008. 'Trading into the Future'. Report of the WTO Public Forum 2008. WTO: Geneva. https://www.wto.org/english/res_e/booksp_e/public_forum08_e.pdf.

———. 2013. 'Ministerial Declaration and Decisions of the Ninth Ministerial Conference, Bali', 3–6 December. https://www.wto.org/english/thewto_e/minist_e/mc9_e/bali_texts_combined_e.pdf.

———. 2017a. 'Principles of the Trading System'. https://www.wto.org/english/thewto_e/whatis_e/tif_e/fact2_e.htm.

———. 2017b. 'Groups in the Negotiations'. https://www.wto.org/english/tratop_e/dda_e/negotiating_groups_e.htm.

———. 2017c. 'Case Summary: EC – Export Subsidies on Sugar (DS265, 266, 283)'. https://www.wto.org/english/tratop_e/dispu_e/cases_e/1pagesum_e/ds266sum_e.pdf.

———. 2017d. 'Technical Information on Safeguard Measures'. https://www.wto.org/english/tratop_e/safeg_e/safeg_info_e.htm.

Woodrow Wilson International Centre for Scholars. 2008. 'Brazil and the United States: Trade Agendas and Challenges of the Bilateral Relationship'. Brazil Institute Special Report, April. http://www.wilsoncenter.org/publication/brazil-and-the-united-states-trade-agendas-and-challenges-the-bilateral-relationship.

Zanella, Matheus A., and Carolina Milhorance. 2015. 'Cerrado Meets Savannah, Family Farmers Meet Peasants: The Political Economy of Brazil's Agricultural Cooperation with Mozambique'. *Food Policy* 58: 70–81. http://www.sciencedirect.com/science/article/pii/S0306919215001438.

INDEX

Lightning Source UK Ltd.
Milton Keynes UK
UKHW010931190122
397359UK00002B/96

9 781839 980244